MASTERY OF TEACHING SKILLS

MASTERY OF TEACHING SKILLS

By

S.B.J.R Chowdary
M.A., M.Ed.
Senior Lecturer
A.N.G. Ranga College of Education
Chilimuru
Guntur Distt., (A.P.)

Naga Raju
M.A., M.Ed.
Lecturer
Al-Momin College of Education
Podili
Prakasam Distt., (A.P.)

General Editor

Dr. Digumarti Bhaskara Rao
M.Sc., M.A., M.A., M.Ed., Ph.D.
Reader & Research Director
R.V.R. College of Education
Guntur–522 006 (A.P.)
&
Member, Board of Studies in Education
Acharya Nagarjuna University
Nagarjuna Nagar–522 510

DISCOVERY PUBLISHING HOUSE
NEW DELHI-110002

First Published – 2004

Reprinted – 2017

ISBN: 978-81-7141-861-9

Mastery of Teaching Skills

Published by:

DISCOVERY PUBLISHING HOUSE PVT. LTD.
4383/4B, Ansari Road Darya Ganj
New Delhi - 110 002 (India)
Phone: +91-11-23279245, 43596064-65
Fax: +91-11-23253475
E-mail: discoverypublishinghouse@gmail.com
sales@discoverypublishinggroup.com
web: www.discoverypublishinggroup.com

Printed at:
Infinity Imaging Systems
Delhi

CONTENTS

PREFACE

Teaching is a very sophisticated profession. It requires a special knack for knowing things and transferring knowledge to others. A teacher also requires an acumen for imparting education and training the minds of the students. In fact, a teacher is the role model for his taughts.

Teaching needs a particular skill and one has to master it, if he or she desires to become an effective teacher. Thus, our teachers—particularly young and those, who are under training—need a comprehensive book enlightening them on teaching skills and helping them master the art of teaching.

Hopefully, this book would serve the purpose.

—Author

1

INTRODUCTION

Teaching-learning process is as old as human beings are on earth. It has been carried out not only by human beings but also by animals to teach their young ones to adjust themselves successfully with their environment. With the passage of time, it has undergone revolutionary changes.

If the teaching-learning process is effective, then the child is able to make the best use of the things in the world around him. If a child has not learnt the art of living harmoniously with others, he will find himself beset with more difficulties than the person who has learnt how to establish social relations with his fellows. So the acquisition of knowledge, skills and attitudes which enable us to adjust ourselves in an effective manner to the environment may be said to be the aim of teaching-learning.

Teaching-learning process is a means whereby society trains its young ones in a selected environment (usually the school) as quickly as possible to adjust themselves to the world in which they live. In primitive societies this adjustment meant conformity with the things as they were. In advanced civilisation of the modern times, effort is made not only to adjust to things as they are but also to make an advance in the improvement of conditions of life by training the young in the modes of thinking and acting which will help to improve the conditions of living that surround them.

Teaching-learning has four aspects: teacher, student, learning process and learning situation. The teacher creates the learning situation for the student. The process is the interaction between the student and the teacher.

Teaching-learning process is a means through which the teacher, the learner, the curriculum and- other variables are organised in a systematic manner to attain p e-determined goals and objectives.

Teaching-learning process simplifies the various elements of the teaching-learning situation have to be brought into an intelligible whole. The teaching-learner activities which are varied and complex have to be harmonised. These elements and activities indude learners and their individual differences, the methods of teaching, the material to be taught, class-room conditions, teaching devices. and aids, questioning and answering, assignments, thinking, enjoying, creating, practicals skills, discussions and many others.

Teaching-learning process is influenced by the totality of the situation. Teaching learning is fruitful and permanent if the total situation is related to the life situations. Teachers can play an important role in, facilitating learning when they take into account the needs of the learners.

Interaction between the teacher and the learners is the core of the teaching learning process. This interaction through a sort of three way communication, results in behaviour changes in the learners.

A learner needs the help of a teacher when he wants to learn any subject and to solve any problem. The process of guiding the learner involves eight steps—communication from the teacher to the learner (steps 1 and 2), from learner to teacher (steps 3 to 5), and again from teacher to learner (steps 6 to 8). Through this 3-way communication, teacher could direct his course of teaching concretely. On the other hand, learner can know how well his learning is progressing and how sure he can make his way of learning. So teacher should establish firmly this 3-way communication between many learners and himself.

The formative evaluation in step 7 and KR in step 8 are important to conduct the effective teaching learning processes. KR is a kind of feedback information which has many types. For example, in responding to his behaviour, teacher, says: "good," "wrong," "no," "well," "hum," "wonderful," "interesting" and some times repeats and summarizes learner's opinions. Sometimes teacher gives many non-verbal KR, nodding, smiling, winking, and making gestures.

Teaching and learning are interlinked. We cannot think of teaching without learning. The teacher teaches and the students learn. Teaching is not in a vacuum. It is therefore obvious that for making teaching learning sound and effective in our educational institute the teaches must look into its various aspects very carefully and critically so that they contribute in making teaching-learning inspirational and relevant. Following are the chief aspects:

Command, planning and organisation of the subject matter or content and activities. There are no two opinions about the important factors that the success of the teaching-learning process greatly depends upon the thoroughness of knowledge of the subject matter to be taught by the teacher. The soul of effective teaching learning is good command of the subject matter. The next aspect is to present the subject matter to the class. Here we enter into the field of organisation of the subject-matter and the use of methods of teaching and teaching technology. The teacher's endeavour will be to use different dynamic and progressive methods of teaching and learning. He should encourage the students to develop proper habits of learning. He should stress self-learning on the part of the students.

Class control and discipline. Appropriate class control and discipline is one of the most important characteristics of a successful teacher. A good teacher is one who can control his class not through fear or high-handedness but by virtue of his interest in the learner, good command on the subject-matter and the ability to present it interestingly and effectively. The learners also appreciate good teaching and cooperate with the teacher in the teaching-learning process.

Psychology of Learners. It must be realized by a teacher that all his knowledge of the subject-matter, his ability to present it methodically and effectively and his ability to control the class situation ably, while teaching will be effective only if he takes into consideration the interests, abilities, aptitudes and limitations of the learners. A teacher must learn to understand his learners and encourage them. He has to be sincere and honest towards his learners. An ideal teacher is always humble. He has to practise tolerance and patience in dealing with the learners. The participation of the learners is very important and necessary if the teaching learner has to have a broader and meaningful process.

Evaluation. Evaluation has an important place in the teaching learner process. A teacher should carefully evaluate his students to find out how they can make more progress. He may use a variety of methods for this purpose. Self-evaluation by both the teacher and the student is very important.

Teaching remains central to both learning and evaluation. There is an interrelatedness between teaching objectives (ends), learning experiences (means) and evaluation (evidence of what is taught and learnt). Evaluation is the process of determining— (1) The extent to which an objective is achieved (2) The effectiveness of the learning experiences provided in the classroom and (3) How well the goals , of teaching have been accomplished.

In evaluation one has to know where students were at the beginning if we are to determine what changes are occurring.

In evaluation one has to obtain a record of the changes in pupil by using appropriate methods of appraisal.

In evaluation one has to judge, how good the changes are in the light of the evidence obtained.

Evaluation may lead to changes in teaching technology and also in learning technology.

Thus, evaluation comes in at the planning stage when teaching objectives are identified. At every point of learning, evaluation is an attempt to discover the effectiveness of the learning situation in evoking the desired changes in students.

Evaluation is integrated with the whole task of teaching and learning and its purpose is to improve learning and not merely to measure its achievement. In its highest sense, evaluation brings out the factors that are inherent in student growth such as proper attitudes and habits, manipulative skills, appreciations and understanding in addition to the conventional acquisition of knowledge.

It has been rightly observed, "The definition of evaluation places it in the stream of activities that expire the educational process; these activities can be reduced to four essential steps: identification of educational objectives, determination of the experiences students must have to attain these objectives, knowing the pupils well enough to design appropriate experiences and evaluating the degree to which pupils attain these objectives."

Objectives provide the starting point on which are based all the learning experiences which in their turn are the material of evaluation.

Teaching Objectives. Our teaching objectives are the changes we wish to produce in the child. The changes that must take place through education are represented in:

1. The knowledge children acquire
2. The skills and abilities children attain
3. The interest children develop
4. The attitudes children manifest

If education imparted is effective, then the child will behave differently, from the way he did before he came to school. The pupil knows something of which he was ignorant before. He understands something which he did not understand before. He can solve problems he could not solve before. He can do something which he could not do before. He revises his attitudes desirably towards things.

Specific Classroom Objectives. These objectives must involve points of in formation,the skills and attitudes to be developed and interests that could be created through the particular topic or subject taken up for work in the classroom:

A statement of classroom objectives:

(1) serves as a basis for the chores of classroom procedures that should provide for suitable experiences to the children.

(2) serves as a guide in seeking evidence to determine the extent to which the classroom work has accomplished what it set out to do.

Learning Experiences. A learning experience is not synonymous with the content of instruction or what the teacher does. Learning results from the active reaction of the pupil to the stimulus situation which the teacher creates in the class. A pupil learns what he does. He is an active participant in what goes on in the class. Changes in a pupil's way of thinking and developing concepts, attitudes and interests have to be brought about gradually. No simple experience will result in the change. Many experiences, one reinforcing another, will have to be provided. They may have to be repeated in increasing complexity or levels in meaningful sequence extended over a period of time. A cumulative effect of such experiences will evoke the desired change of behaviour with reference to a specific objective.

The following considerations will be useful in the selection of such experiences:

1. Are they directly related to goals?
2. Are they meaningful and satisfying to the learners?
3. Are they appropriate to the maturity of the learners?

It is worth bearing in mind that learning is what students do, teaching is what the academic staff does and that improvement in teaching can only be demostrated if there is consequential improvement in learning. On the other hand, improvement in learning may occur for reasons that have nothing to do with teaching, for example, students are able to spend more time, gain better access to libraries and become more strongly motivated.

As observed by proof. R.S Adams and others, "Students may learn what the teacher intended them to; they may not. Furthermore, teachers, like others, are fallible, they may not always teach correctly. It follows then that in any learning situation, students may learn correctly what the teacher taught incorrectly or may learn incorrectly what the teacher taught correctly-or fortunately, the opposites."

Finally, although students certainly do learn because of the instructions they receive, they also learn in spite of the instructions they receive. In the process of accommodating to what is being taught students attempt to 'fit' the new experience—into their past experience in to the knowledge, insights and understandings that they have accumulated previously. It is this capability of human beings to transcend their immediate circumstances, to, add into their 'learning' their past experiences, that complicates the instructional process and makes it difficult for teachers to tailor the learning experience appropriately for their (unusually diverse) students. As a consequence, the instructional strategies are often based on different assumptions. Some deliberately set out to exercise control over the learner by : (i) either trying to exclude outside influences; or (ii) by trying to build beyond them; or (iii) by trying to overpower them. For example some earlier attempts at programme learning tried to confine student attention precisely and exclusively to the material to be mastered. Other more sophisticated mastery learning programmes attempt to both discover and start from what the learner's basic knowledge is and to provide 'branch' programmes catering for individual differences. Operant conditioning, of course, has always represented an attempt to 'override' other influences, however powerful they might be. Outside these more mechanistic strategies, other instructional strategies have been based on other assumptions. For example, where students are expected to learn by emulating their instructors (e.g. as in medical and veterinary training) reliance is placed on observational 'learning.'

Teaching operations and learning operations are interlinked. Nevertheless teaching operations to be successful must take into account the learning operations needed to accomplish the teaching objectives which themselves are based on learning objectives. It is therefore, desirable to consider the learning operations first. Learning operation are as under:

1. Discrimination of stimulus situation.
2. Response or cognition.
3. Assimilation of relationship between specific elements of the situation and the response.
4. Developing application and control over the environment.
5. Definite behavioural changes.

Teaching operations may be enumerated as under:

1. Presentation of stimulus in a specific control.
2. Bringing suitable responses by organising appropriate learning experiences.
3. Elucidation and elaboration.
4. Setting up drill and review exercises for fixing up the behaviour in the repertoire of learning.
5. Evaluating learning outcomes.

Variables and Components in the Learning Process

1. Task to be learned.
2. Characteristics of the task to be learned.
3. Characteristics of the learner.
4. Conditions under which effective learning takes place.

Components of the Teaching Process

1. Instructional goals
2. Entering behaviour
3. Instructional procedures
4. Performance assessment

A close review of the components of learning and teaching processes reveals that there is a close correspondence between the two. Performance assessment becomes a part of the teaching process so as to confirm whether or not the instructional objectives are realised and it provides a feedback to other components and also supplies data for developing teaching technology.

Modern teaching-learning process assigns an important place to student-activity. It calls for a child-centred approach. The most distinctive feature of modern society is its science-based technology which has been making a profound impact not only on the economic and political life of a country but also on its educational system. The changes that occur as a result of the impact are broadly described as 'Modernisation'. This modernisation has affected the teaching-learning process in many ways. The recent changes in the concept of teaching-learning process have led to the development of newer areas of educational endeavour. In a traditional society the aim of teaching-learning was the assimilation of the accumulated-stock of knowledge. But in the modern society, the main aim of teaching learning is not acquisition of knowledge alone. It is the awakening of curiosity, the stimulation of creativity, the development of proper interests, attitudes and values and the building of essential skills such as independent study. Teaching-learning process has to serve as a powerful instrument of social, economic and cultural transformation of the society. Teaching-learning process is conditioned by the nature and demands of society to which the learner should get adapted and attuned. One of the main aims of teaching-learning in the modern society is to keep pace with the advancement of knowledge and skills.

For a pretty long period, the teaching-learning process has been by and large, a process dominated by the institution of professional teachers. Now, the process is to be replaced to a great extent by a process in which the individual learner is expected to take up challenges through an inevitable intellectual revolution. The intellectual revolution has been enabled futher by forces of hardware technologies at low cost, socialization process due to interdependence. Besides, projects, farms, factories, markets, excursions and playgrounds will become classrooms in the new teaching-learning process.

2

THE DIMENSIONS

Kothari Commission begins its report with this remark, "The destiny of India is being shaped in its classrooms no doubt a sound programme of education plays a significant role in nation's development and the quality of education programme is greatly determined by the quality of teachers. Hence, in order to improve the quality of education, it is necessary to have a sound programme of professional education of teachers." In our country we have the B.Ed , programme to train, secondary school teachers. Several training' institution's are production a large number of trained teachers every year. But does this increase in the quantity of teachers, could improve the quality of our education programme? Are they really able to shape the 'Destiny of India in its classrooms? If it is not so than why? Why are they not performing their jobs properly'? What is wrong with them? It means somewhere there must be some lacuna in their professional development. The teachers preparing programme, i.e., B.Ed. programme must be having some deficiencies, resulting in the deterioration of the quality of teachers.

The purpose of this discussion is merely to analyse critically the prevailing B.Ed. programme, pointing out its weakness and providing some suggestions for its improvement.

The purpose of the selection of the candidate is to choose the candidates, who really possess an aptitude for teaching, having a sound knowledge of their subject having a positive attitude towards teaching profession. The present position of selection of candidates for training in India is not satisfactory. The criteria for selection, in a way, is academic record, which are neither valid nor reliable. A student may get good marks merely by chance or by using unfair means, or by memorizing the subject matter. He may be intelligent enough to get good marks but it does not ensure his interest and positive attitude in the teaching profession. It is seen that some candidates come into this line because of certain forces, while they were not intended for it. This type of inadequate selection of candidates contributes to a great extent in the deteriora-tion of the qualities teachers would not only improve the quality of training but also save the personal and social wastage.

Therefore, some elaborate techniques for the selection of candidates for admission should be used somewhat like that of C.I.E. Here are some suggestions to improve the selection procedure:

1. Candidates should be interviewed. The interview should be structured. A well prepared schedule should be used.
2. Intelligence Test, like Raven's Progressive Matrices Test should be used.
3. Test of General Knowledge should be applied.
4. Tests in school subjects showing his competence in his field of study.
5. Language test should be used.
6. Aptitude, interest and attitude inventory should be used.

A well directed guidance service provided in teacher's college will be of considerable help in giving scientific advice to the prospective candidates. It is necessary that candidates who wish to join a teacher's college should be able to analyse themselves, and determine as objectively as possible their own suitability for the teaching job. Selection of student-teachers will become easier with this kind of willing cooperation from these seeking admission.

The second determination of B.Ed., programme -deficiencies is the time period provided for the training of teachers. In our country, the period of training of teachers for secondary schools has all along been of one year after graduation-the effective session being of eight to nine months. The main purpose of teacher-education programme is to develop healthy attitude, broad based interest and values consistent with the dignity of training profession and thereafter, develop a personality too. It is not possible for a training college during the short duration of nine months. Even a slight change in attitude towards pupils and the profession would take longer time. If teachers preparation has be raised from the level of training in certain skills to real education and development of teacher's total personality increase iii the period of training is essential.

The main aspect of teacher-education programme is its organization. The organization of teacher-education programme determines the quality of the programme as well as that of the teachers. The job which is to be performed by the teachers, is needed to be analysed in order to organize the programme for their teaching. A teacher has to teach several groups to students in a school. He stays in the school for at least five to six hours. Besides his classroom teaching, he may have to be incharge of serval class activities. He has to understand and discharge the various organizational and administrative duties of the school as and when required. He is also expected to maintain a pleasant human relations with all concerned.

The existing training programme does not provide adequate, opportunities to the student-teachers to have enough competency to face the varied type of situation faced in their real teaching life. The main reason of it is that the organisers of teacher's training programme are not aware of the real existing problems of schools. They are not in direct contact of schools. The new teachers face those problems in the school and learn by experience only how to solve those problems. Therefore, something that a teacher does in a school, does not get a place in training college and something that training college has got within its curriculum has little bearing on the school practice. This gap between the school and the training institution leads to a number of limitations such as the growth of content stagnates, methodology getting state and contact with academic discipline become weak.

Hence, it is necessary to establish a close matching between the work schedule of the teacher in a school and the programme adopted for teacher-preparation in a training college.

In the. B.Ed. programme, there are some papers which have to be prepared by the student-teachers. Out of which have to be prepared by the student-teachers. Out of which, I would like to analyse the three main papers, i.e... Principles of Education, Educational Psychology and History of Education.

A student-teacher should know the fundamentals of education in respect of socio-political and economic background. The meaning of education, the objectives, the socio-cultural and politico-economic background various agencies that influence education, the principles that guide construction of curriculum are a few items among the thematic content these topics do not have direct relevance to the job of a teacher. Because it is necessary for an adult to know about these things and student-teacher has to learn curriculum. But in a short duration of 9 months, a proper preparation towards a good orientation seems impossible, hence they are treated as topics to be covered very much through lectures.

Therefore, the areas that need improvement are (i) allowing more time to learners to do good reading for a sound build-up of the intellect and attitude, (ii) punning the existing course, (iii) arranging for experiences of exchanges other than merely attending lectures, and (iv) changing completely the mode of testing inputs.

Knowing the child in all his stages of development and in the numerous aspects of his stages of development and in the numerous aspect of growth assumes a big mass of information necessary for the teachers to master. This is for facilitating overall guidance-education personal, social, intellectual and the like-to the child at school. The conditions in the school are such that such valuable experience gained in training college do not find justifiable use in the school. Within the rigid programme of the school, the very implications are forgotten. The book learning fades away as the time advances. Theories of learning prescribed in the course are not of any use in the classroom situations. These theories are not developed on the basis of human experiences and in our education process we have direct concern with the teaching theories rather than the learning theories.

The study of the history of educational development is again not a significant value. What is the use of it to study History, while we have a vast present and future before us? Though it is acceptable that one can analyse the present and can see into the future only when he knows the past. But the short period of nine months and other more significant courses like Education Technology compel not to give more importance to the history of education. It is desirable to study the reports of different education commissions constituted after independence but not the whole history from the very primitive stage.

The general, it is desirable that the content of the teacher-education programme should be taken from the real life situation. It must have direct implications in the daily school teaching. The teaching, practice of the student-teachers should be directly related to their theory courses. It will help them to understand and to make use Of the knowledge provided to them in their theory courses.

The next point of dispute on which the emphasis provided is the theory and practical aspects of teacher-education programme. In most of the institutes more emphasis is given to the theory in respect the marks and time. The ratio of marks generally remains, between theory and practice as that of 5:2. In some institutes practical aspect is given equal importance to that of theory. It is considered that to develop the teaching personality of student-teacher teaching practice plays a significant role along with the sound theory programme.

The main purpose of the teaching practice programme is to help the student-teachers to acquire the power of observation, attention, teaching imagination and a sense of time. He learns how to prepare his lesson independently and how to mark pupil's work.

Requirements for teacher-education in our set up rightfully put emphasis on practice-in-teaching and some sessional practical work. Just the enumeration of the Practical Work is a list-rich and varied-ranging from school assignments, projects, to psychology practicals and visual education. Besides it constitutes craft work, community services and co-curricular activities. The programme of practical work is intended to strengthen the school practice of the student-teacher when he is under training and later to add to the dimension of his role as a teacher-in-service. But the planning implementation of such practical work, makes a very poor show. Usually these activities assume importance so long as the pupil are under training. Very little of the impact of such activities are carried over to the school practice field.

Even after all kinds of elaborate arrangements regarding placing practice-in-teaching are made non-serious to the task of teaching, deficient sense of duty, irresponsibility, aimlessness and indifference to children, lack of innovative measures in teaching are great obstacles in the development of pedagogical skills.

The reasons for these may arise from the improper system of organization of student-teaching and the nature of the supervision of practice-teaching. As regards to the organization of student-teacher, there is no any satisfactory system for it. Generally the department of education large colleges initiate trainees for teaching quite early. They give importance to lectures on general and particular methods of teaching quite early in the session in order to prepare the trainees for the teaching they have to do.

In general a trainee has to teach 40 to 60 lessons spread out during the whole session. The college does not have a system to organize any internship in teaching or even block teaching. Under the guidance of the method master the trainees as early as in august are put into actual contact with children and classroom teaching situation. The class teaching usually starts soon from 10 A.M. to I P.M. and classes of theory papers from 2 P.M. to 5 P.M. The practice-teaching programme spreads out from August to March. The placement of students in schools for teaching undergoes changes. The allocation depends upon the availability of classes in school so much so that sometimes some teachers may have to teach continuously for two terms, Sometimes a student completes teaching lessons in one subject before the takes up teaching in the other. There are some general problems related to the schools provided for practice-teaching. In availability of classrooms, indifference of the students to be taught, generally make the teaching practice ineffective, Some times it is seen that two or more pupil-teachers take their classes under the same roof. This one example may draw a sketch of the prevailing position of the organization of teaching practice.

Criticism lesson is also one part of the teaching-practice. This is aimed to assess the overall teaching personality of the student-teacher after having a sufficient amount of training. This assessment becomes a basis for the final examination of the student-teacher.

To improve the organization of teaching practice, there are some suggestions like: Free-teaching preparation should be made adequate; internship practices should be exercised and the theory classes should be suspended.

SYSTEM AT WORK

The purpose of supervision is the improvement of instruction objective and in the student-teaching situation. The supervisory organization for teaching and the supervisory techniques and practice aimed at bringing improvement in the instructional activity of the student-teachers by familiarizing the student-teacher, on the one hand, with various techniques and practical skills in teaching and on the other, help them to develop confidence in facing the classroom situations.

Supervision before classroom teaching aims at guiding the student-teachers in planning their lessons. They have to learn to organize contents of their teaching, formulate suitable gestures of right type to evoke right of their teaching, formulate suitable gestures of right type of evoke right responses from the students and develop other related abilities and skill that enable to enter and successfully face the class with confidence. In the existing situation, the students are asked to prepare the lesson-plans themselves without introducing them with its proper procedure and the lessons plans are checked superficially. No any type of discussion is made be the subject method specialist. The students are free to enter the classes without, having any type of previous knowledge of facing the classroom situations.

Supervision during the classroom teaching is generally exercised by the teachers of training colleges. The teaching practice is organized in local schools scatted mostly from amongst those in the vicinity of the training institutions. The training colleges arrange a system of team supervising the student-teaching of student-teachers in a school. The team of supervisors may or may not relate from one school to another. The teaching of student-teachers is supervised by either teacher. He may or may not be the method specialist. Therefore, the student to tend to receive a general supervision from the college supervisor who are often neither subject method specialist nor have been the active school teachers of the subject for years. These supervisors mostly offer descriptive type of criticism though constructive type of criticism is desirable one. These remarks are related to the general personality of the student-teachers—

(a) Questioning,

(b) Black-board work,

(c) Class Management and Discipline, and

(d) Overall impression.

The supervisor seldom critically appreciates the student knowledge of the subject and the order of its presentation to the students. The supervisors fail to supervise all the lessons taught by a trainee and in many cases not more than 25% of the lessons are being supervised. The percentage of lessons supervised by the subject method specialist varies from 5% to 25/% of the lessons taught by a student-teachers.

The reasons for the lack of supervision and the faulty staffing pattern resulting in shortage and non-availability of the subject method specialist, uneven distribution of teaching subject among the student' teachers, lack of time and too many lessons to be supervised in a class period, i.e., ratio of student-teacher, teacher-education is inappropriate, defective time table etc.

It is suggested that the supervision of student-teaching be the joint responsibility of the college faculty represented mainly be the method master and the school teachers and major share of responsibility in this enterprise should rest with the school teachers because the supervision of student-teaching requires more than simply the art of teaching. To guide and appraise the student-teacher, the supervisor must obviously have a more through understanding of his field and of such educational discipline like psychology and such a supervisory can generally be available in a college faculty. Therefore, the school teacher should be assisted in his work of supervision of student-teacher by the college supervisor of student-teaching. Frequent conference and consultations between them will not only help to relate them to practice, but will also help the student-teachers to improve the performance in a realistic school setting. The student-teaching will continue to fall short of its potentialities until the method specialists and the successful school teacher are given the highest status in the faculty and are help responsible for highest status in the faculty and are help responsible for organizing supervision and carrying out the student-teaching programme.

At last the two main weaknesses of B.Ed. programme can also be highlightened which are, as the B.Ed, programme does not emphasize on the knowledge of the basic subject meaning there by that there is no provision to increase and strengthen the knowledge of the particular subjects of the student-teacher. The whole teaching practice remains indifferent with regard to the subject knowledge of the student-teacher.

Secondly, the whole B.Ed. programme does not make the student competent enough to complete his whole prescribed syllabus in his real teaching life within the limited time of session. The teaching practices which he exercised during his training period does not help him to take his class-perfectly and-to complete his prescribed course within the period provided.

In teaching practice, the student-teacher should be given a chance to face the real problems of classroom teaching, They should practice the particularly skill needed for their particular subjects. They should know how to complete their course and how to perform other related work other than the teaching.

Lastly, I would like to conclude that the teachers' training programme to produce good teachers has a significant value in our country. So, it is essential to bring improvements in the prevailing B.Ed. programme in order to make the maximum use of the potentialities of our nation.

CURRENT SITUATION

In the post-independence period teacher-education has registered a tremendous expansion. There are at present about 2100 teacher-education institutions. These include State Institutes of Education, Secondary Training Institutions and University Departments of Education, elementary, pre-primary and special branches. In a survey it has been shown that the members of the staff in such institutions are by large inadequately prepared for the job. In the study of secondary teacher-educators it has been observed that only 5 per cent of them have a doctorate degree. The elementary stage presents a still worse situation.

The majority of teacher-educators of this stage are mere graduates with a bachelor's degree in education holders of master's degree are very rare in them. The same is the case with pre-primary training institutions and the special fields, viz; physical education, guidance and counselling, science education, Hindi teaching English teaching, audio-visual instruction and craft education. In the last ones most of the teacher-educators are quite well up in their special branches but they lack the pedagogical background.

The major weakness in the existing system of professional education remains the same as was stated by the Education Commission in 1966. Their, observation quoted as below is valid.

"By and large, training institutions for primary and secondary teachers have remained isolated form the main stream of the academic life of the university, as well as from the daily problems of the schools. The quality of training institutions remains, with a few exceptions, either mediocre or poor. Competent staff is not attached, vitality and realism are lacking in the curriculum and programme of work which continues to be largely traditional, and rigid techniques-are followed in practice-teaching with a disregard for present day needs and objectives.

Some of the glaring defects which persist in our teacher-education programmes may be enumerated as follows:

Artificiality in Courses of Studies Including Theory, and Practice

Teacher-Education courses at different levels are the continuation of the patterns adopted more than a quarter of a century ago. They embody a course content which is not helpful in preparing an effective teacher. The theory courses in particular have no articulation with practical work and teaching skill requirements. The application of theory to practice is reconcile and leaves enough room for revision and restructuring. The weightage on content is negligible. The weightage on content is negligible. The methods courses are routine and wanting in practical bias. The emerging concepts of educational technology have yet to make an impact of them. There is no conceptual framework in the overall course structure.

The practice-teaching course as prescribed has assumed the form of a meaningless ritual and its carry-over potential in the development of a dynamic strategy for handling instruction problems in actual classrooms is very poor.

Ineffective Methods of Teaching

Teacher-educators in our country are averse to innovation and experimentation in use of methods of teaching . They have shown a remarkable allegiance to the traditional method of instruction, viz, lecturing and dictating of notes. Their acquaintance with modern classroom communication devices is inadequate. In many cases the lectures are dull, monotonous and uninspring. As a consequence of this our student-teachers can only talk about the methods by cannot use them with facility and case. The various logical and psychological operations involved in the act of teaching are indicated in non-coherent way. There is absolutely no manifest or learnt concern on the part of teacher-educators to achieve in a planned and systematic way the awareness and control over the instructional technology.

Less Emphasis on Development of Professional Attitude

The entire teacher-education programme is so designed that little emphasis is laid on the development of professional attitude which is so important for a sound programme of teacher-education. Needless to comment that in so The of the states the teacher-education programme has been commercialised and optimum saving is made through the revenue raised through the income elicited from the capitation fee charged from student-teachers of B.Ed. classes. This practice has necessarily resulted into substandard facilities in the colleges. This is generally reflected in the policies followed in the recruitment of teacher-educators too. The 'poor quality of teacher-educator coupled with the sub-standard provision of facilities, is largely responsible for lack of vigorous and dynamic programme on the campus. The effort to build a proper democratic attitude through a community life gets undermined. The net result is that no importance is attached to development of sound professional ethics during the period of teacher-education.

No Impact on School Practices

The Education Commission has rightly observed the teacher's education, both a primary and the secondary level, has become isolated from schools and current development in school education. The method of teaching followed in the schools, their curricula and various requirements are totally different from those advocated and actually implemented in the teacher-education departments. There is no genuine concern for bridging this gulf between what the schools do and what the teacher-education department strive for. The school consider the teacher-education department as a alien institution and not a nursery for the professional development of school teacher. The teacher-education departments in their turn just observed the formality of finishing the prescribed number of lessons little caring for the soundness of pedagogy involved in the procedure.

Poor Academic Background

In most of the institutions proper admission procedures are not observed. The student-teachers have to use public pressure and underhand methods for securing a seat in the teachers' colleges. In a large number of instances those applying for admission to teacher-education departments, do not have the requisite motivation and the academic background for a well deserved entry in the teaching profession. Such student-teachers remain indifferent to work and studies'. In some of the states the girls get admitted in quite a sizeable proportion because of their merit. But due to their family circumstances and other handicaps, they never enter into the teaching profession and in any case are not willing to serve in the rural areas. This has partly created the ghost problem of untrained teacher backlog. In some of the states the female teachers, because of lack of mobility, are available for being hired on considerable reduced rates of emoluments. This in its wake has engendered mal-practice of several forms.

Lack of Proper Facilities

The teacher-education programme is given a step-motherly treatment in most of the general Arts Colleges and in the University Departments. About 20 percent of the teacher-education institutions are being run in rented buildings and there is no facility for an experimental school or laboratory, library and other equipment necessary for a good teacher-education department. In most of the teacher-education institutions there is no separate hostel facilities for student-teachers.

No Effort to Regulate Demand and Supply

The State Education Departments have in majority of cases no control in the starting of post-graduate teacher eduction departments. The teacher-education departments on the other hand have no data what so ever on the basis of which they may work out the desired intake for their institutions. There is a considerable lag between the number of teachers required and the number of teachers made available to the market. This has contributed to the problem of unemployment and under-employment of a varying magnitude.

Little or No Interaction

The teacher-education departments in the states are like cut off isolated and at present there is nothing very exemplary in them on the basis of which they may function as models for the University Departments. It is also a fact that other university departments treat the teachers' training section as something inferior. They run away from the idea of collaborating in any programme sponsored by teacher-education section. Even in areas such as evaluation, teaching methods and curriculum development , teacher-education departments have not been able to make any dent.

Research in education is considerable neglected. Whatever research is being reported is of a very inferior quality. The teacher-education programmes have not been properly studied by undertaking any systematic research. The result is that unwarranted suggestions based on mere speculation become the guiding principles in conducting teacher-education programmes.

There is little stimulus provided to the teacher-educators for their professional growth, because of which even the' Summer institutes which are being run' with the help of UGC and NCERT are not able to deliver the goods. Most of such programmes are being conducted in a routine and un-imaginative manner. Even the association of teacher -educators has deteriorated in quality as far as its deliberation's are concerned. It has not contributed anything so for towards developing of a sound professionalisation of teacher-education in the country.

Inadequate Financial Provision

In most of the states teacher-education is still-being -run by the fee collected from student-teachers. The share of state grant is much too small, This has told upon the financial health of teacher-education institutions and most of them are in a bad shape. It is largely because of this that the facilities in teacher-education departments are of a sub-standard nature.

RIGHT DIRECTION

A scrutiny of the statement of problems will reveal that what is needed is a vigorous and planned actions which should be supplemented with an in ameliorating the situation as it exists today:

(1) The courses of studies both in theory and practice should be reorganised. For this a pragmatic research should be conducted by some universities to see what is the course structure which will be helpful for realisation of the goals of teacher-education. The ratio of theory and practical work-should be specially studies and a special programme should be developed for recording various type of practical work/practical activities which are required to be conducted in school. A comprehensive hob analysis of teaching in our schools should be necessarily made the basis for re-casting of courses in teacher-education.

(2) The method of teaching in the teacher-education departments should be such I that it inspires a sense of appreciation among other departments of the university and colleges. A teacher-education department should, therefore, conduct special innovative programmes in the following directions. Seminar, combining of 'seminar and discussion's with lectures, term teaching, panel discussions, and projects sponsored by the faculty members for improvement of learning in various spheres.

(3) A strong break-through should be made by organising M. Phil. (Education) for such students who hold Master's Degree in other disciplines. This course should be both terminal and preparatory.

(4) For development of professional attitude it will be advisable to recognize the colleges of education as unit in themselves. Such an institution should be equipped with facilities for organising various type of activities such as daily assembly programmes, community living, social work, library organisation and other curricular activities which promote democratic spirit of mutual appreciation and fellow feeling.

(5) The practising schools have to be taken into confidence. For this the members of the staff of teaches, colleges

should be closely associated with the schools. It will be better if the faculty members of teacher-education departments work in schools on regular 'basis from time to time. Similarly the senior teachers of secondary schools should be brought in the fold of teacher-education department mid mutual dialogue should be initiated. The courses of studies and the practical work and, practice-teaching can be easily moderated in such a way that they will have useful implications for improving school practices.

(6) The admission procedures of B.Ed. should be completely systematised and necessary steps should be taken to make it full proof against tempering and meddling as far as possible. It will be advisable to evolve suitable admission procedure through studies, but at present the whole problem is that of restoring confidence in procedure of admission.

(7) It will be in the fitness of things if at the time of setting up a teacher-education department, a demonstration school is made integral part of it and a definite norm should be followed for certain facilities such as laboratories, libraries and other important audio-visual equipment.

(8) There should be a planning unit in each State Education Department. The function of this unit should be to regulate the demand and supply of teachers at various levels of schools. This unit can also be given the responsibility of projecting future requirements of teachers 'in categories.

(9) The teacher-education department should be made a nucleus for research on teaching curriculum and, evaluation, in the regular university departments. It can also be entrusted the 'responsibility of sponsoring programmes for extension such as bringing the community into close contact with the university academicians. The' teacher-education departments may be: improve suitable

with the help of the university professors of eminence. There should be a free exchange of scholars from one department of the other particularly in the subjects of nature and biological science and languages. This will improve the quality of teacher-education programme immensely.

(10) Teacher-education programme should be organized on the basis of evidence obtainable from research in such areas as follows:

(a) Teacher behaviour.

(b) Developing a conceptual framework and a theory of instruction.

(c) Innovative practices of teaching such as Micro-teaching, Stimulation and interaction analysis.

(d) Theory courses to be prescribed at various issues.

The findings of such researches should be implemented wherever there is a scope and thus, the entire teacher-education programme should be vitalised with the help of research.

(e) The professional association of teacher-educators should be streamlined by broad-basing its present composition. It should include eminent scholars from different disciplines and teachers of various levels so that its professional strength is increased. For professional growth of teacher-educators there should be seminars, summer institutes and research symposia at more frequent intervals.

(f) The state Government should make adequate provision for funds for teacher-education departments. They should be treated at par with other colleges and departments of the university for all sorts of grants. Special assistance should be given for running an experimental school and holding of practice-teaching sessions in various schools.

(g) As in the case of agriculture, there should be at last one school of education in each state which should provide different levels of teacher-education programmes.

(h) There should be a staff college for in-service education of training college and university teachers.

(i) There is a paucity of sound text-books and auxiliary reading material, including reference books in Hindi and regional languages, in the field of teacher-education. Statewise organisations be set up along the lines of Hindi Granth Academies in close cooperation with teacher-education institutions and departments to encourage and provide good professional literature to students of education.

(j) Universities should have independent Faculties of Education so that teacher-education institution and departments enjoy greater autonomy and freedom in formulating programmes.

Correspondence courses in teacher-education should be provided, with a strict and high screen for admissions and a rigorous manner of assessment. As matter of fact this should apply to the regular attendance courses too.

(k) Libraries in the teacher-education institutions are generally very poor. In each state there should be a special library for teacher-education which must have complete and comprehensive Reference Section equipped with all available journals for must be set up to code all research material.

Now NCTE is working in the direction to improve our teacher-education programmes to remove these defects at national level.

Exercise

1. Enumerate the problems of teacher-education problems and their causes.
2. Suggest some remedial measures for solving these problems.
3. Indicate the problems of teacher-education and identify the causes Suggest some practical ways and means for the improvement.
4. Write short note on the following:
   (a) Problem of Methodology of teaching.
   (b) Problem of Admission Criteration.
   (c) Problem of Student-teaching
   (d) Problem of Theory and Practical.

3

ROLE OF EDUCATION

Teaching is an essential part of education. Its special function is to impart knowledge, develop understanding and skills. It generally excludes inculcation of values like truth. It is usually associated with the in parting of knowledge of 3 R's - Reading, Writing and Arithmetic- representing various school subjects. Education, on the other hand, has a wider connotation. It implies 7 R's - Reading, Writing, Arithmetic, (All three denoting school subjects), Rights, Responsibilities, Relationships and Recreation (Requirements and ideals of a modern democratic state). In teaching we limit our outlook omitting those more important means of education which are involved in the school as a systematically organised social community, including its tone or general moral environment, its government and discipline, and that potent influence - the personality of the teacher. James Welton observes, "We treat teaching by itself, because it is an aspect of school life which can be singled out in thought, though it cannot be separated in reality, from the whole of which it forms a part and because it covers a fairly consistent body of doctrine. It is true that the value and success of all school teaching depends on those wider and deeper elements of school life-tone, discipline, etc. - which are omitting. But it is true that whilst the latter may be excellent the former may be of poor quality.

BASIC IDEAS

Albert Einstein (A Swiss Physicist 1879-1950): The supreme art of teaching is to awaken joy in creative expression and knowledge.

American Educational Research Association Commission in 'Handbook of Research on Teaching' (1962): Teaching is a form of interpersonal influence aimed at changing the behaviour potential of another person.

Amidon and Hunter (1967): Teaching is an interactive process, primarily involving classroom, which takes place between teacher and pupils and occurs during certain definable activities.

Anatole France (French novelist 1844-1924): The whole art of teaching is only the art of awakening the natural curiosity of young minds for the purpose of satisfying it afterwards.

B.O. Smith (1963): Teaching is a system of actions involving an agent, an end in view, and a situation including two sets of factors those over which the agent has no control (class size, size of classroom, physical characteristics of pupils etc.) and those that he can modify (ways of asking questions almost instructions and way of structuring information or ideas gleaned.)

Burton (1963): Teaching is the stimulation, guidance, direction and encouragement of learning.

Clark (1970): Teaching refers to activities that are designed and performed to produce change in student (pupil) behaviour.

Floyed Well (1958): Children are notoriously 'curious about everything except the things people want them to know. It then remains for us to refrain from forcing any kind of knowledge upon them and they will be curious about everything.

CaWeo Calieleo (Italian astronomer 1564-1652): You cannot teach a man anything, you can only help him to find it himself.

HE. Morrison (1934): Teaching is an intimate contact between a more mature personality and less mature one which is designed to further the education of the latter.

Israel Sheffler (1966): Teaching may be characterised as an activity aimed at the achievement of learning and practised in such a manner as to respect the student's intellectual integrity and capacity.

John Dewey (1859-1952): One might as well say he has sold when no one has bought, as to say he has taught when no one has learned.

John Bmbacher (1939): Teaching is an arrangement and manipulation of a situation in which there are gaps and obstructions which an individual will seek to overcome and from which he will learn in the course of doing so.

John Chapman (1960): The gift of teaching is a peculiar talent, and it implies a need and craving in the teacher himself.

Joyce and Well (1972): Teaching is a process by which teacher and students create a shared environment including set of values and beliefs (agreement about what is improvement) which in turn colour their view of reality.

J. Wilton: To know where the pupils are and where they should try to be are the first two essentials of good teaching.

Michael Oakeshort (1966): Teaching is two-fold activity of communicating information and communicating judgement.

N.L. Gage (1962): Teaching is a form of interpersonal influence aimed at changing the behaviour potential of another person.

Ned. A. Flanders (1970): Teaching is an interaction, process. Interaction means participation of both teacher and students and both are benefited by this. The interaction takes place for achieving desired objectives.

Paul Goodman (1980): A good teacher feels his way, looking for response.

Thomas P. Green (1971): Teaching is the task of a teacher which is performed for the development of a child.

W.R. Ryburnt (1946): Teaching includes the training of emotions of the child. It is one of the means of giving right feeling to the children.

William Lyon (1970): In my mind teaching is not merely a life work, a profession, an occupation, a struggle, it is a passion. I love to teach, as a painter loves to paint, as a musician loves to play, as a singer loves to sing, as a strongman rejoices to run a race.

Yoakm and Simpson: Teaching is a means whereby society trains the young in a selected environment as quickly as possible to adjust themselves to the world in which they live.

In the type of teaching as mentioned by Morrison, teaching is reduced to what the teacher does. There is interaction but the flow of instruction is from the teacher. In this type of teaching, the learners may become passive listeners

Brubacher's definition of teaching assigns more place to the learner. This approach tends to be child or learner-centered.

B.O. Smith seems to be more pragmatic in his approach to teaching. He accepts certain limitations of the learner in the teaching learning process.

Smith's definition contains the following three elements:

(a) Teaching is a system of action.

(b) Teaching is a goal-directed action.

(c) Teaching takes place in a situation comprising the controlable and uncontrolable set of factors.

A review of the definitions given above reveals that to play his role competently in teaching, a teacher is expected to understand the significance of the following:

Who is to teach. The teacher is to teach and he must .. understand himself thoroughly—his strengths and weaknesses and strive to present a reasonably good model before his students.

Whom to teach. The child is to be taught. Therefore, a teacher should understand him thoroughly - his abilities, aptitudes, attitudes, manners and temperaments and accordingly cater to the individual differences of students.

Why to teach. The teacher should always keep in view that the aim of education is to develop harmonious personalities, who are culturally refined, emotionally stable, ethically sound, mentally alert, morally upright, physically strong, socially efficient and spiritually enlightened. He should not forget even for a moment that the traditional 3 R's have been replaced by 7 R's, that is, reading, writing, arithmetic (representing various disciplines), rights, responsibilities, relationships and recreation.

Where to teach. The teacher ought not to visualise the school to be merely a place of imparting information but a place where men of tomorrow are trained to take their place as enlightened citizens in the society and contribute to national development.

What to teach. The teacher must have mastery over the subject he teaches.

How to teach. The teacher must use new teaming-learning technology to make his teaching. Effective and inspirational.

When to teach. Appropriate steps need to be taken by the teacher to develop motivation of the student in the entire work.

TEACHING INSTRUCTIONS

Instruction is primarily concerned with the development of knowledge and understanding in the pupil about a thing, system or process. Imparting of knowledge and understanding merely represents one of the several objectives which we want to achieve through teaching. Teaching is concerned with all the domains of pupil's behaviour, i. e., cognitive, conative and affective. Instruction is a part of teaching.

The distinction between teaching and instruction may be seen from another angle. The face to face interaction of the teacher and taught found in teaching is not so much essential in the process of instruction . In instruction, a teacher may be replaced by the programmed material, computer, teaching machine, radio and television etc. A teacher cannot be replaced by these aids. Of course, in teaching a teacher makes use of them. Thus, instruction is one of the several modes of teaching.

THE SIGNIFICANCE

Teaching is giving Information. There are many things that the students cannot find out for themselves. There are many things that they can never know unless they are told. There are many things the use of which they do not know. These things they have to be told. So one essential part of teaching is communicating knowledge. Knowledge must be given in a systematised manner. Teaching should be-made interesting. It must, however, be stressed that knowledge aspect should not be unduly emphasized.

Teaching is Causing to Learn. It is wrong to think, that knowledge can be passed on from one person to another like money. Knowledge will be received only when the students are prepared to receive it. Real teaching consists in persuading the child, by one method or the other to learn for himself. The teacher is an instrument in helping a child to learn how to do things for himself.

Teaching is a Matter of Helping the Child to Respond to his Environment in an Effective Manner. F.N. Freeman observes, "It is not what is presented to the child which educates him, but rather the reaction that he makes to what is presented. Certain children may fail entirely to respond to a lesson, or may respond in a wrong manner. If a child's response to his geography is to memorize the words, without any understanding of the facts they represent, the lesson is ' educative for him (he has not been taught), although it may be educative for the child next to him who reacts properly."

Teaching is Helping a Child to Adjust himself to his Environment. A child is reacting in some way or the other to his physical and social environment, from his very birth. His reactions are both fruitful and harmful. Teaching should help the child to make successful adjustment. This may be done in two ways. Sometimes we modify the environment and at other times strengthen the child. Teaching should make the child socially efficient, that is, a worthy member of society, making his contribution to the common good. Yoakam and Simpson: write, "Teaching is a means whereby society trains the young in a selected environment as quickly as possible to adjust themselves to the world in which they live. In primitive societies this adjustment means conformity with things as they are. In more advanced civilizations, such as ours, effort is made not only to adjust to things as they are" but also to make an advance in the improvement of conditions of life by training the young in modes of thinking and acting which will help to improve the conditions of living that surround them."

Teaching is Stimulation and Encouragement. Teaching should fire the enthusiasm of the child. It is to encourage the child in the development of his natural desires to work, and to be active.

Teaching is Guidance. Teaching is to guide the pupils to learn the right things in the right manner and at the right time. Teaching is to guide the students to do things in such a way that time, material and energy are not wasted.

Teaching is Training the Emotions of the Child. Ryburn observes, "It is also the encouraging and training of the emotion all life. This is an aspect of teaching which is very commonly neglected', at least in practice. But our teaching will be only one-sided and distorted unless we take into account the 'necessity for helping the child to develop a stable emotional life." Teaching is to develop the emotional life of the child by providing an atmosphere of love, affection and freedom. Teaching is to provide such activities as will sublimate their instinctive urges to action.

Teaching is Both a Conscious and an Unconscious Process. Teaching is both a conscious and an unconsciously process and the most effective part of it is generally the part of which we are unconscious. The personal relationships between the teacher and the taught have a great bearing on the growth of the child.

Teaching is a Means of Preparation. Though preparation for future is not the only aspect of teaching, yet it is an important aspect: Teaching is to help the immature child to develop physically, intellectually, emotionally and spiritually to participate effectively in the life of the community.

Teaching is Formal as well as Informal. Formal teaching is deliberately planned, systematically organised and is always purposive. Teachers are just formal agents of teaching. School is not the only agency of teaching. Informal teaching is carried on by the parents, brothers and sisters at home, playmates, student community outside the classroom, etc. The few hours of the school are insufficient for the full development of the child. Formal and informal teaching must coperate, if good results are to be achieved. School should 'supplement' not 'supplant', the training imparted by the home and *vice-versa*.

Teaching as a Skilled Occupation. Every successful teacher is expected to know the general methods of teaching and instruction in creating suitable learning situations. He is also expected to be familiar with the general objectives of education.

Teaching is an Art. Art implies the intelligent action of a human being through which it is possible to modify an ordinary course of events. Teaching is an art which can be improved through research.

Teaching is a Form of Social Service. The teaching profession is regarded to be a sort of social service and the teachers as servants of society in whose hands has been entrusted the task of shaping and developing the behaviour and conduct of the young children for maintaining and improving the social patterns.

Teaching as a Relationship. Teaching is a, relationship which is established between three focal points in education, the teacher, the child and the subject. Teaching is the process by which the teacher brings the child and the subject together. The teacher and the taught are active, the former in teaching and the latter in learning.

Teaching as a Skilled occupation. Every successful teacher is expected to know the general methods of teaching and instruction in creating suitable learning situations. He is also expected to be familiar with the general objectives of education.

Teaching is Both an Art and Science. Silverman (1966) has expressed the nature of teaching in these words, "To be sure teaching-like the practice of medicine-is very much an art which is to say, it calls for exercise of talent and creativity. But like medicine, it is also a science, for it involves a repertoire of techniques, procedures and skills that can be systematically studied, described and improved. A good teacher, like a good doctor, is one who adds creativity and inspiration to the basic repertoire."

ROLE OF TEACHING

1. Creating learning situations.
2. Motivating the child to learn.
3. Arranging for conditions which assist in the growth of the child's mind and body.

4. Utilizing the initiative and play urges of the children to facilitate learning.
5. Turning the children into creative beings.
6. Inspiring children with the nobility of thoughts, feelings and action.
7. Giving information and explaining it.
8. Diagnosing learning problems.
9. Making curricular material.
10. Evaluating, recording and reporting.

TEACHING STANDARDS

Sri Aurobindo describes the marks of good teaching in these words, "The first principle is that nothing can be taught. The teacher is not an instructor or task master, he is a helper and guide. His business is to suggest and not to impose. He does not actually train the pupils's mind, he only shows him to perfect his instruments of knowledge and helps and encourages him in the process. He does not impart knowledge to him, he shows him how to acquire knowledge for himself. He does not call forth the knowledge that is within, he only shows him where it lies and it can be habituated to rise to surface. The distinction that reserves this principle for the teaching of adolescent and adult minds and denies its application to the child, is a conservative and unintelligent doctrine. Child or man, girl or boy, there is only one sound principle of good teaching. Difference of age only serves to diminish or increase the amount of help and guidance necessary, it does not change its nature."

John Dewey (1859-1952) states, "The more a teacher is aware of the past experiences of students, of their hopes, desires, chief interests, the better will he understand the forces at work that need to be directed and utilized for the formation of reflective habits." Further he writes, "The teacher is a guide and director, he steers the boat but the energy that propels it must come from those who are learning."

Albert Einstein (1879-1955) has observed, "It is the supreme art of the teacher to awaken joy in creative expression and knowledge.

Montaigne, a French philosopher (1533-1592) advises, "A tutor should not be continually thundering instruction into the ears of his pupil, as if he were pouring it through a funnel, but, after having, put the lid, like a young horse, on a trot before him, to observe his paces, and see what he is able to perform, should according to the extent of his capacity, induce him to taste, to distinguish, and to find out things for himself, sometimes opening the way, at other times leaving it for him to open."

Joseph Payne (English educator, 1808-1876) writes, "The teachers part in the process of instruction is that of guide, director or superintendent of the operation by which the pupil teachers himself."

Swami Vivekananda (1863-1902) describes the role of the teacher in teaching as, "The true teacher is he who can immediately come down to the level of the student."

Following are the marks of good teaching :

Good teaching recognises individual differences—Good teaching treats each child as unique. Good teaching recognises that catering to individual differences brings strength. It must be remembered that standardized procedures do not fit every pupil.

Good teaching is causing to learn—Good teaching enables the child to learn for himself. It is not stuffing the mind of the child with information. Good teaching is what we can make the child do for himself.

Good teaching provides opportunities for activity—The child is inherently active. Passiveness on the part of the child implies that he is not in good physical and mental health. A good teacher keeps the students active. He is aware of the fact that to keep the students disciplined, he must fill the time with work and he does so accordingly.

Good teaching involves skill in guiding—A good teacher motivates his teaching. He stimulates " through his personality and his activities the personalities and activities of the pupils." He creates such situations as lead to desired types of learners.

Good teaching is kindly and sympathetic—Good teaching must create an environment of acceptance, sympathy and understanding.

Good teaching decreases the distance i.e. to either teacher and the taught—Teachers should come out of their ivory tower and come as close with the students as possible.

Good teaching is not tied to any method—Methods, techniques and devices should be adopted to local situations and considered as servants and not masters.

Good teaching is cooperative—Good teaching is an active and living process. A good teacher seeks the cooperation of the learners.

Good teaching is kindly and sympathetic—A good teacher always creates. A cordial atmosphere in the classroom. He always ensures his pupils's emotional stability and security. He is loving, kind, affectionate and sympathetic to his pupils. He bears in mind this fact "love the child and he will love you, hate him and he will hate you." He avoids scolding and sarcasm.

Good teaching involves careful planning—Good teaching keeps in view that everything cannot be taught to children at every time. A good teacher carefully studies the mental make-up of the pupil he teaches, studies the individual differences of pupils and then prepares his subject-matter. An unplanned lesson often results in a failure and involves a waste of time, energy and money also.

Good teaching is democratic—A good teacher always respects the individuality of his pupils. He keeps democratic ideals, contents, methods and objectives in view.

Good teaching provides desirable and selective information—The good teacher does not try to teach all the available information that he gathers form books and experience. On the other hand he makes a judicious selection and teaches all that is useful to live a good life as responsible member of the society.

Good teaching helps the child to adjust himself to his environment—Man has been struggling against natural forces since ages. He is expected either to adjust himself to these natural forces or to adjust the forces to himself. A good teacher helps the child in both directions.

Good teaching is progressive—A good teacher aims at improving his modes and techniques steadily. He also helps the child to make suitable progress in life.

Good teaching leads to emotional stability—There are very powerful inherited urges which always cry for expansion. A good teacher knows that unguided expression leads to wilderness, and therefore, helps in providing his pupils suitable opportunities which assist in training and sublimating their urges and emotions.

Good teaching is both diagnostic and remedial—A good teacher makes use of the various measuring instruments which have been provided by psychology and discovers the intelligence, aptitudes and interests of children and accordingly plans his work.

Challenge of Education-A Policy Perspective (1985). A publication of the Ministry of Education, and a forerunner of The National Policy on Education-NPE 1986, has something worth quoting, on quality of education. It states, "It is difficult to define quality, particularly with reference to educational processes. However, it could be stated that a quality conscious system would produce people who have the attributes of functional and social relevance, mental ability and physical dexterity, efficacy and readability and above all, the confidence and the capability to communicate effectively and exercise initiative, innovative and experiment with new situations. To these personal attributes one could add the dimensions of a value system conducive to harmony, integration and the welfare of the weak and disadvantaged."

Quality teaching also known as effective teaching is the chief instrument of quality education. It is essentially concerned with translating the objectives of education into action and practice. It is concerned with how best to bring about pupil learning by various activities. Quality teaching may be defined as the teacher's ability to stimulate students intellectually and move them emotionally to instill in them love for learning and develop suitable skills and attitudes.

Quality teaching is based on the premise 'All teachers should teach well and all students should learn well'.

An understanding of the following facts would go a long way in quality teaching:

1. Effective teaching is a comprehensive concept. Several variables are involved in teaching.

2. All types of variables play their part in teacher-learning situation.
3. 'What' and 'how' of effective teaching should be carefully comprehended.
4. There are several models of teaching and each should be considered in the overall context of teaching.
5. All models are complimentary to each other.
6. A teacher should adopt an electric approach in the selection of a model.
7. Developing a personal model of teaching in consonance with the requirements of quality teaching should become the cherished goal of every teacher.
8. Skill in creating intellectual excitement has two components: The clarity of an instructor's communications and their positive emotional impact on students.
9. Quality teaching results from a teacher's skill attracting both intellectual excitement and positive rapport with students.
10. The development of good rapport is based on three qualities in the teachers interaction with students: the teacher cares for student progress, the teacher has consideration for students as learners and the teacher respects students as individuals.
11. The three elements involved in teaching competence while contribute to teacher's authority and prestige are: Mastery over the subject, interest in the subject and effective learning situations and experiences.
12. Quality teaching presupposes an understanding mind; a feeling heart and a lofty personality.
13. In quality teaching the environment is of mutual cooperation and of purposefulness. A play-way spirit is the chief characteristic of the work.

A *'A'* is for alertness on the part of the teacher to the multifarious needs of the learners. Alertness is very helpful in taking appropriate decisions and timely corrective measures.

'A' is also for adaptability in handling several situations.

B 'B' is for businesslike attitude. It is to be ensured that every learner in the class, remains busy in realizing the goals set.

'B' is for balanced behaviour.

C 'C' stands for cooperative teaching-learning. The learners must be made active partners.

'C' is for clarity of purpose. The teacher and the learners must be clear about the goals for the achievement of which they are working.

'C' is for clarity of the subject-matter taught. A teacher must make all possible efforts to make his lesson clear. Difficulties of the learners must be appreciated and clarified.

D 'D' stands for democratic classroom environment.

'D' is for discovery. Children should be guided to find out new facts, ideas and principles. It helps children in becoming independent and resourceful learners.

'D' stands for democratic discipline.

E 'E' stands for expectancies. Each learner should be expected to learn. No learner should be considered without any potential.

'E' stands for enthusiasm. The teacher himself must demonstrate enthusiasm for his work.

'E' stands for appropriate etiquettes.

F 'F' is for feedback. Feedback helps the teacher and the learners to take timely corrective measures for the completion of the task.

'F' stands for faith of the teacher in himself.

G 'G' is for goal-setting. Appropriate goals should be set for the learners. They should also be made clear about the suitability of goals. Efforts may be made to associate the learners with the setting of goals.

H 'H' is for hard work on the part of the students as well as teachers. .

'H'is for humour. Humour on the part of the teacher releases fatigue and tension.

'H' stands for human touch.

I 'I' stands for involvement of all the learners in classroom activities and experiences.

'I' stands for impartial attitude.

'I' stands for inspirational teaching-learning.

J 'J' stands for just attitude.

'J' stands for judicious rewards and punishments.

K 'K' stands for knowing children's abilities, aptitudes and interests.

'K' stands for the knowledge of the sub-matter.

L 'L' stands for linking present, past and future knowledge.

'L' stands for leadership qualities.

M 'M' stands for motivation.

'M' stands for management of the class.

N 'N' stands for needs of the learners and their satisfaction.

O 'O' stands for open-mindedness.

'O' stands for out of class activities.

'O' stands for objectivity in approach.

P 'P' stands for praise. Verbal and non-verbal praise of children can motivate them to hardwork.

'P' stands for personal contact with every learner.

Q 'Q' is for quiz. From time to time, quiz competitions may be arranged in the class.

'Q' stands for quality teaching.

'Q' stands for question-answers.

R 'R' stands for review of the lesson.

'R' stands for relationships.

'R' stands for resourcefulness.

S 'S' stands for success experience. Success motivates the learner to achieve more.

'S' stands for scientific temper.

'S' stands for self-analysis and self-control

T 'T' stands for technology of teaching.

'T' stands for tutoring which involves removing difficulties, individually or in small groups.

V 'V' stands for undivided attention to teaching.

'V' stands for unbiased attitude to the treatment of controversial issues.

V 'V' stands for visual aids.

'V' stands for variety of experiences.

'V' stands for voice-modulated.

'V' stands for variation in the presentation.

W 'W' stands for welcoming attitude.

'W' stands for warmth towards students.

X 'X' stands for X-ray of the teaching process. It implies finding out of the difficulties and potentials of the students.

Y 'Y' stands for yardstick i.e. same standard basis of making a judgement on the performance of the students.

'Y' stands for you, implying that you (student) are the most important element in the teaching-learning process.

'Y' stands for zenith or excellence.

Either J. Swenson in The Teacher's Letter (1952) states that each of the following seven wonders brings a new challenge to the classroom teacher:

First wonder. How much children are ready know before they come to school. They bring with them rich resources of knowledge, skill and understandings-mostly self-learned.

First challenge. How much do I know of these rich resources? How far do I go in searching them out? How do I use what I find?

Second wonder. Children's eagerness to learn. It is natural for children to inquire, to discover. It is unnatural for them to be passive, disinterested.

Second challenge. How do I use this eagerness to learn? In what direction should it be channelled? Am I feeding it or killing it?

Third wonder. The never-ending process of learning. Every hour of the day, no matter where he is with whomever or whatever he works, the child learns.

Third challenge. Is he learning what is best for him, now and later? Am I setting the stage for constructive learnings?

Fourth wonder. The infinite variety of abilities, personalities, needs, and interests of pupils. He who says, "I know children" has not taken time to study the marvels of their growth.

Fourth challenge. Do I know as much as I should about each child's abilities, personalities, needs, interests? How can I learn more? Do I accept differences or rebel against them?

Fifth wonder. The concomity of learning. Simultaneously, children learn subject matters, traits of personality, habits of working, attitudes and appreciations-many of them permanently.

Fifth challenge. Do I push so hard toward a single goal that I push the children away from another of equal importance? Do I leave these "marginal learnings" to chance?

Sixth wonder. The faith, respect, loyalty and tolerance to children. When a teacher treats them well—sometimes even when' he does not—they will respond with respect and understanding.

Sixth challenge. Do I have an equal faith in them and in their motives? Am I as loyal to them and their welfare? Do I treat them with respect and understanding?

Seventh wonder. The ability of children to teach. Each child learns form the other, and even the teacher can learn much from children. .

Seventh challenge. Do I use my opportunities to learn from children? Do I listen, literally and figuratively, to the lessons they can teach?

TEACHING CONCEPT

Several attempts have been made to analyse activities involved in teaching with a view to understand it scientifically, design teaching materials and methods for realising the specific objectives efficiently, and to evaluate and modify it in the light of the feedback.

Plenlders, Ned. S. (1959) of the University of Minnesota was the first educator to categories all the sets of verbal behaviours (teaching activities) of a teacher in the classroom while interacting with students. He classified these activities into three categories:

1. Teacher Talk. 2. Pupil Talk and 3. Silence/confusion.

1. Teacher talk was further categorised as under:

(1) Indirect influence which includes (a) Accepts feelings (b) Praises or encourages. (c) Accepts or uses pupil ideas (d) Asks questions.

(2) Direct influence which includes (a) Lecturing (b) Giving directions (c) Criticising or justifying.

2. Pupil talk which induced (a) Pupil talk response (b) Pupil talk initiation.

3. Silence or confusion.

Komesnr, N.P. (1966) tried to analyse teaching into various specific activities like introducing, demonstrating, contrasting, explaining, proving, justifying, explaining, defining, appraising, amplifying, rating, interpreting, questioning, elaborating, identifying, conjecturing, confirming etc.

Gagel NL. (1968) attempted .to analyse teaching in terms of technical skills. According to him, "Teaching skills are specific instructional techniques and procedures that a teacher may use in the class room. They represent an analysis of the teaching process into relatively discrete components that can be used in different combinations in the continuous flow of the teacher's performance."

Clarlcs, S.CT. (1970) analysed teaching in terms of some specific activities that are designed and performed to produce change in student's behaviour. Those activities may be of cognitive, affective or conative nature and belonged to different levels.

Brown, B.B. (1968) analyses teaching by considering it as a manysided activity which includes several activities like questioning, giving information and listening etc.

Modern Technology	*Traditional Technology*
1. Based on modern scientific principles and discoveries.	1. Based on old techniques of teaching.
2. Emphasises the development of critical thinking power of the learner.	2. Stresses memorisation.
3. Uses team teaching.	3. Teaching by individual teacher.
4. Stresses group activities.	4. Listening to lectures of teachers.
5. Uses individualised techniques	5. It is a technique of mass instruction teaching.
6. It defines objectives of teaching clearly.	6. Objectives are usually vague.
7. Teaching material is thoroughly prepared.	7. Little preparation is done.
8. Time required to master the material may vary across students.	8. Time for completion is same for all students.
9. The teacher's role is not to teach in the sense of subject matter presentation but to manage the instructional environment, diagnose students, direct the use of available resources.	9. The teacher is primarily responsible for all subject matter preparation and also must prepare and administer tests and mange the 'house keeping' details.
10. Materials used in the class-room include new media, measurement techniques and they are coordinated.	10. General guidelines are given by the administrator.
11. Objectives of instruction are subject to review.	11. Generally there is very little review.
12. The purpose of student evaluation (tests and other measures) is to help the student by providing feed back on performance, diagnosis of strengths and weakness and providing information for making decisions such as extra help, environment programme etc.	12. When tests are supposed to be used for diagnostic purposes, they are generally used only to establish grades.
13. It is, by and large, student-centred.	13. It is, by and large, teacher-centred.
14. Classroom environment reflects freedom and spontaneity.	14. Classroom environment reflects authoritative attitude of the teacher.

Passi, B.K. (1976) states that teaching constitutes a number of verbal and non-verbal teaching acts like questioning, accepting pupil response, rewarding, smiling, nodding to pupil response, movements, gestures, etc. These acts, particularly in combination, facilitate the achievement of objectives in terms of pupil growth.

Jnngira, N.K. and Singh Ajit (1982) present the analysis of teaching as, "Teaching can be analysed in terms of teacher behaviour at least at three levels viz, component teaching skills, competent teaching behaviours and atomistics teaching behaviours."

ROLE OF TECHNOLOGY

Teaching technology involves the mechanism of instructional process in the classroom situations, levels of teaching, theories of teaching, principal teaching operations and establishing relations between theories and teaching operations.

Teaching technology as a concept can be classified into four well-defined components. These components are: (i) Manpower, (ii) Methods, (iii) Materials, and (iv) Media.

As a method, it implies making use of a few devices such as programmed learning, team teaching, micro-teaching, personalized system of instruction, etc.

As materials, it comprises instructional materials, comprising programmed text-books, manuals, guides, text and other written/ print materials, which expose to the learner the contents of these sources of materials.

As media, it implies audio or visual or both audio-visual media such as radio, tape recorders, films, educational television as teaching aids to supplement effective teaching and to promote better learning.

Whatever be the method, material or media, it requires man-power to operate/utilise in the teaching learning environment. Thus, the four M's constitute a whole sequence of chains of; inputs/facilities in teaching technology.

Exercise

1. "To know where the pupils are and whom they should try to be are the first two essentials of teaching." Explain this statement.
2. What are the most essential things that a teacher should know to make his teaching effective?
3. "Teaching is a tripolar process or relationship." Elucidate this. "Good teaching is giving information." Do you agree with this view? Give arguments in support of your answer.
5. Explain the marks of good teaching.
6. What is quality teaching? On what factors does it depend?
7. State the factors which determine effective teaching.
8. List any ten activities involved in classroom teaching.
9. Explain the 4 M's of teaching technology. How does modern teaching technology differ from the traditional one?

4

THE TRENDS

The objective of such a course for the B.Ed. students are:

(a) To orient the incoming students to the nature, scope and significance of their respective training programme.

(b) To orient them according to the needs and responsibilities of the Education Department.

(c) To orient them according to the specific course choice available in their respective programmes.

(d) To develop closeness and familiarity with their classmates and advisors.

The course is organized for a period of 4 to 6 days depending upon the needs of the students. The syllabus for the entire programme is developed in advance and is circulated among the students and the members of the staff. The entire course is conducted through group discussions under the leadership of students.

This is a new technique for in-service teachers. Correspondence, courses are being successfully done by different professional groups in serval countries of the world. Experts who have visited U.S.A., U.S.S.R. and Australia have reported that correspondence courses are regarded in these countries as a normal vehicle of education in many areas. In 1961, the experts of India strongly recommended that selected Universities in India should experiment with correspondence courses. University of Delhi was the first to start correspondence courses. 'The N.C.E.R.T. consti-tuted a study group which reported in 1904 about correspondence courses in Training, Colleges. The group pointed out the correspondence method it if may be applied to the professional education of teachers should be adopted to meet two special requirements of teacher-education; first, to adequate facilities for the development of teaching skills through practice-teaching and secondly continuous contact between the student-teacher and the institution.' The four regional colleges of Education and the' Central Institute of Education, Delhi have undertaken the bold experiment of correspondence courses of the Regional Colleges of Education, there is a provision of two summer courses of 2 months each. It is too, early to predict the result of such an experiment.

ROLE OF RESEARCH

Action Research has been found to be a very commendable technique for trying out a number of programmes of qualitative improvement in various spheres of school education. In Teacher-education, some experiments have been planned and conducted to improve the actions and decisions related to the various aspects of the programme. University College of Education, Dharwar has already done a pilot study with regard to improving to content knowledge of the student-teachers and making them more efficient in teaching than what they usually are. Some of the conclusions of the study are :

(a) Seminars, discussions and workshop, even though of short duration, will help to improve the content knowledge of the student-teachers.

(b) Acquainting the trainees with the techniques of teaching and demonstration of skills and involving them in a series of rehearsals of teaching at the beginning does not seem to help to improve their skills of teaching more quickly than the usual practice. It could, however, be concluded from the findings of the self-evaluation test that favourable attitude could be created through such methods.

SIMULATION FACTOR

Phillip W. Perdew defines simula.tion as activities which are similar to teaching and observing but which are not, in fact, carried M" the regular classroom.

This may involve the use of new media such as audio or video-tapes of teaching situations, intermittent photography,, and micro-teaching with video play back. It may also include more traditional approaches such as the college student-teacher his fellow students, as if they are high school pupils.

Better Supplementation to Laboratory Experiences : In fact, if this technique is of interest to teacher-educators not only as a tool for research but also as a means of enriching, supplementing and replacing inadequate aspects of laboratory experience.

Provides Better Rehearsal Ground : In fact, these techniques achieve their maximum potential in the pre-student-teaching learning experience and may become a new kind of demonstration laboratory prior to student-teaching.

INTERACTION ASSESSED

In the field of teacher-education, teacher's classroom interaction has also been taken as target and attempts are made to analyse it and to quantify it.

Thus, we see that most intensive long range programme of this dimension has been conducted under the leadership of Ned, A. Flanders. In his study Flanders found that the verbal patterns of teachers in high achieving classroom were significantly different from those in low achieving classrooms.

Advantage: The following are the main advantages—

(1) It is an objective and exploratory device for analysing classroom interaction.

(2) Teacher behaviour may be improved when it is used along with micro-teaching.

(3) It is highly used for in-service teachers for evaluating them and for improving.

(4) It also acts as feedback mechanism.

(5) It helps in formulating due self-concept and proper self-evaluation of teachers.

COLLECTIVE EFFORTS

Team teaching is also called cooperative teaching. It occurs when two or more teachers share in planning and conducting instruction that is offered to the same group of students, whether they may be at elementary, secondary or college levels.

A great variety of organizational patterns, included under the label of 'Team Teaching. Teams vary in size from 2 elementary teachers who share the instruction offered to 40 or 50 students of teams made tip of many as 8 teachers and over 200 students.

Teacher assignments for the teams represent a considerable number of role and specializations. Team roles include those of team leader, master teacher, part time teacher, intern teacher, teacher aid and team clerk.

Anderson (1966) has listed seven characteristics of team teaching that represent contributions by various authors, and that may be considered as advantages:

(1) Specialization in teaching functions.

(2) Flexible sub-grouping of pupils.

(3) Flexible, efficient use of school resources.

(4) Ease of using professionals and non-professionals as supplementary teachers.

(5) Wider range of resources and technologies used.

(6) Ease of training apprentices and beginning teachers.

(7) Stimulation of professional growth of team members.

PROGRAMMED TEACHING

Programmed instruction is a revolutionary device in the science of learning, now-a-days, its use in the field of teacher-education has also attained importance. Now-a-days, there is a new trend in teacher-education to use the technique of programmed instruction for such areas as an expedient. Teaching of school subjects, educational statistics and some aspects of educational psychology have been given for trial and as a result of this, a few really good programmes are variable for student-teachers.

The Advantages—The following are the main advantages:

(1) Here the student remains active and proceeds according to his own pace.

(2) It makes optimum use of all the scientific principles of efficient learning.

(3) Here learning becomes efficient, pleasant and permanent.

(4) It may be adopted for home study, and can save the teacher from devoting time to the correction of home work.

(5) It makes learning faster, definite and more through.

The Education Commission (1964-66) has also realized the importance of teaching various subjects with the help of programmed instruction.

READING PROGRAMME

Reading proficiency is important at all ages. Reading is so inter-related to the whole educational process that educational success requires successful reading. It is pointed out that if the first button of a man's coat is wrongly buttoned all the rest are certain to be crooked. Reading is the first button in the garment of education. As such, if this is not developed in school and if it is still a drawback at the tertiary level, the college students will find it difficult in proceeding at a fast pace in academics due to reading deficiencies. Reading comprehension, reading speed and critical reading become the vital tools for the success at the collegiate level more than at the school level.

Reading is a meaningful interpretation of verbal symbols. It is an extension of oral communication and builds up on listening and speaking skills. In the early stage, learning to read means learning to vocalise the written symbols or marks. The child may say the words loud or he may say them to himself. In either case, reading means saying the correct words. The discovery that printed words 'talk' is the first step in learning to read.

While meaningful response is the very heart of the reading process, it should also embrace all type of thinking, evaluating, judging, imagining, reasoning mid problem solving.

As the child advance in his grade, from the task of recognising words, he is led to understand a new range of ideas, concepts and master new forms of expression. An efficient reader learns how to comprehend what he reads, to distinguish major form minor points to follow directions, to interpret, to summarise and make an outline. Finally reading becomes reflective and evaluative. A student must be able to grasp the meaning of a writer's ideas; and mature reader relates his previous knowledge and experience to his present reading and compares the facts and arguments presented by one with the other. The nature of the reading task, therefore, changes as the learner progresses from less mature to more mature levels. Reading is not one skill but a large number of inter-related skills that develop gradually over a period of time.

Growth and development of reading depends on two broad aspects:

1. Personal, which in turn depends on
   (a) adequate experiential background
   (b) adequate language background
   (c) adequate maturation
   (d) adequate physical development
   (e) adequate intellectual development
2. Environmental, which depends on
   (a) adequate motivation
   (b) adequate instruction
   (c) adequate work habits
   (d) adequate social and emotional development.

The effect of inhibiting factors in multiplicative rather than additive. It is illogical to expect to produce a successful reader by growth and development in only certain specifies. The teacher of remedial must given consideration to all aspects of development.

There is usually a group of interacting factors, each in its own way contributing to the reading disability or preventing future growth. The teacher must make sure that the learner is reading on a variety of subjects and must provide for readiness in all areas. He can do this only if he knows the learners assets and liabilities.

Difference in learning ability of learners are not only related to biological potential but also to the environmental opportunities. Some student get into the state of having reading disability because the environment does not call for their potential. It is almost impossible to predict the learning of the student without knowing the structure of his environment the types of behaviour that are rewarded and the kinds of rewards provided. The student from a middle class home has an advantage because his home contains 'hidden curriculum', which permits him to deal appropriately with the first school experience. The first generation learner or the student from a home where there is meagre experiential background is likely to have difficulty in reading. Some of the other causes are poor visual perception, poor auditory acuity, immature eye-movement habits, left handedness, low academic aptitude, lack of interest, emotional factors, poor sight vocabulary, lack or training in phonics, etc.

While discussing reading disability, it should be pointed out that good readers invariably read widely while poor readers seldom read anything. In order to be good tennis player, one must play a great deal of tennis. Similarly, to become a skilful and effective reader, one must do a lot of reading. A sure cure for retarded reading is to get the student to read. Lack of interest is the most frequent concomitant factor for poor reading performance. The diagnosis should, therefore, attempt to discover why a learner has no interest in reading. It should also try to discover any basic non-reading interests the learner may have that can be used as foundation for developing reading interests.

There are different types of reading programmes recommended for different readers. These can be classified as—

1. Developmental reading programme
2. Corrective reading programme
3. Remedial reading programme

FACTORS OF DEVELOPMENT

This programme emphasizes reading instruction that is designed to systematically develop skills and abilities considered essential at each level of reading advancement it, thus, encompasses also the corrective and remedial programme, and is carried on in the regular classroom. The developmental reading programme is systematic and continuous involving all the skills at all levels by all teachers.

This consists of remedial activities usually carried on by the regular teacher within the framework of regular classroom instruction. Corrective instruction is provided when the entire class or small groups of students are deficient in a particular skill. Corrective reading deals with the problems of those type of students who can identify words and comprehend what they read, but only with great difficulty.

There are two kinds of corrective reading instruction; one is for general retardation and the other for specific retardation.

General Retardation : The reading level of these students is substantially lower than their mental 'age, but no other specific problems exist. They learn only after a great deal of effort. They are like underweight children whose eating habits are not conducive to gaining weight but will if they follow a proper diet. They may not have been reading for initial reading experiences, and thus fall farther behind as their schooling is continued. Instruction may have been above the students level of ability. They perhaps were not stimulated to learn because instruction was below their ability level, or perhaps-they were absent from school at critical periods. The reading profile of the generally retarded student is relatively uniform. They need more experience in reading including systematic instruction at their level of ability. There is a need for major adjustments in materials and instruction and a reading programme that will motivate them to learn.

Specific Retardation : In specific retardation there is a definite weakness in a given area and it is usually a weakness in a specific skill. Such reading retardation is not generally complicated by neurological difficulties. Learning capacity is adequate but deficiencies in regard to certain specifics such as word analysis or comprehension indicate that they have not profited from regular class work as well as they should have. Although each student presents a distinct pattern of acquisition and remediation, there will usually be others in the class with a similar problem. Their overall reading performance may be adequate, but deficiency in a given area may impede appropriate growth. The- reading profile may show them to be high in over all ability but diagnostic testing will reveal a low sub-score on a test. There is usually a need for training for total remediation in the basic skills. The students should be kept in the regular classroom in which special help is provided to those with reading problems.

Remedial Instruction : Remedial instruction consists of remedial activities taking place outside the framework of regular class instruction and usually conducted by a special teacher of reading. Remedial instruction should thus be restricted to a small clinical group with severe symptoms of retardation in reading. It is the group that has difficulty in remembering whole word patterns that does not learn easily by the regular method and show orientational difficulties, i.e. this programme is designed for the student who is not benefiting from the corrective programme because the class teacher is either not able to or does not have the time to deal with the problems. The disability is either total or at least of an extreme nature.

FACTORS FOR TREATMENT

The type of remedial treatment given to the student depends on the character of the diagnosis made. If physical factors are responsible remedial attention should be provided. If the diagnosis should reveal that the learner has, low mental ability as indicated by non-reading and reading types of intelligence test, this factor should be taken into account while remedial programme is planned. There are students who are emotionally maladjusted, who lack interest in reading , who are deficient in general experiential background and who suffer from lack or reading practice. In every case of reading disability, the data gathered during the diagnosis should be utilized in planning the remedial programme.

A first step in a remedial reading programme is to identify students who need attention. The following procedure may be followed for this purpose:

(a) Observing student while they study

(b) Studying eye movements during reading

(c) Using interest inventory

(d) Grade text-books

(e) Standardized/teacher made tests silent and loud reading.

Informal teacher made tests can be used effectively for both diagnostic and remedial purpose. Types of questions that can be employed in evaluating reading comprehension are:

1. Questions which measure ability to understand stated facts.
2. Questions which measure ability to comprehend facts that are implied.
3. Questions which-test whether the pupil is able to gather the central idea of the passage.
4. Questions which test whether the pupil, is bale to gather the central idea from a paragraph.
5. Questions which evaluate the ability to read and understand questions.
6. Questions which check the pupils knowledge of word meanings.

The specific type of the remedial treatment to be given to a student will depend on the diagnosis made of his reading and other personality variables. Some of the general rules of procedure are:

1. Begin from where the learner is.
2. The learner should be frequently informed of his progress.
3. The remedial work must be real and vital to the learner.

4. Definite satisfaction on the part of the learner, should accompany the work.
5. A large variety of exercises and activities should be provided.

A suggestive list of a few general procedures that help in improving the reading disabilities/weakness are given below—

Improving Vocabulary—Sight vocabulary (recognise a minimum number for words at sight), wide reading, use of dictionary, systematic work study, study of derivation of works, studying unfamiliar words, etc.

Improving the Speed of Reading—Wide reading of easy and interesting material, use of time limit, Metronsocope, push card method, reading boards, reading accelerators, etc.

Improving Reading Comprehension—Reading for main ideas, writing the central idea of the paragraph, composing newspaper headlines, etc.

Skimming a book, chapter or article.

Reading for details.

Reading ability is not a unitary trait but one of a complex skills each of which must be developed by appropriate practice.

Samples of passages for remedial reading for college students of the first year are presented in Appendix D (i). The first sample has relevant questions on the reading passage so as to assess the reading comprehension of students whose achievement level is rather low. College teachers can select passage and frame questions to suit the reading level of the students. The given passages are in no way an indication of the level of the college students, not even the low achievers. They are meant to be samples based on which the teacher may prepare reading comprehension test for passages, two and three, similar to that to passage one.

In the basic skills given which will help in identifying low achievers. Their problems in terms of lack of knowledge in basic skills of addition, subtraction, multiplication and division specially in respect of fractions, decimals and use and value remedial programme carried out as per the diagnosis. Working out additional exercises and problems to get through knowledge of basic skills would enable the students to overcome their weaknesses. When a college teacher gets an orientation to this concept he will be able to help his students in a pragmatic manner.

Comments : Reading is an essential aid today to personal development and social progress. It is an indispensable factor in modern culture interwoven with work, recreating and other personal and social activities. It provides a permanent record of human experience that can be examined and studied time and again in arriving at convictions and valid generalizations. Many of these values cannot be attained so effectively through the use of mass media such as radio, cinema and television because the reader is not free to pause and deliberate at will. For many purposes there is no substitute for books and other printed materials.,

Many aids to learning which are now available create new instructional problems. Two facts should be kept clearly in mind (1) Instruction must make efficient use of all pertinent aids to learning, and (2) Attention to reading problems must keep pace with increasing demands for greater competence in critical interpretations for higher levels of culture, and for greater personal and social efficiency among youth.

Consistently throughout the high school and college years effort should be made to help develop functional reading skills, mature reading habits and positive attitudes, towards reading. But beyond these more or less traditional objectives considerable greater emphasis should be place on the development of:

1. The disposition to read in order to solve basic personal and social problems. `
2. The ability to interpret with critical accuracy the significant meanings contained in various written presentation.
3. The ability to make clear discriminating judgements and to translate decision into actions.

For such success, for mature personal-social adjustment and for keen enjoyment and emotional release, young people need to read widely and critically.

The teacher is concerned primarily with helping each student develop into a harmoniously adjusted personality. Reading is considered as one avenue through which the attainment of that objective may be facilitated.

REMEDY FACTOR

In the teaching process, teaching becomes effective only when learning takes place in students. It generally observed that not all students achieve the level that their teacher expect them to reach. Students' achievement, especially low-achievement is 'Invariable reflected in their performance in class and term tests or half yearly and annual examinations, in addition to their daily output and behaviour in the classrooms. The cumulative effect of a-student's inability to comprehend what happens in a class or his consistent low performance in tests result in not being able to meet the standards or norms of a college for moving form class to class. Because of the inability to secure the minimum level of performance required for this purpose, a student cannot pass or be promoted from one class another and stagnation at the same class for another year takes place. Such students are generally termed as non-achievers.

The term 'low-achiever' is difficult to define as it represents students with many types of achievement. It is in reality an 'umbrella term' which encompasses various kinds of achievement, with different degrees in each category. Some of the terms commonly used to denote a low-achiever are below average, dull, slow learner, under achiever, learner disabled, mentally retarded, socially and culturally deprived, under-privileged, etc. The correct connotation of some of these terms are given below:

Below Average : In terms of achievement of a particular class, the students who achieve below the average performance of students of that class are categories as below average..

Mentally Retarded : Children having an IQ (Intelligence Quotient) to 70-70 are referred to as mentally retarded. The mentally defective are feeble-minded and the severely retarded group consists of morons with 5069 IQ, imbeciles, 25-49 IQ and idiots 0-24 IQ. The morons come under the group educatable mentally retarded and the imbeciles, trainable mentally retarded. A low IQ in a child (mentally retarded) indicates that the average mental maturity level will probably never be attained and that mental development proceeds at a rate that is slower than the average. These types of student seldom reach the tertiary level.

Slow Learners : Generally slow learning students are some what below average in achievement mid general mental ability. In intelligence, they are higher than the mentally retarded (IQ 70-80) and are marked by their deficiency in some specific way-memory, imagination, attention, speed of forming association, reading difficulties, lack of basic skills and so on.

Under Achievers : An under achievers one who does not work up to his capacity mid whose achievement is far below his potential mid capacity. Under achievers as contrasted to achievers, tend to be characterised by more withdrawal behaviour and by less social work-oriented interaction with peers (Perkins 1965), by more negative self-concepts (Shaw, Edsan, and Bell 1960) by more negative self-concepts (Shaw, Edsan, mid Bell 1960) by higher mechanical and artistic interests and by lower verbal and mathematical aptitude mid by membership in lower status occupational groups. (Frankel 1960). The under-achievement syndrome could start very early in the academic life and it can also be in specific subjects.

Learning Disabled : learning disabled children differ from mentally retarded children in that they are not retarded generally. They have usually average intelligence mid able to learn in most areas but with a learning difficulty in one area. This field of learning disabilities is relatively new mid has multi-disciplinary approach including medicine, psychology and education. Three major disabilities, included in this category are : (1) Dyslaxia—a disorder relating, to language, skills or reading, writing and spelling, commensurates with intellectual abilities, (2) Dyscalculia—failure to perform the operations of arithmetic, and (3) Hypertension—children with this difficulty manifest a consistently high level of activity in situations in which it is clearly inappropriate, along with an inability to inhibit the activity on command.

Culturally Disadvantaged : This term culturally deprived implies a lack or opportunity to learn. It generally refers to students with low socioeconomic background, who live in poor conditions. Their verbal ability may be limited, even though they may excel other children in mechanical abilities. Their home provide markedly inadequate intellectual stimulation.

A brief explanation of the different categories of low achievers should enable a college teacher in trying to identify the low achievers in this class. The category of under-achievers at the tertiary level a vulnerable group that needs attention and remedial care as well as group that can attain the greatest benefit from remedial teaching.

Under Achievement : The students who are classified as under-achievers, function as though their mental capacities were unusually low but who, in fact, have considerable unused ability. 'They may be unable t o express themselves clearly in terms of standard language and in ideas and, concepts. Invariable under-achievers are isolates, lacking friends. The poor performance may be due to various causes other than lack of potential ability. These causes may be physical, intellectual, emotional and environmental.

Physically this group of students could have defective eyesights, difficulty in hearing and lacking in stamina problems that have not been rectified. Certain type of handicaps such as orthopaedic, speech and personality, need special attention and care.

Emotional causes could be intense fears, deep emotional conflicts, feelings of inferiority, insecurity and inadequacy, conflict with accepted values, unhealthy and unwise companions, high or low expectations, feeling of hatred, jealousy and revenge mid adjustment problems.

In the intellectual category would come factors such as lack of motivation, improper learning habits, dependence on memory alone, dislike for certain teachers or subjects, and lack of communication skills. Faulty teaching methods of the, teachers can also contribute to the lack of interest in' a subject leading to under achievement.

Some of the home conditions and situations like lack of adequate facilities for learning, sibling rival additional home responsibilities, attitude of parents and their preferences, lack of love and affection, quality of language used at home and parents' unfulfilled ambitions and desires could also contribute to wider achievement.

When an area is over-crowded and unhygienic, lacking in recreational facilities, and a value system hardly has a social climate, the student from such locality and environment is placed at a disadvantage position for achieving normal academic standards, if not academic excellence.

The causes listed are many but even a few or, a combination of some of them could lead to wider achievement. Unless a teacher is alert, such students potentials could not be brought to light and in turn they are not able to perform according to their potentials. How can a college teacher identify these under-achievers out of the 60 or 100 students in his class'. 'Some of the indications are listed below:

Learns well by rote, unable to reason. Short span of concentration. Learns slowly but forgets quickly. Lack motivation to achieve. The is no consistency in achievement, subjectwise in general. Imagination is generally limited but there are rays of brilliance every now and then. Reading rate is low. There are language problems. Students is immature. Personality is imbalanced. Frequently absents from class. Output in a course fluctuates.

According to the feedback from the teacher or from teacher to teacher, we also see if a student has poor self image/self concept. Negative attitude to study. Wide fluctuations in the marks/grade points obtained in class test and annual examination.

As can be from the cause and factors of identification, the under achievements syndrome develops in school and continues in college too, when the underachiever has not been provided with a suitable remedial programme to achieve according to his potentials.

In order to carry out remedial teaching for the wider achievers, the college teacher may adopt some of the recommended approaches and programmes. If the teacher can identify the under achievers and a separate group formed special remedial classes can be conducted for this group formed, special remedial classes can be conducted for this group. However, certain general principles of remedial teaching can be adopted in regular classes so that not only under achievers but also normal and over-achievers can benefit from them. College teachers should avoid introducing too many new concepts in one and the same class. Concepts are built and ideas already comprehended and developed. Unless there is clear explanation., quoting examples and giving applications values wherever mere narration of concepts and giving applicational values wherever mere narration of concepts will not lend for effective learning. The teacher has to take time to build on concepts and atleast 90 percent of his students must profit from his explanations and aids. In each class it is good for the teacher to outline specific objectives of the unit to be covered during that period and if possible put these down in one comer of the black-board so that students are able to follow different aspects of the lessons taught. Further, the teacher should not only motivate the students to study their lessons regularly but also encourage their special interest and aptitudes through further references, reading, writing of assignments, reports and doing of practical work in their interested areas. The students should achieve a feeling of accomplishment in what they choose to work on.

The under achievers need attention in small groups. Their language and communication skills should be improved so too their reading ability. It is not a psychologically healthy procedure to compare the achievement of under achievers with their classmates or siblings. They must be protected from undue comparison and undue pressure. It is a good policy to avoid creating frustration and emotional conflicts. The teacher should emphasize more of practical work than abstract thinking. The under achievers find fulfilment in doing short and specific assignments and these should be evaluated and feedback given as constructive remarks for further progress. Some of these approaches would enable the wider achievers to work towards their potential level and thereby remove the stigma of being grouped as under achievers.

SLOW PROCESS

One other group of low achievers, some of whom, enter the portals of colleges is the slow learners. Slow learners and under achievers have many common characteristics and in reality many a wider achiever is categorised as slow learner. However, the major difference is in the fact that an under achiever's potential capacity is high but he/she is not achieving that level and a slow learner is slow in specific areas in addition to having, in all probability, a low IQ, (80-90 IQ) between the mentally retarded and the average. Those slow learners who can learner well by rote but have low reason in power could enter the tertiary level classes and continue there as long as their rote memory helps them to proceed from one class to another. When other mental faculties are needed such as reasoning, problem solving, reflective thinking, etc., their rote memory fails them, and they are not able to profit from college education. However if their slowness was due to reading difficulties, lack of concentration power, and inadequate acquisition of basic skills, these can be remedied by a well-planned and successfully executed remedial programme. An effective guidance and counselling programme or student's personal service would go a long way in helping the low-achievers.

Exercise

1. Explain the term, 'Current practices' and innovation practices. Enumerate the main current practices and innovative practices, used in teacher-training.
2. Indicate the need of reading programme. Describe process of reading.
3. Explain the term 'Remedial Teaching' and indicate the methods of teaching for wider achievers, low achievers and slow learners.
4. Write short notes on the following :

   (a) Intership Teaching

   (b) Orientation Course

   (c) Simulated Training

   (d) Supervised study.

5

THE OBSERVATIONS

Teaching is an interaction process between a teacher and taught. The classroom teaching activities and events can be studied objectivity by observing these situations. Recently a number of systematic observational techniques have been developed. The classroom teacher behaviour can be measured objectivity by employing these techniques. Prior to this systematic observation, the classroom ratings have been used for observing and evaluating classroom teaching. The purpose of the rating is to be diagnosed by the use of classroom rating. Thus, the teaching can be graded but can not provide the basis for improving and modifying teaching activities or teacher-behaviour'.

The systematic observation techniques are used for analysing the teaching activity systematically and objectively. The flow of classroom events can be recorded and analysed. It provides the structure to teaching events and flow to teacher-behaviour. Thus, the teaching activities are diagnosed and provide the awareness about the teaching events and components, but teaching or teacher-behaviour has originated the concept of interaction analysis of teaching.

SIGNIFICANCE OF BEHAVIOUR

The systematic observation is a set of procedures. It uses a system of categories to encode and quantifies classroom behaviour of teacher and students.

Systematic observation is an accepted method of organizing observed teaching acts in a manner which allows any trained person who follows stated procedures to observe, record and analyse interaction with the assurance that others, viewing same situation, would agree to a great extent with his recorded sequence of behaviour.

The systematic observation represents a useful means of identifying, studying, classifying and measuring specific variables as they interaction within instructional learning situation'.

The systematic observation techniques require that observed activities and events of teaching should be encoded or classified by the use of non-evaluative related objectives set of categories which describe the specific behaviour or activities. An observational system has the pre-requisites that it includes and describes specific variables which are a part of classroom setting.

The purpose of developing the observational system is that a teacher can be trained to use them for analysing classroom behaviour and for planning and studying his own teaching activities. The basic purpose of systematic observation is to help operationalize teaching objectives in teaching strategies.

PRACTICAL ASPECTS

Since 1960, the efforts have been made in this direction to develop the systems of observation. The works of With all (1949), Flanders, and Amidon (1960), Medley and Mitzel (1948) and Galloway (1968) have developed system of observation for studying the classroom teaching activities. The observation system are of two types: 1. Sign System, and 2. Category System

Sign System : A sign system is composed of a list of behaviour. The observer simply checks or notes in some manner behaviour which occurs during a given period of time. The behaviour is marked only one during the observational period. The sign system of the Florida Taxonomy of cognitive behaviour consists of fifty five items with are grouped in seven level as defined by Bloom (1956):

(1) Knowledge, (2) Translation, (3) Interpretation, (4) Application (5) Analysis, (6) Synthesis and (7) Evaluation. The behaviour is marked only once as it occurs per six minutes observation period.

Category System : A category system is composed of a discrete set of categories. A behaviour unit is classroom events which occur during a three second of duration, e.g., Flander's ten categories system of interaction analysis consists of three major units of behaviour: A-teacher-talk, B-pupil talk and C-None of these or both. Each unit of behaviour is calculated in number of categories. The teacher-talk has been classified into seven categories, and pupil-talk into two categories.

The category system is of two types:

(a) The Reciprocal Category System (RCS), (b) The Equivalent Talk Categories (ETC.).

Reciprocal Category System (RCS) : Richard Ober (1967) of the University of Florid has put forward a modification of the Flander's Interaction analysis System known as Reciprocal category System (RCS). There Are nineteen categories in this system. The none categories are applicable to either teacher or student in a reciprocal manner and tenth category is silence or confusion. The nine categories are : warms, accepts, amplifies elicits, responds, initiates, directs, corrects and cools-make the classroom climate easy and formal. The RCS, therefore, not only enables use to estimate the nature and type of teacher-pupil interaction but also estimates the social-economical climate in the classroom by noting the warning and calling behaviour of teacher.

Equivalent Categories (ETC) : E. L. Bentley and E. Milber have developed the Equivalent Talk Category (ETC) in (1970). There are ten categories in this system; The categories emphasise the type and degree of intellectual interchange between the teacher and his pupils enabling use to determine the available opportunities for pupils to think and to infer in the classroom. This appears to be rather limited value. It makes possible to observe and measure cognitive interaction in a classroom between teacher and students. The informing and responding are basic functions which are observed by this system.

ROLE OF DISCIPLINE

The system of observation is a recent development in the field of education. The researches have introduced the system of classroom observation since early (1930, 1945, 1946) and their associates have initiated work in this direction. They were interested to explore process of interaction between teacher-taught in the classroom teaching.

Lippitt and White (1943) have studied the influence of democratic behaviour with the help of Kurt Lewin. It has a great significant from development point of view.

Withal (1949) has classified the verbal statements into seven categories, and studied social and emotional climate of classroom. Robert Wales (1950) has made a significant contribution in the area of social and emotional climate of classroom teaching.

Ned A. Flanders (195 1) was interested to study the classroom influence of a teacher on student's achievements. He developed a ten category scale for observing the classroom verbal interaction. His category system is most popular in this area.

Richard L. Ober (1968) has modified the Flander's ten categories system. He has added nine more categories in -the Flander's ten categorises. Thus, Ober has given nineteen categories. This modified system includes action and reaction both type of categories. Therefore, It is called Reciprocal Category System (RCS).

Brown, Ober and Soar (1968) have also developed Taxonomy of Teacher Behaviour.

Thus, the work of Withall (1949), Flanders and Amidon (1946) and Gallowy has pioneered the utilization of observational system in the study of classroom teacher-behaviour.

Interaction analysis is a specialized research procedure that provides information about only a few of the many aspects or provides information about only a few of the may aspects of teaching. It is an analysis of spontaneous communication between teaching. It is an analysis of spontaneous communication between teacher and pupils, and it is of no value if the many aspects of teaching. It is an analysis of spontaneous communication between teacher and pupils, and it is of no value if no one is talking or if teacher talks continuously, or if student reads from a boom. Unless additional records are kept the following kinds of information will be ignored right wrong, good or bad content information whatever is being discussed, the variety of instructional material being used the various class information during learning activities ; the preparation of the teacher as received by lesson plan and anything else not directly revealed by verbal communication.

The entire process of interaction analysis becomes a measure of teacher-influence because it makes an assumption that most of teacher influence is expressed through verbal statements and mode of non-verbal influence is positively correlated with verbal. Those, who have worked with this technique, are disposed to accept this assumption.

Interaction analysis is an observation procedure designed to minimize these difficulties, to permit a systematic record of spontaneous acts and to utilize the process of instruction by taking in account of each small bit of interaction.

ANALYSIS TECHNIQUE

Flander has developed ten categories of system. The first seven categories are used when teachers are talking and next two categories are used when any pupil is talking and the last category is used to indicate the silence or confusion in the classroom. So far as the communication is concerned, these three conditions—(a) teacher talk, (b) pupil talk, and (c) silence or confusion are said to exhaust all possibilities. It is an objective and systematised technique for evaluating the classroom performance of a teacher.

Interaction analysis is nothing more and nothing less than an observational technique which can be used to obtain a fairly reliable record of spontaneous verbal statements and to determine their quality.

Flander's instruction Analysis is concerned primarily with verbal behaviour. This can be observed with high reliability than non-verbal behaviour. An assumption is made that verbal behaviour of the teacher is an adequate sample of his total behaviour in the classroom, we must assume that the verbal statements of the teacher are consistent with his non-verbal gestures, in fact, his total behaviour. This assumption can not be easily tested since it will take too long a period to develop a reliable measure of nonverbal behaviour.

IDEAS AND FACTS

Various theoretical assumptions which are basic to very idea of interaction analysis are as follows:

1. In a normal classroom situation, it is verbal communication which is predominant.

   (Flanders 1965)

2. Even though the use of spoken language, might be resort to non-verbal gestures in classroom, verbal behaviour can be observed with higher liability than most non-verbal behaviour and also it can reasonably serve as an adequate sample of the total behaviour in classroom.

3. We can normally assume that verbal statements of a teacher are consistent with his non-verbal gestures and, in fact, his total behaviour. This assumption was sustained in terms of experience in Minnesota studies.

   (Flanders, 1966)

4. The teacher exerts a great deal of influence on the pupils. Pupils behaviour is affected to great extent by this type of teacher behaviour exhibited.

   (Anderson and others, 1946)

5. The relation between students and teacher is a crucial factor in the teaching process and must be considered an important aspect of methodology.

   (Haggerty, 1932)

6. It has been established that social climate is related to productivity and to the quality of interpersonal relations. It has been proved that democratic atmosphere tends to keep work of a relatively high level even in the absence of the teacher.

   (Lewin and other, 1939)

7. Children tend to be conscious of a warm acceptance to the teacher and to express greatest fondness for the democratic teacher.

   (H. V. Perkins, 1950)

8. The role of classroom climate is crucial for the learning process.

   (Perkins 1956)

9. The teacher's classroom verbal behaviour can be observed objectively by the use of observational technique designed to 'catch' the natural modes of behaviour which will also permit the process of measurement with a minimum disturbance of normal activities of the group of individuals.

   (Wrightstone J. Wayne, 1958)

10. Modification of teacher classroom behaviour through feedback is possible (Flanders 1963), though how much change can occur and more knowledge relating to the permanence of these changes will require further research.

    (Flanders, 1963,1966)

11. Teacher influence is expressed primarily through verbal statements. Non-verbal acts of influence do occur, but are not recorded through interaction analysis. The reasonableness of this assumption rests upon the assertion that the quality of the nonverbal acts is similar

to the verbal acts; to assess verbal influence, therefore, it is adequately a sample of all influences.

These assumptions focus our attention on the verbal participation of teachers and students in teaching-process.

THE CATEGORIES

The Flander's system attempts to categories all the verbal behaviour to be found in the classroom. It has two main categories: teacher talk and pupils talk. A third category covers other verbal behaviour, i.e., silence or confusion. The first main category is subdivided into two direct and indirect teacher's talk. Indirect influence is that subdivided into the more specific categories—(1) accepting, feeling, (2) Praising or encouraging, (3) accepting and using, ideas and (4) asking questions. Direct influence is subdivided into three categories: (5) teaching, (6) giving directions, and (7) criticising or justifying authority. Pupil's talk is divided into two categories: (8) responding to teacher, and (9) initiatory talk category (10) is usually referred to silence or confusion. All categories are mutually exclusive but subsume all type of verbal behaviour. The categorise or verbal interaction are based upon the following two major activities initiates 'initiation and response' of both the agents of classroom teaching.

An interchange between initiation and response forms the classroom verbal interaction. The non-verbal interaction takes place through on task and off task activities caused by teacher or students.

NON-FORMAL ATTITUDE

It involves the following four categories:

Category 1. Acceptance of Feelings—The teacher accepts feelings when he understands how the children feel, that they have children for their feelings. These kinds of statements often communicate to children both acceptance and clarification of the feeling.

Category 2. Praise or Encouragement : In this category jokes are included that release tension, but not those that threaten pupils or are made at the expense of individual pupils. Often praise is a single work : 'good' yes 'fine' or such as : 'Continue'. Go ahead with what are your saying 'Um hm'; go on; tell us more about your ideas.

Category 3. Accepting and using Ideas: This category is quite similar to category 1, however, it includes only acceptance of student ideas, not acceptance of expressed emotions. When a student makes a suggestion, the teacher may paraphrase the student's statements, restate the idea more simply, or summarized what the student said. The teacher may also say, well that's an interesting point of view. I understand what do you mean, Statements belonging to category are particularly difficult to recognize, often the teacher will shift from, using the student's idea to stating the teacher's own idea.

Category 4. Asking Questions : This category includes only question to which a teacher expects an answer from the pupils., If a teacher asks a question and then follows it immediately with an opinion, or if he begins lecturing, obviously the question is not meant to be answered. A theoretical question is not categorized as a question.

Direct Teacher Behaviour : This includes the following three categories.:

Category 5. Lecturing : A lecture is the form of verbal interaction that is used to give information, facts, opinions or ideas to the pupils. The presentation of material may be used to introduce, review or focus the attention of the class on an important topic.

Whenever the teacher is explaining, discussing, giving option or facts or information, category 5 is used. Rhetorical questions are also included in this category. Category 5 is the one of the most frequently used in classroom observation.

Category 6. Giving Directions : The direction about where or not top classify the statement as a direction or command must be based upon the degree of freedom that the pupil has in response to teacher's direction. When the teacher says, will a of you stand up and stretch? He is obviously giving a direction.

Category 7. Criticizing or Justifying Authority : A statement of criticism is one that is designed to change students behaviour from non-acceptable to acceptable. If the teacher is explaining himself of his authortity, defending himself against the pupil, or justifying himself, the statement falls into this category. Other kinds of statements that fall into this category are those of extreme self reference or those in which a teacher is constantly asking the children to do something as a special favour to the teacher.

Pupil Talk : It involves the following two categories:

Category 8. Pupil Talk-Response : This category is used when the teacher has initiated the contact or has solicited pupil statements, when the pupil answers a question asked by the teacher or when he responds verbally to a direction the teacher has given anything that the pupil says that is clearly in response to initiation by the teacher, belongs to category.

Category 9. Pupil Talk-Initiation : If the pupil raises his hand to make a statement or to ask a question when he has not been prompted to do so by the teacher, the appropriate category is.

Category 10. Silence or Confusion : This category includes anything else not included in the other categories. Periods of confusion in communication, when it is difficult to determine who is talking, are classified in this category.

Accepts Feeling : Accepts and clarifies and attitude or the feeling tone of a pupil in a non-threatening manner. Feelings may be positive or negative. Predicting and recalling feelings are included.

Praises or Encourages: Praises or encourages pupil-action or behaviour. Jokes that related tension, but not at the expense of another individual; nodding head or saying 'Um hm'? or go on' are included in this category.

Accepts or Uses Ideas of Puplils : Clarifying building, or developing ideas suggested by a pupil. Teacher extension of pupil ideas are included but as the teacher brings more of his own ideas into play, shift to category 5.

Asks Questions : Asking a question about content or procedure based upon teacher ideas, with the intent that a pupil with answer.

Lecturing : Giving facts or opinions about content, or procedure expressing his own ideas, giving his own explanation or criticizing or justifying an authority other than a pupil.

Giving Directions : Directions command or order to which a pupil is expected to comply.

Criticizing or Justifying Authority : Statements intended to change pupil behaviour from non-acceptable to acceptable Pattern ; bowling some one out : stating why is the teacher doing what is the doing : extreme self-reference.

Pupil Talk-responses : Talk by pupils in response to teacher. Teacher initiates the contact or solicits pupil statements or structures the situation. Freedom to express own ideas are limited.

Pupil Talk-Initiation : Talk by pupils which they initiate. Expressing own ideas; initiating a new topic ; freedom to develop opinions and a line of thought like asking thoughtful questions; going beyond the existing structure.

Silence or confusion : Pauses, period of silence and periods of confusion in which communication can not be understood by an observer.

Major features of this ten category system lies in the analysis of 'initiation' and 'response' which is a characteristic of interaction between two or more individuals. To lead, to begin, to introduce an idea or concept for the first time is to express one's own will.

To response means to take action after an initiation, to counter, to amplify or react to idea which has already been expressed, to confirm or even to comply of the will expressed by others. We except the teacher, in situation, to show more initiative than the pupils, With the ten category system, an estimate of the balance between initiation and response can be inferred ,from the percent of time of teacher talk, pupil talk and silence or confusion.

THE FUNCTIONING

Encoding and decoding are the two processes of interaction analysis. The encoding process is used for recording classroom events and preparing observation matrix by observing the numbers of ten category system. The decoding is process of interpreting observation matrix. These processes have been discussed in the following paragraphs.

Encoding Process : The first step in the process of encoding is to memorize the code numbers, in relation to key phrase of words which are indicated in capital in relation to key phrase or words which are indicated in capital in ten-category system. The trained observer acts like an automatic device highly discrimination and does without hesitation at the instant an event is recognized. An observer sit on the last bench of the classroom and observer, a teacher when he is teaching. At an interval of every three seconds he writes down that category number which best represents are communication event just completed. For instance, when teacher is lecturing the observer puts 5; when he asks question he puts 4; when student replies he puts 8; when teacher praises he puts 2; when teacher asks to sit down he puts 6; when again the teacher starts lecturing he puts 5. The procedure of recording events goes on at the rate of 20 to 25 observations per minute.

Because of the complexity of the problems involved in categorization, several ground rules have been established. These rules of observation aid in developing consistency in vying to categorize teacher classroom behaviour.

Rule 1: When it is not certain in which of two or more categories a statement belongs, choose the category that is numerically farthest from category 5, e.g., if an observer is not sure whether it is 2 or 3 or choose 2. If in doubt between 5 and 7., he chooses 5.

Rule 2: If the primary tone of the teacher's behaviour has been consistently direct or- consistently indirect, do not shift into an opposite classification unless a clear indication of shift is given by the teacher, e.g., clearly he must also be ready to change when the teacher obviously moves all the way along with the system ;

i.e., to 1 or 2 from 6 or 7, or when the teacher moves all the way to 6 or 7 from 2 or 3. This rule is often called the rule of the biased, unbiased observer.

Rule 3: An observer must not be concerned with his own biases or with the teacher's intent. If 'a teacher attempts to be clever, pupils see his statements as criticism of pupils, the observer uses category 7, rather than category 2. This rule has particular value when applied to the problem of helping teachers to gain insight by their own behaviour., e.g., 'I was trying to praise them; 'I wanted them to answer that question.'

Rule 4: If more than one category occurs during the three seconds' interval, then all category used in that interval are recorded; therefore, record of each change in category. If a change occurs within three seconds, repeat category number. The fourth rule, therefore, 'is that a category number is recorded in every three seconds unless the teacher changes categories within the three seconds interval.

THE ROLE PLAYERS

The interaction analysis technique is considered scientific and objective for observing and analysing, classroom teaching events. The precision and accuracy of the observation depend upon an observer who encodes the classroom activities. Therefore, trained and experienced observers become the major importance in observing the classroom behaviour.

This intra-inter observer agreement is estimated, both the observers practice for encoding the interaction of student-teachers through ten category system dung the early days of teaching practice. They observe the same class simultaneously for fifteen minutes in a classroom situation. It is necessary to count the number of tallies recorded for each category for both the rates. Thus, the tallies per category counted, added and checked against the total number of tallies on the data collection sheet. The ratio and percentage are computed for tallies of each category and recorded on work-sheet. The obtained tallies, ratio and percentage of the rates have been summarized in the table.

Observer Frequency, Ratio and Percentages of Categories Recorded in 15 Minutes Classroom Teaching

Category	A			B			
	f	Observer Ratio	%	f	Observer Ratio	%	Difference of Percentages
1. Accepts Feeling	0	.00	0	0	.00	0	0
2. Praise or enocouragement	6	.019	2	7	.023	2	0
3. Accepts and uses idea of students	16	.053	5	15	.049	5	0
4. Ask questions	20	.065	7	18	.060	6	1
5. Lecturing	80	.258	26	85	.282	28	2
6. Giving directions	42	135	14	35	.116	12	2
7. Criticizing or justifying authority	010	1	0	0	0	0	1
8. Students' talk response	115	.371	37	118	.391	30	2
9. Students' talk initiation	2	.006	1	0	0	0	1
10. Silence or confusion	26	.084	8	24	.079	8	0
N	310	1.001	101	302	1.000	101	9 or

Rate = .09

P_0 = 1.00—disagreement. P_e = 1.00—.09 = 0.91

The difference of percentage column is added, mid Iis obtained to be. It represents the total disagreement between the two observers and is used for calculating PO, the agreement between the observers. The greatest possible agreement would be 100 percent.

Thus, the reliability coefficient 0.887 is obtained for the raters aggreement. Generally the reliability' 0.7 can better be achieved by most serious Reciprocal Category System (R.C.S.) of students. In workshop objective's reliability .60 is frequently established as an acceptable level of reliability. However, an obtained reliability (.89) index shows significant agreement between observers who have, completed the schedule of classroom interaction-analysis.

Decoding Process : After encoding the classroom events into ten category system 10 x 10 matrix table is prepared for decoding the classroom verbal behaviour. The observation matrix table consists of 1.0 rows and 10 columns. The generalized sequence of the pupil-teacher interaction can be estimated in this matrix table. It indicates, what form a pair, of categories. The first number in the pair indicates the row and the second number shows, the column. For example (10-6) pair would be shown by a tally in the cell formed by row 10 and column 6.

The record sheet of classroom observation is used for preparing this matrix table. Before marking the tallies in matrix table, category 10 is added in the beginning and at the end of the categories of a record sheet. Thus, the observer from the pairs for making tallies in the matrix-table.

Tabulation is now made in the matrix to represent pair of numbers so the sequence of events may be located that, which events follow. The first pair is (10-6) the second is (6-10) etc. The particular cell in which tabulation of the pair of numbers is made, is determined by using the first number in the pair to indicate that row and the second number in the pair of the column. Thus, (10-6) will be shown by a tally in the cell formed by row 10 and column 6. The second pair, and each excepts the first and the last, is used twice and pair indicates the cell. It is for this reason that 10 is entered as the first number and the last in the record. This number is chosen as it is convenient to assume that each record begins and ends with silence. This procedure also permits the total of each column to equal the total of corresponding row.

The observation matrix table indicates the frequency of each category separately in margin total. The cells-frequencies represent the flow of event which proceed and follow. It may be seen form the table values that the total of category 2 is 12. It reveals that teacher has praised his students 12 times in his classroom teaching. The cell (5-4) has 7 tallies, it indicates that the lecturing is followed by questioning seven times in his classroom verbal interaction. The Pupil talk (PT) amounts 35 percent whereas teacher talk (TT) amounts 62 percent.

When the observation matrix is prepared, two numbers are taken at a time and one tally is entered the 10 x 10 matrix. The first number stands for row and second number for column; thus each number in a series once becomes row and once becomes column, but it is interesting to note that 10 categories are added in the beginning and at the end of the obtained series of coded categories before preparation of 10 x 10 matrix. The procedure is followed for preparing the matrix, after making the tallies for the series, each corresponding row and column total should be equal if there is no error in tabulation. The tabulation is interesting but very time consuming affair.

There are three arithmetic procedures that are commonly used in order to make comparison between two or more matrixes. They all share in common the setting up of proportions so that direct comparison of number can be made regardless of how long a particular observation is lasted. The most elegant method, and one which is generally used in research project that have access to a computer, is to convert all matrixes-usually these are composite matrixes involving thousands of tallies to a common base of 1,000. This is called a millage matrix. It might be considered improper to convert a row tally matrix into a millage matrix, unless it contained more than 700 or 800 tallies. A second method, for using more frequently because it - is convenient, to convert all column totals into percent of the matrix total mid then calculated certain interaction ratios. A third method is used only when two matrixes are involved and there is no need to refer to normative expectation. This method requires a simple ratio based upon two matrix tables.

Once such a ratio sets up on a slide rule, a number from one matrix can be increased or decreased either alternative being available, so that it can be compared directly with another. In this book, the second method is considered for obtaining the interaction variables.

The second method is to convert all columns and rows tallies of matrix into certain behaviour ratios which are used generally for research purposes. These behaviour' ratios have been explained and formulas for these ratios are, organized in a tabular form. This method requires a simple ratio based upon the average of two observations of matrix, In this, Fifteen behaviour ratios are considered, the formula for each behaviour is provided.

Teacher Talk (TT) : The FIAC system of interaction analysis is referred to categories 1, 2, 3, 49 5, 6 and as indicative of teacher -talk (TT). It may be defined as action taken by the teacher that reflect the tendency of teacher-talk. These teacher-talk (TT) is calculating by adding the frequencies 1 to 7 categories multiplying by 10 and dividing by the total tallies (N) of the matrix. It may be written as:

$$TT= \frac{(1+2+3+4+5+6+7)}{N} X\ 100$$

Indirect Teacher-Talk (ITT) : The indirect teacher influence may be defined as actions taken by the teacher which encourage and support student's participation. According, Clarifying, praising and developing the idea, feeling expressed by the pupil will support students activities. Indirect teacher-talk can be operationally defined by nothing down the percentage of teacher statements including into categories 1, 2, 3 and 4. The indirect influence multiplying by 100 and dividing by total number of matrix tallies (N) which can be presented as:

$$ITT= \frac{(1+2+3+4)}{N} X\ 100$$

Direct Teacher-Talk (DTT) : The direct teacher influence may be defined as actions taken by the teacher which restrict students participation. Expressing one's own views through lectures, giving directions and criticism with the expectation of compliance to restrict pupils-participation. Direct influence may be operationally defined by counting the percentage of teacher statements falling into 5,6 and 7 categories, The direct influence is computed by adding the tallies of 5..6 and 7 categories, multiplying by 100 and dividing by the total tallies. It can be written as:

$$DTT= \frac{(5+6+7)}{N} X\ 100$$

Pupil Talk (PT) : Pupil-talk is defined as talk by pupils in response to teacher. A pupil who asks to approve, his work in order to make sure that it is satisfactory before going to next step. Pupil-response can be operationally defined by noting down the percentage of student-talk falling into categories 8 and 9. Pupil-talk can not be c-inculated, by adding the tallies of 8 and 9 categories, multiplying by 100 and dividing by total tallies of the matrix. It can be written as:

$$PT= \frac{(8+9)}{N} X\ 100$$

Silence or Confusion (SC) : The silence or confusion is defined as any event not included in other categories. Period of confusion in communication which is not understood by an observer or when it is difficult to determine who is talking is classified in this category. The silence or confusion can be defined operationally by noting down the tallies of category 10. The SC can be computed by counting the tallies of category 10 multiplying by 100 and divided by total tallies. It can be presented as:

$$SC= \frac{10 \text{ X } 100}{N} \text{ X } 100$$

Indirect to Direct Ratio (I/D Ratio) : It is customary in this area, using Flander's techniques, to involve such measures, as I/D ratio to seek estimated for teacher's direct and indirect influence behaviour pattern it can be defined operationally by noting down the proportion of indirect influence and direct influence of teacher. It can be computed by adding the tallies 1, 2, 3,4 of categories and multiplying by 100 and dividing by the total tallies of 5, 6 and 7 categories. It can be written as:

$$ID = \frac{(1+2+3+4)}{(5+6+7)} \text{ X } 100$$

Pupil Initiative Ratio (PIR) : Pupil initiative ratio (PIR) is proposed to indicate what proportion of pupil talk is judged by the observer to be percentage of category 9. It can be calculated by multiplying the tallies of category 9 by 100 and dividing by the sum of all pupil talk or total tallies of categories 8 and 9. The PIR is computed by counting the tallies of category 9, multiplying by 100, and dividing by total tallies of 8 and 9 categories. It can be presented as:

$$PIR = \frac{9 \text{ X } 100}{(8+9)} \text{ X } 100$$

Teacher Response Ratio (TRR) : The teacher response ratio (TRR) is defined as an index presenting the tendency of a teacher's tendency to react the ideas and feelings of the pupils. The TRR can be obtained by adding the frequencies of categories 1, 2, 3, multiplying by 100 and dividing by the sum of categories 1+2+3+6+7. The formula is designed so that the index will be a figure percentage never higher than 100 and never less than zero. The formula can be presented as:

$$TRR = \frac{(1+2+3)}{(1+2+3+6+7)} X\ 100$$

Teacher Question Ratio (TQR) : A teacher question ratio (TQR) is defined as an index representing the tendency of a teacher to use questions when guidance the more content oriented part of the class discussion. The TQR is percentage of all the, statements, related to category 4 and 5 which are classified in category 4. It -is calculated by multiplying the category 4 frequencies by 100 and dividing by the sum of-categories 4 and 5. The TQR varies teacher, solicits pupil reaction for ideas which the teacher considers important or as lie checks their understanding by asking questions. It can be computed by using the following formula:

$$TQR = \frac{4\ x\ 100}{(4+5)} X\ 100$$

Content Cross Ration (CCR) : The content cross ratio (CCR) is an indication that the main focus of the class discussion becomes on the subject-matter, that attention to motivation and discipline problem is minimum. The CCR is found by calculating the percentages of all tallies that lie within the columns or rows of categories 4 and 5. It can be computed by adding the tallies of 4 and 5 categories and multiplying by 100 and dividing by total tallies of the matrix. It can be written as

$$CCR = \frac{(4+5)}{N} X\ 100$$

Vicious Circle (VC) : As the phrase suggests the occurrence of category six and seven both in a sustained fashion and as shifts between, undersirable and will have the effect of curbing the freedom and initiative of the students. Such restrictive behaviour on the part of the teacher as would make them potently authoritarian is termed as Extended Direct Behaviour. The relevant sequence are be found within the quadrangular area namely calls (6-6). (7-6), (7-7) and (6-7). It 'Can be computed by adding the cells (6-6), (6-7), (7-6) and (7-7) tallies and multiplying by 100 and dividing total tallies of matrix. It can be presented as:

$$VC = \frac{(6\text{-}6)+(6\text{-}7)+(7\text{-}6)+(7\text{-}7)}{N} \times 100$$

Pupil Steady State Ratio (PSSR) **:** The pupil steady state ratio (PSSR) is an even more sensitive index to the rapidity of the teacher pupil inter change when pupil talks the average or about average. The PSSR is calculated by adding the frequencies in the (8-9) + (9 - 9) cells, multiplying by 100 and dividing by all pupil talk tallies, i.e., (8+9). This can be presented as :

$$PSSR = \frac{(8\text{-}8)+(9\text{-}9)X100}{8+9} \times 100$$

Instantaneous Teacher Response Ratio (ITRR 89) **:** The instantaneous teacher response ratio is defined as the teacher tendency to praise or integrate ideas and feelings in the, class discussion as the moment the pupils stop talking. The ITRR 89 can be calculated by adding the cell frequencies in rows 8 and 9 columns, 1, 2 and 3 multiplying this sum by 100 and dividing the product by the total tallies in the cell frequencies in rows 8 and 9 columns 1, 2, 3, 6 and 7. This can be presented as:

$$PSSR = \frac{(8\text{-}1)+(8\text{-}2)+(8\text{-}3)+(9\text{-}1)+(9\text{-}2)+(9\text{-}3)}{(8\text{-}1)+(8\text{-}2)+(8\text{-}3)+(8\text{-}6)+(8\text{-}7)+(9\text{-}1)+(9\text{-}2)+(9\text{-}3)\ \ (9\text{-}6)+(9\text{-}7)} \times 100$$

The Instantaneous Teacher Question Ratio (ITQR 89) **:** The instantaneous teacher question ratio (ITQR 89) is defined as the tendency of teacher to respond to pupil talk with questing based upon his own ideas, compared to his tendency of lecture. The ITQR 89 is calculated by adding the tallies in, (8-4) + (9-4) cells. This can also be written as :

$$ITQR = \frac{(8\text{-}4)+(9\text{-}4)}{(8\text{-}4)+(8\text{-}5)+(9\text{-}4)+(9\text{-}5)} \times 100$$

Steady State Ratio (SSR) : The steady state ratio (SSR) reflects the tendency of teacher and pupil talk to remain the same category for period longer than- three seconds. The higher is the ratio, the lesser rapid is the interchange between the teacher and pupils on an average.

The SSR can be determined by calculating the percentage of all tallies that lie within steady state cells. The SSR can be computing by noting down the tallies of steady state ratio cells, multiplying by 100 and dividing by total tallies of the matrix. It can be presented as:

$$SSR = \frac{\text{SSC (steady state cells)}}{N} \times 100$$

Where :

SSC = (1-1), (2-2), (3-3), (4-4), (5-5), (6-6), (7-7), (8-8), (9-9), (10-10).

The behaviour ratios are computed by using the above formula. The indices of these behaviour ratios are meaningless. These can not be interpreted as such. The normative expectations are developed as standards for these behaviour ratios. The obtained behaviour ratios can be interpreted with the help of these norms.

The normative expectations of the behaviour ratios have been developed by the author in the Indian conditions and Ned A. Flanders in U.S.A. for grade VI, VII and VIII separately. The behaviour ratios can not be used for analysing the nature of teaching whether teaching is democratic and authoritarian.

The teachers who have the greater values of pupil-talk, teacher response ratio, teacher question ratio, pupil intuition ratio, indirect teacher influence be and pupil steady state ratio than the normative values are considered to effective teacher. On the other hand teachers who have highher teacher-talk, silence or confusion, steady state ratio, content cross ratio, and direct teacher behaviour than their normative values are stated. The interaction analysis technique is an exploratory device. It provides the flow of class-room verbal behaviour but quality of teaching can not be passed.

The research findings in the area of teacher behaviour are also taken in consideration the following manner:

Normative Expectation of Behaviour Ratios (Based upon FIACS)

Behaviour Ratio	VIII Class		VII Class		VI Class	
	India	U.S.A.	India	U.S.A.	India	U.S.A.
1. Teacher Talk (TT)	67	70	64	61	60	53
2. Pupil Talk (PT)	21	19	24	28	27	32
3. Silence/Confusion (SC)	12	11	12	11	13	15
4. Teacher Response Ratio (TRR)	26	35	27	41	36	52
5. Teacher Question Ratio (TQR)	19	20	20	26	22	26
6. Pupil Interaction Ratio (PIR)	12	15	16	32	23	34
7. Steady State Ratio (SSR)	46	52	47	54	45	48
8. Pupil Steady State Ratio (PSSR)	37	26		55	46	53
9. Content Cross Ratio (CCR)	72	68	54	55	49	47
10. Instantaneous Teacher Response Ratio (ITRR 89)	48	67	54	75	65	77
11. Instantaneous Teacher Question Ratio (ITQR 89)	42	39	44	45	56	45
No. of Teachers observed	137	16	173	16	155	30

The process factor of teacher-effectiveness is an important aspect. The quality of interacting can be assessed by developing the norms. The normative behaviour have been provided in the table.

The second type of verbal behaviour is obtained as interaction variables. These variables have been used by Flanders himself for extracting the factors for classroom interaction.

The flexibility is counted variation in behaviour in terms of frequency in specific activities. The arithmetic difference between the larger i/d ratio over all time used categories and the smallest i/d ratio for all time used categories.

QUALITY ASSESSED

The computation of behaviour ratios and interaction variables do not reveal the structure and flow of verbal interaction. The clockwise flow analysis and box flow diagrams are prepared with the help of matrix-table. The qualitative and visual interpretation can be made with the flow analysis. The interaction models of the teacher can also be located from the clockwise flow chart.

A flow diagram can form a visual display which may be more acceptable for understanding the, nature and structure of the verbal behaviour. It is necessary to provide a feedback to teacher by analysing their observation matrices in flow diagrams. Some kinds of comparison are made with the help of flow diagrams. Two matrices may be compared in order to find similarities and differences between two segments of interaction. Sometimes a single matrix is compared with normative expectations in order to decide whether a particular interaction is typical or non typical. It is also possible to compare the patterns within a single matrix to a value model, i.e., a desired or preferred state of affairs, described in form of a matrix, which the teacher is attempting to develop.

The inferences about the sequence of events (what precedes and what follows) can also be made. By understanding the relationship between rows and columns, probability statements can be made by the flow pattern which can be shown by arrows within the matrix.

In order to make a flow diagram from a matrix knowledge of clockwise rotation of events and the difference between columns and rows, are essential. It is required to draw a blank matrix from consisting of ten rows and ten columns, each properly labelled. The highest cell frequency of a matrix is located for preparing the flow diagram. The cell of highest frequency is the sequence of pair which occurs most often. The highest frequency is circled. This marked cell will be the starting point of presenting ,the flow of event. Most of the matrix with the highest frequency will be the (5-5) cell. However, it is possible for another cell to have the highest frequency and to become the starting point.

Once the starting point located, the next is to identify the event which is most likely to flow. This is done by observing the row which is designated by the second number in the address of the starting cell. The highest frequency in the row other than the second point. The starting point is looped by an arrow. By inspecting the column of second point, the highest frequency of the cell is noted and encircled. It is connected by an arrow with the second step. The highest frequency should be noted only do upward side from the second step, so that clockwise flow may be presented. After locating the third point, the highest cell frequency is noted by inspecting the row towards the right side of the column and in marked by circle. The four the point is connected by drawing a little looping arrow from the third step. This procedure is followed for preparing the clockwise flow diagram. These marked cells and arrows help to clarify the sequence of events and make the matrix display more understandable. This obtained diagram is termed as clockwise flow of classroom interaction. It has been shown by the observation matrix table.

The clockwise flow diagram of classroom interaction is still incomprehensible to the teacher, it is possible to draw a diagrams which looks just a little less complicated. It attempts to use space in way that are proportional to the communication pattern. The steady state pairs are drawn separately related to teacher talk and pupil talk. The size of steady state pairs box is proportional to the number frequencies of the cell. These boxes are connected with a looping arrow by inspecting the frequency of matrix, what precedes and what follows. The thickness of connecting arrow should also be proportional to the frequencies of the cell. Thus, a box flow diagram is prepared. It has been shown in the diagram. It may be helpful for understanding the nature and structure of verbal behaviour of teachers. The following rules should be observed in preparing flowchart. .

1. The size of boxes and arrows should be proportionate to their frequencies.
2. The steady state cells frequency should be limited in preparing box flow-diagram. The larger frequencies should be included in flow-diagram.
3. Sometimes a cell of having lower frequencies is included for the interchange of events, because arrows frequencies are greater.
4. The steady state cells of teacher or students are marked in different tow domains. The boxes are connected with the interchange events of any cell. There may be interchange within the same domain.

The interaction models of critical teaching behaviour have been described by Flanders himself by using interaction analysis categories in his research. Flanders has defined a critical teacher behaviour as a pattern of acts or interaction models that: (a) are logically related to a certain educational outcome, (b) follow a certain sequence with measurable probability and (c) seem crucial in terms of a theory of teacher influence verified by past research. He has developed seven interaction models of critical teaching behaviour, these are quite typical of common practices in-classroom, based upon his research data.

A Summary of Interaction Models of Critical Teaching Behaviour

Models	Teaching Behaviour
Teacher Initiation Models	
(1) High content emphasis under close-teacher direction.	The teacher communicates content and occasionally asks questions to which the students can reply briefly. It is most frequently occurring pattern of teaching.
(2) Teacher directed quick drill.	The teacher asks short-questions mid short responses are given by pupils. The direct (8-4) to (4-8) communication is shown by the double arrows.
(3) Drill combined with lecture demonstration.	In it, basic drill is interrupted occasionally by teacher explanation. The teacher lectures in response to a student explanation.
Pupil Initiation Models	
(4) Teacher gives directions with some clarification.	The teacher gives direction in sustained situation and followed by the student initiation. The initiation for seeking clarification.
(5) Stimulating independent student thought.	The teacher asks questions for a longer period and it is followed by student initiation and responses in sustained situation. It is followed by question.
(6) Attending to Student feelings.	The teacher accepts the feeling of students when he initiates and also encourages or praises student-teacher effective used to be in classroom.
(7) Teacher Tranasition from an affective to an intellectual emphasis.	The teacher moves from affective realm to the intellectual realm of classroom communication. Teacher accepts the emotional to ne of the class frequently. More use of category 1, 2 and 3.

The first three model (1) High-content emphasis wider close teacher direction, (2) Teacher directed quick drill, and (3) Drill combined with lecture demonstration, are involving in more active teacher's role. These three models are more teacher initiated. The last four models (4) teacher gives direction with some clarification, (5) stimulating independent student thought, (6) attending to student feelings, and (7) teacher transitions from an affecting to an intellectual emphasis are involving in more students initiation. The four models are creative models and more pupil's initiated. A summary of the models has been given.

THE RESULT

Nomination of Critical Behaviour : There are a number of behaviour patterns that occur in teaching at critical decision points. These are now mentioned in the same order or on their relative importance to effective teaching.

First, teachers must decide when and why should they turn from providing information and begin to invite student's verbal participation by the use of questions.

Second, Teacher must known how to ask broad and narrow questions and to predict the consequences of asking either type of question.

Third, Teacher must known when to restrict freedom of student's participation by close supervision and guidance such as occurs in teacher directed drills and giving assignments.

Fourth, Teacher must known when to support the expression of student ideas and feeling, how to select particular expression for fourth development and application, and how to guide such activities without developing unwanted excessive dependence. Here dependence refers to the tendency of students to solicit teacher direction mid approval in situations in which more self-directing activities should gradually be developed.

Fifth, Teachers must known how to make constructive use of the effective aspects of student behaviour. Part of motivation concerns with the development and organization of positive attitudes and feelings in relation to educational goals and individual tasks.

THE SUGGESTIONS

The Flanders Interaction Analysis is an observational method of classroom teaching which can be used to obtain a fairly reliable record of spontaneous verbal statements. The following precautions should be observed in the use of this technique :

1. The classroom encoding work should be done by an observer who is familiar with entire process and knows its limitations.
2. It is an exploratory device therefore, value judgements about good and bad teaching behaviours are to be avoided.

   This technique is not an evaluator device of classroom teaching.
3. The questions regarding classroom teaching can only be answered by inspecting the matrix table. The observer can not answer the question relating to teacher behaviour.
4. A comparison between the two matrices can be made in terms of behaviour ratios, interaction variables and percentage of frequencies in each category and, calls frequency but value judgement is not possible.
5. The accuracy of the observation depends upon the reliability of the observer. The classroom recording should be done after estimating the reliability of observers.
6. At least two observers should encode the classroom interaction for analysing teaching and teacher behaviour.

Exercise

1. Define the term observation system and differentiate between sign system and category system.
2. Distinguish between equivalent category system and reciprocal category system.
3. Define Flanders interaction analysis and describe its basic assumptions.
4. Explain Flanders ten category system and explain its encoding procedure and rules of classroom observation.
5. Explain the decoding process and preparation of matrix table and its use in analysis teaching behaviour.

6

ORGANISED TEACHING

NEW DIMENSIONS

Programmed learning is one of the important invocations of the 20th century in the teaching-learning process. It is a self-instructional technique for providing individualized instruction or learning experience to the learner. In programmed learning, the subject matter or learning experience is logically sequenced into small segments. The learning experience is self-corrective.

The English writers prefer to use the term programmed learning and the American authors prefer the use of programmed instruction.

It is held by some educators that 'Gita' is the first example of programmed learning. They hold that the text of the 'Gita' has several ingredients of programming: initial behaviour, small steps, active participation of the learner, terminal behaviour, immediate feed-back and self-evaluation by the learner.

Several educators regard Socrates as the earliest programmer. Socrates used to guide his followers to gain knowledge by conducting them conversationally along a path from fact to fact and insight to insight.

Programmed learning emerged in the beginning of the 20th century from the efforts of American psychologists. E. L. Thorndike

(1874-1949) was the first psychologist whose findings bear direct relevance to programming. Other important psychologists who have made significant contribution in the field are Sidney L. Pressy, Robert M. Gagne, Robert Mager and B. F. Skinner.

Programmed learning is related with the 'Law of Effect' as explained by Thorndike. Sidney L. Pressey, a psychologist of Ohio State University, is credited for developing in the middle 1920's practical machines which could teach as well as test. The teaching machines as developed by Pressey present a series of questions to a student and inform him immediately whether his response is right or wrong.

In 1943, Skinner and his two other colleagues started programming by teaching a pigeon to roll a small bowling ball by operant conditioning. By 1954, Skinner and James G. Holland devised the auto-instructional methods which have served the present generation as the basis for present work in programmed instruction. In Skinnerian programmed instruction, whether mechanised or otherwise, the learner is initially asked a question which he can easily answer correctly without any previous study of the particular lesson. The learner is taught by the sequence of questions. He is asked more and more as the lesson proceeds in very small steps.

In 1955, Norman A. Crowder developed what he calls "automatic tutoring by intrinsic programming" as against "extrinsic programming" developed by Skinner.

Robert Mager (1958) gave a new concept known as "Learner Controlled Instruction" which is a kind of Socratic dialogue in reverse, in which the learner led the instructor. The instructor remained silent until the learner himself stimulated the instructor with questions that suggested the needed illustrations, demonstrations, practice or some other help.

Stoluron, at Illionis, aimed at developing a process which should provide for greater individualization by measuring needs and developing programmes that require a computer to assist instruction.

In 1962, T. F. Gilbert gave formalized expression of his technology of education called Mathetics. Pennington and Slack expressed in 1962 further detailed methods of preparing lessons om mathetic principles.

BASIC IDEAS

Programmed learning is a process of arranging material to be learned in a series of small steps designed to lead a learner through self-instruction from what he knows to the unknown of new and more complex knowledge and principles. A programme takes the place of a tutor and leads the learner through a set of frames of specified behaviour designed and sequenced to make it more probable that he will behave in a given derived way.

In programmed learning, it is said that the most efficient, pleasant and permanent learning takes place when the student proceeds through a course by a large number of small, easy-to-take steps. Wilbur L. Schramm (1962) lists the essential elements of programmed instruction as: (*a*) an ordered sequence of stimulus items, (*b*) to each of which a student responds in some specific way, (*c*) his responses being reinforced by immediate knowledge of results, (*d*) so that he moves by small steps, (*e*) therefore, making few errors and practicing mostly correct responses, (*f*) from what he knows by a process of successively closer approximation, toward what he is supposed to learn from the programme.

Following definitions provide a comprehensive view of programmed instruction.

Dale, Edgar (1962). Programmed learning is a systematic, step by step, self-instructional programme aimed to ensure the learning of stated behaviour.

Das, R. C (1993). Programmed instruction is a method of individualised instruction where each individual learns by himself at his own rate. Programmed learning consists of elements of new knowledge called 'steps' which are arranged in a sequence in such a way that a student can easily learn by himself.

Espich, James E. and William B (1965). Programmed instruction is a planned sequences of experiences, leading to proficiency in terms of stimulus response relationship.

Gulati and Gulati (1990). Programmed learning as popularly understood is a method of giving individual instruction in which the student is active and proceeds at his own pace and is provided with immediate knowledge of results. The teacher is not physically present. The programmer, while developing programmed material has to follow the laws of behaviour and validate his strategy in terms of student learning.

Jacobs and Others (1966). Self-instructional programmes are educational materials from which the students learn. These programmes can be used with many types of students and subject-matter either by themselves, hence the name "self-instruction" or its combination with instructional strategies.

Kampfer (1970). Programmed learning is a device which presents an exercise or a problem to a student, inducing him to respond; and revealing to him whether or not his response is correct.

Leith, G. O. M (1966). Programme is a sequence of small steps of instructional material (called frames), most of which require a response to be made by completing a blank space in a sentence. To ensure that expected responses are given, a system of cueing is applied, and each response is verified by the provision of immediate knowledge of results. Such a sequence is intended to be worked at the learner's own pace as individual self-instruction.

Luonsdaine Arthur, A (1964). An instructional programme is a vehicle which generates an essentially reproducible sequence of instructional events and accepts responsibility for efficiently accomplishing a specified change from a given range of initial competencies or behavioural tendencies to a specified or terminal range of competencies or behavioural tendencies.

Marke, Susan (1969). Programmed learning is a method of designing a reproducible sequence of instructional events to produce a measurable and consistent effect on the behaviours of each and every acceptable student.

Navi, N. S. (1984). Programmed instruction is a technique of converting the live instructional process into self-learning or auto-instructional readable material in the form of micro-sequence (the segments of subject-matter) which the learners are required to read, make some right or wrong response, correct wrong responses or confirm right responses and attain the complete mastery of the concept explained in the micro-sequences.

May, K. O. (1965). Educational programming is the scheduling and control of student behaviour in the learning process.

Smith and Moore (1962). Programmed instruction is the process of arranging the material to be learned into a series of sequential steps. Usually it moves the student from a familiar background into a complex and new set of concepts, principles and understandings.

Stolurow (1966). Programmed learning can be described as a process in which a teacher presents (*i.e.*, communicates), a subject matter to a learner so that he responds to it (i.e. communicates to the teacher) the next item of information to be presented.

THE SIGNIFICANCE

From the above mentioned definitions of programmed learning, following characteristics may be derived:

1. It is a method of individualized instruction.
2. In this technique, instructional material is logically sequenced and broken into suitable small steps or segments of the subject matter called 'frames'.
3. For sequencing a particular unit of the instructional material, the programmer has to pay due consideration to the initial or entering behaviour of the learner.
4. In actual operation, the beginning is made by presenting a 'frame'. The learner is required to read or listen and then respond actively.
5. Programmed instruction system has an adequate provision for feed-back.
6. The interaction between the learner and the learning material or programme is very important.
7. Programmed learning provides self-pacing to the learner.
8. Programmed learning provides for continuous evaluation.

There are three basic types of programmed instructional material—The teaching machines, the programmed textbook and scrambled textbook.

The teaching machine. A teaching machine is intended to function as a private tutor. It is simply a mechanical devise or piece of apparatus designed to present to the student a sequential programme of learning activities comprising instructional items which requires the student to make an overt response and which provides the student with immediate knowledge of the accuracy of his response. It represents the practical application of laboratory technique of education.

Programmed textbook. Each page of the programmed textbook consists of usually four or five panels. The student begins with the top panel on page one, responds to it, turns to page two to get his answers confirmed on the top panel, goes to the top panel on page three, responds to it, confirms the answer by turning the page, and so on.

The scrambled textbook. In a scrambled textbook, branching or intrinsic technique is used.

PRINCIPLES IN APPLICATION

Principle of Small Steps. It is shown by experiments that even the dullest students can learn as effectively as the brightest students if the subject matter is presented to them in suitable small steps. When we divide the task to be learnt into very small steps, and ask the students to learn only one step at a time, then probably all the students will be able to learn one small step at a time and sequentially learn all the steps. It is a difficult task to climb a mountain but once steps are built even a child can climb the mountain very easily. This is known as the 'Principle of small steps'.

Principle of Active Responding. The second psychological principle is that the students learn better and faster when they are actively participating in the teaching-learning process. In our classroom teaching the teachers to ask a few questions and the students respond. But is not possible for the teachers to ask all the students to respond at each small step. A teaching machine text or a programmed text contains a large number of questions—one question at each small step and the students respond actively. The principle of active responding is used for the programmes. The teaching machines and programmes have proved to be superior because they provide opportunity to every learner to respond at every small step.

Principle of Reinforcement. Every response even approximately correct must be reinforced immediately. Delayed reinforcement fails to work. This is possible only when a teacher has to teach only one student at a time. The most ideal situation is when the teacher can cater to the needs of his students individually. But in classroom teaching this is hardly possible. No teacher, however efficient and sincere he may be, can reinforce each correct response of each of his students as soon as it is made in a classroom situation where he has to teach abut 40/50 students. The teaching machines and the programmes do the job more efficiently.

Principle of Self-Pacing. The programmed instruction is based on the basic assumption that learning takes place effectively if the learner is allowed to learn at his own pace. Therefore, a good programme of the material always takes care of the principle of self-pacing. A learner moves from one frame to another according to his own speed of learning.

Principle of Student-Evaluation or Student Testing. Continuous evaluation of the student and the learning process leads to better teaching-learning. In the programmed instruction, the learner has to leave the record of his responses because he is required to write a response for each frame on response sheet. This detailed record helps in revising the programme.

Important stages in the Development of the Programmed Instruction

Preparation. This is the first stage in the development of the programme. It includes:

(*i*) Selection of the topic.
(*ii*) Writing assumptions about learners.
(*iii*) Defining objective in behavioural terms.
(*iv*) Writing the entry behaviour (present status) of the learner.
(*v*) Developing specific outline of the content.
(*vi*) Preparing a criterion test.

Construction or writing of the programme. The programme is written under these heads (*i*) Writing draft frames in a sequence i.e. from simple to complex. (*ii*) Editing the draft frames by a team of experts usually comprising a subject-matter expert, a skilled writer and the programmer.

Try Out Revision. It includes (*i*) Trying out the programme on a few individual learners and finding out their reactions and making necessary changes in the light of reactions, (*ii*) Trying out the programme on a group of learners and making necessary changes on the basis of their reactions; and (*iii*) Trying out the programme in the field.

Evaluation. This implies finding the success or the failure after implementing a programme.

CIVICS-CLASS X

Introduction. This a programme meant for you for the study of salient features of the Constitution of India.

In this programme you will find paragraphs which are called frames. Study each frame carefully and write down what is required. Answers are given at the end. After stating you answers, check them. If your answer is wrong or you do not understand anything, you can again go back to the frame. It is not a test but instead it is a self-study programme.

Frame 1. The Constituent Assembly of India was set up under the provisions of the Cabinet Mission Plan to frame the Constitution of India which was formally adopted on 26th Nov. 1949 and came into force on 26th January 1950. It took nearly three years to complete the work.

(*i*) What was the work assigned to Constituent Assembly?

(*ii*) Under whose provision was it formed?

(*iii*) When did our Constitution come into force?

(*iv*) When was it adopted?

(*v*) How much time did Constituent Assembly take to complete its work?

Frame 2. The Preamble of the Constitution has a great significance but is not a part of the Constitution. The Constitution was framed by the people of India through their representations. It stresses the fact that the reign of the land lies with the people of India.

(*a*) Is the Preamble a part of the Constitution?

(*b*) By whom was the Constitution framed?

(*c*) In whose hands does the reign of law of India lie?

***Frame* 3.** The Preamble of our Constitution is as under:

We the people of India having solemnly resolved to constitute India into a Sovereign Socialist Secular Democratic Republic and to secure to all its citizens:

Justice, social, economic and political;

Liberty of thought, expression, belief, faith and worship

Equality of status and of opportunity; and to promote them all;

Fraternity assuring the dignity of the individual and the unity and integrity of the Nation.

In our Constituent Assembly this twenty-sixth day of November, 1949, do hereby adopt, enact and give to ourselves this Constitution.

Note—Three new terms—Socialist, Secular and Integrity were added to the original text of the Preamble when it was amended in 1976 with the 42nd Amendment.

The Preamble stresses the democratic basis of the Constitution by stating that the People of India gave to themselves this Constitution. It also states objectives like justice, liberty, equality and fraternity.

(i) Who has given the Constitution of India?

(ii) What kind of justice has been ensured by the Preamble?

(iii) What type of Republic is to be constituted?

(iv) What kind of equality has been given to its citizen?

(v) How many types of liberty can a citizen enjoy?

***Frame* 4.** Another important feature of the Preamble is that the people themselves adopted and enacted the Constitution. Thus, the representatives of the people frame the laws of the country and they have the power to change or amend the Constitution.

(*a*) Who frames the laws of the country?

(*b*) What has the power to amend the Constitution?

Frame 5. The Constitution of India has many unique features which distinguish it from Constitutions of other countries. The framers of the Constitution freely borrowed ideas but took care to adapt these to the needs of the country.

The Constitution makes India a Sovereign, Socialist Secular, Democratic Republic. The word Sovereign means that India is completely free from external control. No outside power has the right to interfere either in her internal administration or direct her in the conduct of her foreign policy.

This was emphasised to ensure that India was no longer 'dependent' on the British Empire as she had been before Indian Independence Act 1947 or 'dominion' as she had been from 15th August, 1947 to 26th January 1950.

(*a*) What kind of status did India enjoy during 15th August 1947 to 26th January 1950?

(*b*) Was India sovereign between 15th August 1947 to 26th January 1950?

(*c*) What is the meaning of the word 'sovereign'?

(*d*) Does the Constitution of India have unique features?

(*e*) Did the framers of the Constitution borrow ideas?

ANSWERS

1. (i) To frame the Constitution of India.
   (ii) Provision of the Cabinet Mission Plan.
   (iii) 26th January 1950.
   (iv) 26th November 1949.
   (v) Nearly 3 years.
2. (*a*) No.
   (*b*) People of India through their representatives.
   (*c*) People of India.
3. (i) People of India.
   (ii) Social, economic and political.
   (iii) Sovereign Socialist Secular Democratic.
   (iv) Equality of status.
   (v) Five.

4. (*a*) Representatives of the people.
   (*b*) Representatives of the people.
5. (*a*) Dominion.
   (*b*) No.
   (*c*) India is completely free from external control.
   (*d*) Yes.
   (*e*) Yes.

Merits of programmed instruction. 1. A well-programmed instruction is a great thrust in the direction of individualised instruction, as it is tailored to the needs of the individual learner in the class. 2. It permits individual learner to progress at his own speed. An intelligent learner needs no longer to be bored or allowed to lose interest on account of his slow progress of other learners of the class. He can make progress as he is capable of. 3. Since a programme requires continuous response from the learner, it overcomes the inertia and passivity on the part of the learner. 4. The teacher can give explanation in the classroom if the error is common or he may arrange individual conferences on specific points. 5. Learning material in a programmed instruction is presented in such a way that learning becomes an interesting game and the learner is motivated to meet the challenges set by his own capabilities. 6. Programmes are developed by experts. They are empirically tested and modified till they are standarised. A number of learners can use a single good programme and thus evade textbooks. 7. In programmed instruction the learner is immediately reinforced to correct his response and this reinforcement sustains the motivation of the learner. 8. The self-instructional technique presents material in which its complexity is simplified through the analysis of the subject-matter into small and more easily assimilated segments of information. 9. The introduction of programmed instruction is of great significance for developing countries which are set on the path of educating millions of learners and are short of teachers. 10. Good teachers are freed from the boredom of routine classroom teaching and they are in a position to devote more time to more creative activities. 11. The programmed instruction has been used more successfully in teaching the discernment of the logic of various disciplines and inspiring students to creative thinking and judgement.

12. Certain motor skills and intellectual abilities normally taught by frequent drills and rote memorisation can be very efficiently taught by self-instructional devices. 13. Self-instructional materials have been found to be very useful in the West in revolutionisng the social setting of the classroom. Problems of discipline have been solved and a new hope for eliminating emotional and social problems has been generated. 14. Programmed instruction enables the teacher to diagnose the problems of the individual learner. 15. The introduction of programmed instruction is very helpful in certain situations where human instructors are not easily available in the required number, for instance small schools in the isolated or hill areas.

Programmed materials have been severely criticised as a threat to replacing the teacher.

It is also argued that there is too much emphasis in learning facts and very little emphasis on the mastery of principles and concepts.

Some critics of programmed instruction maintain that the user of a programme does not now where he is headed to.

They also point out that the learners are not aware of the organisation and programmed instruction is unrelated to other aspects of instruction.

It is also argued that the programmed instruction material is very costly and only rich nations can afford it.

It is also stated that the development and use of programmed instructional material require expert knowledge and training. An average teacher finds it very difficult to make use of this device.

As a result of experimental studies and research, following types of programmed instruction have emerged.

1. Linear or Extrinsic Programming
2. Branching or Intrinsic Programming
3. Mathetics Programming
4. Rules System of Programming
5. Computer Assisted Instruction (CAS)
6. Learner Controlled Instruction. (LCS)

The first three styles—linear, branching and mathetics are the basic formats. The rules system represents the deductive and inductive approach to teaching. The other two types, Computer Assisted Instruction (CAI) and Learner Controlled Instruction (LCI) are not the basic format of Programming. They are, infact, the ways and means of providing instruction. Here we have taken up only the basic type of programming.

B. F. Skinner is the originator of linear programming. It is also called a single tract programme. According to Skinner, a creature, a bird or a human being can be led to a desired behaviour by means of a carefully constructed programme consisting of small steps leading logically through the subject-matter from topic to topic, provided each step is reinforced by some kind of favourable experience or reward. The increments in information which the learner is expected to absorb are small. The favourable experience or response increases the probability of the same response to occur again in the future. The process of rewarding the correct response to a stimulus increases the general tendency to give a response.

The sequence of frames and path of learning in programmed learning is systematic and linear. That is why, this type of programming is referred to as linear programming. Hence all the learners have to proceed through the same frames and in the same order.

In a linear programme, learner's responses are controlled externally by the programmer sitting at a distant place. Hence linear programming is also termed as extrinsic programming. In branching programming, learner's response is controlled by the learner himself internally. It is, therefore, also called intrinsic programming.

Merits. 1. Immediate knowledge of results acts as a great motivator and releases anxiety and tension. 2. The smallness of the frames brings the sub-goals within the reach of the learner and thereby facilitates secondary reinforcement. 3. Repetition strengthens the responses and ensures learning. 4. Easy nature of the programme provides 'success experience' to the learner.

Limitations. 1. In linear programming, the learning process becomes quite dull on account of the following reasons (*a*) Subject matter is broken into very small pieces, (*b*) Responding is quite mechanical and restrictive, and (*c*) The learning process is quite slow. 2. The use of linear programming is limited to some subjects and topics. 3. Linear programming cramps the imagination of the learner and initiative for creative, integrative and judgement learning. 4. Linear programming encourages guessing. 5. Linear programming does not develop the discriminating power of the students.

Branching or intrinsic programming was developed by Norman A. Crowder (1954) an American technician. According to Crowder, branching or intrinsic programme is one which adopts to the needs of the learners without the medium of any extrinsic device such as a computer. It is not controlled extrinsically by the programmer.

Norman A. Crowder was a technician who was working in the United States Air Force. He was faced with the problem of efficiency of vocational training. His programme is based on intuition. His approach at the most is practical. This type of programme employs multiple choice response patterns. The learner is required to select one right answer out of several responses presented to him.

Merits. 1. Big size of a frame as well as the branching minimises unnecessary repetitions and responding, thus reducing the amount of learning time and fatigue. 2. The pitfalls and consequences of erroneous logic are usually explained in the remedial frames so that the learner not only gets the correct responses but also understands why some other response is not correct. 3. Instead of simple response it provides alternatives in the form of multiple choice. 4. Through its broad frames, branching programme provides for more freedom to respond and scope of choosing one's path of learning according to one's need. Thus, it helps in maintaining the interest and initiative of the teacher. 5. Branching programme is helpful in the development of the power of discrimination of the learner. 6. Branching programme helps in the development of creativity and problem-solving ability. 7. Branching is most useful in the areas beyond facts, definitions and basic skills. 8. The frames being of a large size contain a good deal of information and this may enable the programmer to enrich the style and expand his ideas.

Programmed Instruction	*Traditional Method*
1. It is an individualised technique of instruction.	1. It is a group technique.
2. It is based on the teaching principles that have been known for years.	2. It becomes difficult to apply teaching principles in crowded classrooms.
3. It presents the instructional matter step by step in logical order.	3. It presents the instructional matter as a whole.
4. The size of the unit of information presented to the pupils is a small bit of information.	4. The unit is a lengthy one. There is very little provision for response from the students in the form of answers to questions.
5. Immediate feedback is given to the learner.	5. The learner does not get immediate feedback.
6. Objectives are defined very clearly in operational terms.	6. Objectives are not well-defined and are usually vague.
7. The programmer prepares his programme with care and precision.	7. Very little preparation is made.
8. Programme is prepared in such a way that the student automatically participates actively by making responses continually.	8. The student usually remains a passive listener and the teacher himself does the summarising and reviewing.
9. A programme is developed empirically through a series of tryouts and refined gradually. Effective sequences students reaction of frames are retained and ineffective ones discarded.	9. It is usually found to be very difficult to modify traditional instruction.

Limitations. 1. The multiple choice questions provided in this programming may lead to guess work on the part of the learner and he may not understand the subject matter of the frame. 2. The setting of appropriate multiple choice questions suiting to the entire material of the frames proves a difficult task. 3. No branching method can provide infinite branching to take care of all possible needs of every individual student. 4. The cost of branching programme is very high when compared with traditional teaching approaches. 5. The branching programme is not suitable for small children as they are unable to express symbolisation. 6. The programme needs revision after every five years. 7. It is difficult to cover the entire subject matter of the curriculum in the stipulated time. 8. The diagnostic questions framed by the programmer may or may not suit the needs of the individual learner. 9. The programme cannot shape the behaviour of the learner.

Teaching Instruction and Programmed Instruction. According to Edger Dale, "Teaching' is a broad, vague, ill-defined term and instruction' is a purposeful, orderly, controlled sequencing of experience to reach a specified goal. 'Programmed instruction' is a sub-head under instruction and represents a more rigorous attempt to develop a mastery, over specified goals to secure 'insured' learning."

RESPONSIBILITY OF TEACHERS

Programme learning cannot replace the teacher. Any innovation in the school programmes and practices must remain in the hands of the teachers. The radio and T V did not displace the teacher. Similar is the case with programmed instruction. It is upto the enlightened teachers to take up the challenging task of preparing programmes. We have got a wide market. The programmes can be sold all over the country. A student who is convinced that he can learn better, achieve more with the help of this programme, will definitely prefer instead of buying this programme to buying a text book. By taking up this challenging task we will not only help the cause of education, help our fellow teachers by setting them free from the routine task of information, giving help to the students to achieve more, but we will be helping ourselves also.

It may also be remembered that these gadgets can be used mainly in the cognitive field and possibly in the psycho-motor field to develop certain abilities and skills of the students as an individual. A teacher is something more than all these gadgets put together. He has to bring about socialization of the individual; he has to promote socially desirable attitudes and interests and mould the personality of the students. The effective domain is almost reserved for his care. At present the teacher is not able to devote his energy and time to this important task as most of his time and energy is consumed by his routine job as an information giver. We always talk of education for three 'H's'—the head, the hand and the heart. But it has almost remained a mere slogan. Programmed learning, teaching machines and other gadgets will set teacher free from routine work. These are labour-saving devices for the teacher so that he may function more effectively in a field of his own choice.

Technique involved in programmed instruction can be used in teaching different subjects. Teaching of mathematics, science, social studies and elements of Indian languages can be done effectively with the help of this new technique. The teacher has to formulate objectives of teaching a particular subject, undertake content analysis of the subject matter in the light of objectives, frame a chain of questions which will lead the pupils in the direction of the objective and present the questions to his pupils who are expected to try their hand at answering the questions independently. The teacher will have to play the role of a friend, guide and philosopher in the class when the pupils are engaged in solving the riddle and at the same time acquiring knowledge or skill. The question of class discipline may not arise as the pupils will be found busy doing the task assigned to them by the teacher. The teacher will have to do remedial or corrective teaching as the weakness of his pupils will be located in the very act of learning. The pupil will also undergo a process of self-evaluation as he completes his work.

Role of the teacher in the changed context of Programmed Learning may be stated as under :

1. Teacher as an advisor in helping students in the selection of programme learning material.
2. Teacher as a discussion leader for focussing the attention of the learners on important points.
3. Teacher as a guide to clarify doubts and elaborate on various points asked by the learner.

4. Teacher as an evaluator of the learning outcomes.
5. Teacher as a consultant to the various agencies engaged in production of programmed material.

The programmed learning approach can be adopted in normal classroom teaching in the following ways:

1. A teacher can make use of the principles of programmed learning such as active responding, minimal errors and confirmation while teaching various subjects in the conventional manner.
2. A teacher can define behavioural objectives in advance of teaching.
3. A teacher can validate the instructional systems of a class in terms of the performance of learners immediately after teaching is over.
4. A teacher can regulate questions and answers. The answer of a learner can be immediately reinforced by informing or telling whether it is correct or incorrect.
5. A teacher can plan the entire instructional programme of a classroom and can treat the terminal behaviour, the pre-requisite skills and content analysis in advance.

Komoski (1960) an expert has observed "Two thousand years ago the world's first public administrator, a gentleman by the name Quintilian wrote what might be called a handbook for teachers." In it he has one bit of advice which will serve as an excellent starting point for a discussion of programmed learning and its potential uses. His advice is: "Do not neglect the individual student. He should be questioned and praised."

Programmed instruction is still in its infancy in India. Programmed instruction as an optional or elective paper has been included at the B. Ed./M.Ed. level in a few universities in India. It also forms a part of the paper of Educational Technology/Educational Innovation. However, as regards its classroom use, it may be observed that it is almost nil. As far back in 1966, the Kothari Commission suggested to develop programmed material in different subjects to test the suitability of the technique in Indian conditions. An Association of Programmed Instruction has been formed to coördinate the research being done at different centres in the country. The association also disseminates the information on new studies through its journal issued from time to time. The National Council of Educational Research and Technology has also done some work in the field. In spite of all these efforts, it may be stated that the application of programmed instruction has not yet made an appreciable impact on our classroom teaching. Our methods of teaching still remain traditional, by and large.

Following are the important factors which stand in the way of introducing programmed instruction in Indian schools:

1. Resistance to change.
2. Lack of good programmes.
3. Lack of facilities.

A Dictionary of Education (1981) by Derek Rowntree considers child-centred approach to education/teaching, as, "Rather wordly slogan, but its main point is made by teacher who claims 'I teach children, not subjects'. Implies care for the 'whole' child-his Personality, Needs and Learning Style and not just for his or her academic process."

The Concise Dictionary of Education (1982) by G.R. Hawes and L.S. Hawes defines child-centre education as, "An educational theory or system that emphasises the pupil and his or her individual characteristics as central in conducting instruction instead of focusing on subject matter, external authority, and educational requirements. Curriculum is constructed according to the pupil's interests and needs."

In their book *A Critical Dictionary of Educational Concepts (1986)* Robin Barrow and Geoffrey Mitburn observe, "The essence of child-centred education is, self activity, that the child should be at the centre of concern. ...Explicitly or implicitly, child-centred educationalists tend towards a view of *Education* being a process of leading out rather of imparting knowledge."

Child-centred education stresses the need for taking care of the child, its growth and development. It requires 'individualisation' of approach, so that one must study each child carefully, keep observations over a period of time, study the growth and development in sensory—motor area, intellectual area, emotional area, social area, language area, and so on.

The Aim. The aim is development of the total personality of the child.

Programme. Programme is to be activity-based with different teaching strategies.

Pace of Learning. It is to be based on children's needs and abilities.

Teaching-Learning. Teacher's role is that of a facilitator in learning and development.

Discipline. It is to be achieved through the maintenance of positive human relationships between teachers and pupils.

The Need. 1. The child is agent in his own teaming. Out of the three components of a learning situation; the child, the teacher and the components of a learning situation environment, pride of place is to be given to the child. He must become the most important agent in his learning. It means that curriculum must be thought of in terms of activities and experiences which appeal most to the child. 2. Children learn best when they are active. When we consider the child an agent in his own learning, we must provide for him to be active. The medium of learning is the activities undertaken by the child. Learning takes place through a continuous process of interaction between the learner and his environment. 3. Knowledge or information is not the goal. Self-realization is the goal. Personality and character are more important than the subject matter. To possess all the knowledge of the world and lose one's own self is an awful fate in education. 4. Child-centred approach is more psychological than logical. It emphasises the process rather than the product. 5. Child-centred approach gives freedom to the child under the creative and sympathetic direction of the teacher. 6. One single exposure to an experience does not affect all the necessary coordination of the physical and mental faculties of a child to preserve the net value of exposure. Hence there has to be repetitive exercises and drills to give a certain knowledge and the efficiency and tenacity of a skill and value. It is here the child becomes a trainee and the teacher becomes a trainer or the child an educand and the teacher as an educator. 7. A child is a unique being and can function only by remaining in the world in which it has a specific role to play.

The teacher's role in the world in which it has a special role, both in its spirit, is to help the child to conform to its unique habitual values, choices and consistent behaviour patterns. 8. The child's sense of wonder and astonishment and his natural curiosity lead to a learning process which should be encouraged by teachers.

The Limitations. Child-centred education has a few limitations which must be taken care of by the teachers. Too much freedom is likely to engender ego-centricism in children. Children may grow to be unwilling to accept reasonable authority. If all the times and at all places, likes and dislikes, preferences, whims and interests of children are elevated above the mature judgements of parents and teacher, it may result in undesirable outcomes. Adams, therefore, wanted that both the children and their teachers should be on the same footing of importance.

Pragmatically speaking, learning cannot be child-centred always in absolute terms. Child-centred education implies that each child may have a separate learning activity besides a few group activities. Perhaps no nation can afford to spend so much money, resources and time on child centred education. Child-centred learning is confined to the learned discourses of educational thinkers. There are so many children under the charge of a teacher that it is rather impossible to attend to the specific needs of children individually.

Corrective Measures. Of course emphasis on child-centred education tends to free the child from the tyranny of the traditional approach to education which meant 'chalk and talk', 'bookish knowledge' and the 'supremacy of the rod'. Implicit in all the positions of child-centred education is that the teacher must be prepared to give initiative to the learner in the educational encounter. The teacher as well as the child must remain active in the teaching-learning activity. The teachers must take the initiative and find out the limitations of the learner's own spontaneous and undirected activity. The teacher has an obligation to assess the limitations of child's choice of educational activity. The teacher's legitimate role in encouraging self-disciplinary function cannot be over-emphasised.

The role of the teacher in child-centred education.

1. Motivation of children.
2. Developing trust and confidence in children's capacity to learn.
3. Becoming as a resource for creating meaningful learning experiences.
4. Accepting the individual and the group.
5. Participating as a member of the group in guiding learning.
6. Becoming sensitive to the child's needs and interacting in a way that would provide a sense of feeling and security.
7. Recognising and reinforcing the individual contribution.

The educators and philosophers have emphasised certain principles of teaching which the teachers are expected to bear in mind for making their teaching effective, efficient and inspirational. Sometimes these principles are classified as psychological and general principles. This classification is however very arbitrary and both types overlap.

Principle of activity or learning by doing. Children are active by nature and any process or method that is not based upon the student activity is not in accord with the progressive educational theories. Rousseau considers the child as a "hero" in the drama of education and as such he must be allowed to play the dominant role. So the first principle is to keep the class active.

Children have been endowed by nature with tremendous vitality. In the words of T.S. Avinashilingam, "The great Ganga of life flows majestically on. But if anyone tries to retain and dam it, the dam will break unless attempts are simultaneously made to divert it into other channels. The waters can only be diverted, but cannot be dammed indefinitely. If anyone tried to do the impossible, it would be at his peril, for the dam will break, sooner or later. So is the nature of children. The great vitality of our children cannot be permanently restrained without providing a positive purpose. Thus, providing for various types of activities which will interest the children and give them opportunities for observation and the use of their hands is to offer them the fulfilment and satisfaction which nothing else confers."

Activity does not mean mere physical activity. If a pupil is to develop all sides of his personality, then it is necessary for him to be active in all ways, to exercise all the powers he has.

Principle of playway. This principle is closely related to the principle of learning by doing. According to Froebel play is the chief activity of childhood. It gives joy, freedom, contentment and inner and outer peace. It holds the source of all that is good. But "without rational conscious guidance," says Froebel, "childish activity degenerates into aimless play instead of preparing for those tasks of life for which it is designed."

Play is a natural activity just as a poet cannot refrain himself from writing a poem, a musician from singing, a dancer from dancing and an actor from acting, so too a child cannot refrain himself from playing. Play comes from within. It is a voluntary activity and is the manifestation of creative urge. It gives joy, freedom, contentment, inner rest and peace with the world. This implies that a spirit of playway should prevail in classroom work.

Principle of motivation. The teacher will do his best to motivate all children in the lesson. Motivation arouses the interest of children and once they become interested, they are willing to concentrate and work. Motivation is developed by the following techniques:

(i) Utilising the instinctive tendencies of the children in an effective manner.

(ii) Satisfying the curiosity of children.

(iii) Utilising all the senses of children.

(iv) Relating closely body and mind.

(v) Linking teaching-learning with life.

Principle of self education. Best teaching is enabling the child to learn by his own efforts. Teachers must fire the imagination of their students. Children, we are told, must be left free to express themselves, for the best education is self-education. Teachers, we are told, must stand aside. They must talk less, explain less and direct less. Adamson states, "The whole business is between the individual and his world's and the teacher is outside it, external to it. He may facilitate it, turning his attention to one or other member of the wedded pair. He may approach the individual and his avenues of approach will be one or other of the instincts or emotional dispositions which are the prime movers of mental life. He may try fear, pugnacity, curiosity, or sympathy or a combination of them, to quicken the current which seems to him sluggish or he may approach the factor truth, whichever of the three words it belongs to, and see whether anything can be done by lighting it up, or lining in main features and blotting out detail to facilitate adjustment. But whatever he tries, subject or object or both together, he remains outside the process, a spectator, a manipulator, perhaps a disturber; he is never in it and of it. Within that mysterious synthetic activity through which the individual is at once appropriating and contributing to his environment, forming and being formed by it... the teacher has neither place nor part."

The statement implies that the essential activity in teaching is not the adjustment of child to teacher but is to enable him to adjust himself to the environment and also to change the environment to adjust himself. Teaching must enable the child to work independently and without the teacher at a later state.

Dr. A.G. Hughes and Dr. E.H. Hughes remark, "It must be emphasised, however, that teachers are not as superfluous as some enthusiasts suggest, teaching is not the baneful evil it is sometimes represented to be. It is true that children are by nature curious, assertive and creative, but they are also submissive, imitative and ready to appeal for help. It follows, therefore, that we are not necessarily working contrary to child nature when we teach. We must, however, know when to teach and when to stand aside, when to explain and when to leave children to make discoveries, when to demonstrate and when to leave children free to experiment, when to require children to listen and when to give them scope for free expression." The two important aspects of teaching are stimulation and inspiration. The teachers must fire the enthusiasm of their pupils. They must encourage them in the development of their natural desire to work and to be active and guide these desires into worthwhile channels. The late President Eliot of Harvard once said, "The supreme value of a teacher lies not in the regular performance of routine duties, but in his power to lead and inspire his students through the influence of his own mental and moral personality and examples."

Principle of individual differences. No two children are alike. Teaching to be effective must cater to individual differences of children.

Principle of goal setting. A definite goal must be set before each child according to the standard expected of him. Short-term or immediate goals should be set before small children and distant goals for older ones. It must be remembered that goals should be very clear and definite and the children must understand these goals.

Principle of stimulation. Burton has said, teaching is the stimulation, guidance, direction and encouragement of learning. Ryburn emphasises this aspect in these words, "the guidance of the teacher is mainly a matter of giving the right kind of stimulus to help him to learn the right things in the right way."

Principle of association. Thorndike points out that things we want to go together should be put together. Many different things or ideas which we want to go together should be associated with each other. They should form a part of one process. Then it becomes easier to make the students understand their relationship.

Principle of readiness. This principle is indicative of learner's state of mind to participate in the teaching-learning process. Readiness is preparation for action. A teacher must be alive to this principle.

Principle of effect. This principle states that a response is strengthened if it is followed by pleasure and weakened if followed by displeasure.

Principle of exercise or repetition. According to it, the more a stimulus induced response is repeated, the longer it will be retained. Other things being equal, exercise strengthens the bond between situation and response. Conversely a bond is weakened through failure to exercise if it is the principle it has two sub-parts, (i) Principle of use and (ii) Principle of disuse.

Principle of change and rest. Psychological experiments in learning have demonstrated that fatigue, lack of attention and monotony can be overcome by making appropriate provision for change, rest and recreation. While framing the time table it is kept in view that subjects and activities are provided in such a way that the students do not experience boredom and fatigue. Usually two consecutive periods of a subject are not provided in a class.

Principle of feed-back and reinforcement. Learning theories point out that the immediate knowledge of the results and positive reinforces in the form of praise, grade, certificates, token money and other incentives can contribute to make the task of learning joyable.

Principle of training of senses. Senses are said to be the gateways of knowledge. The power of observation, discrimination, identification, generalisation and application can only be appropriately developed through the effective functioning of senses.

Principle of group dynamics. Under the influence of group behaviour, appropriate changes in the behaviour of the members of the group can take place. Individuals composing the group think and feel as the group feels, do as the group does. A suitable climate for group dynamics is to be created in the classroom environment.

Principle of creativity. Opportunities should be provided to the students to explore things and events and find cause-effect relationships. This principle envisages that every student possesses some element of creativity which must be explored and developed to the maximum extent.

Principle of correlation. Gandhiji was of the firm view that Correlation should be the basis of all work. He advocated that correlation of the learning task should be established with the craft, physical and social environment.

Successful teaching necessitates that the teacher comes down to the level of the pupils and at the same time assists them in rising above it. To a great extent, the principles of teaching to be followed depend upon the age of the pupils, the subjects and topic of the lesson. However, there are certain general principles which should underline the teaching of all subjects. As already stated, there is no clear-cut dividing line between psychological and general principles of teaching.

Principle of definite goals or objectives. Destination or goals of teaching-learning must be clear to the teachers and students. Goals and objectives keep the teachers and students on the track. Definiteness of goals helps in planning executing and evaluating every step, phase or act of the teaching-learning process.

Principle of child centredness. The entire teaching endeavour is for the child. Therefore, it is essential that teaching strategies should cater to the aptitude, interest and abilities of the students. In the drama of education, child should be assigned the role of 'hero.'

Principle of linking with life. Teaching can never be performed in a vacuum. It is always in a social context. In the teaching of all the school subjects, examples from everyday life should be given their due place.

Principle of correlation. Knowledge is one 'whole.' Various ideas and events are interrelated. There exist links among various subjects. Correlation of the present events can be made with the past. Similarly future can be visualised on the basis of the present happenings or state of affairs. Gandhiji propounded his system of Basic education with correlation as its cornerstone-correlation with the craft, correlation with the physical environment and correlation with social environment.

Principle of active involvement and participation of students. Teaching-learning is a two-way traffic. Traditional teaching was almost teacher-centred. There was very little scope for the involvement of the students. The teacher taught and the students listened to him passively. The new teaching emphasises that the students must actively participate in all the stages and steps of teaching-learning.

Principle of cooperation. Classroom environment becomes lively when the teacher and the taught work in unison, helping each other in carrying out the task of teaching and learning. All the participants have the same common interest. Naturally, they must cooperate with teacher.

Principle of remedial teaching. All students do not learn with the same speed and accomplishment. Some lag behind and need extra coaching. The teacher has to find out where the fault lies and think for positive measures. He may have to arrange for remedial or compensatory or extra teaching for any particular group of students for removing their specific difficulties.

Principle of creating conducive environment. Physical as well as social environment of the classroom plays a vital role in motivating the learners. Arrangement of light and furniture etc. should be properly attended to. There should be proper discipline and order. The teacher should be sympathetic but firm.

Principle of planning. Planning determines the quality or success of any task. Planning in teaching involves the preparation of the lesson notes, provision of teaching aids, and working out strategies to be adopted in the delivery of the lesson.

Principle of effective strategies. Teaching process to be effective must adopt proper means, strategies and tactics. A teaching strategy is a generalised plan for a lesson which includes structure, desired learning behaviour in terms of goals of instruction and an outline of planned tactics necessary to implement the strategy.

Principle of flexibility. Strategies should serve as guides for effective teaching. Strategies may have to be changed if the classroom situations so warrant. Teaching is a complex task and a live phenomenon. The possibilities of alternation in planned strategies cannot be ruled out at the execution state. A teacher must be quite imaginative and resourceful for adopting himself and his teaching to the requirements of the teaching-learning environment.

Principle of variety. A variety of teaching aids and strategies should be adopted to motivate and sustain the interests of the students. Variety serves as great tonic for creating fresh environment and checking boredom and lethargy.

Significance. The maxims of teaching are very helpful in obtaining the active involvement and participation of the learners in the teaching learning process. They quicken the interest of the learners and motivate them to learn. They make learning effective, inspirational, interesting and meaningful. They keep the students attentive to the teaching-learning process. A good teacher should be quite familiar with them. Now we proceed to discuss them.

Proceed from the known to the unknown. The most natural and simple way of teaching a lesson is to proceed from something that the students already know to those facts which they do not know. What is already known to the students is of great use to the students. This means that the teacher should arouse interest in a lesson by putting questions on the subject matter already known to the pupils. The teacher is to proceed step by step to connect the new matter to the old one. New knowledge cannot be grasped in a vacuum. A civics lesson on the powers of the President of India may start from the powers of the President of Municipal Board or of the President of Village Panchayat. A lesson on profit and loss in arithmetic can easily be taught to the pupils by referring to the shopkeepers who make profit. A history lesson on Lord Ram may be taken up with the celebration of Ram Lila.

Proceed from simple to complex. The simple task or topic must be taught first and the complex one can follow later on. The word simple and complex are to be seen from the point of view of the child and not that of an adult. We would be curbing the interest and initiative of the children by presenting them complex problems before the simpler ones are presented. In a lesson on nature study, for instance, a child will understand the concept of a flower first and thereafter its various parts. Similarly in a geography lesson the teacher will take up the general study of a region or country first and later on a detailed and specific study.

Proceed from easy to difficult. We must graduate our lessons in order of ease of understanding them. Students' standard must be kept in view. This will help in sustaining the interest of the students. In determining what is easy and what is difficult we have to take into account the psychological make-up of the child. Logically viewed one skill may be easy but psychologically it may be difficult. There are many things which look easy to us but are in fact difficult for children. The interest of the child has also to be taken into account. Lines are very easy to draw but a child may not like to draw lines. He may try to draw an animal. There is no doubt that it is difficult, but it is more interesting to him and so is easy for him. We should encourage him to do so and our approach will be psychological instead of logical.

Proceed from the concrete to the abstract. A child's imagination is greatly aided by a concrete material. "Things first and words after" is the common saying. Rousseau said, "Things, Things, Things." Children in the beginning cannot think in abstractions. Small children learn first from things which they can see and handle. Very young pupils learn counting with the help of pebbles, etc. A child understands an aeroplane with the help of a model. Actual visits to canals and rivers provide a clear idea of them.

A lesson in geography can be made interesting with the help of models, pictures and illustrations of bridges, rivers and mountains, etc. Care must be exercised to ensure that the students do not remain at the 'concrete stage' all the time. This is only the initial step for children with a view to reach the higher stage of 'abstraction' as they advance in age.

Proceed from particular to general. Before giving principles and rules, particular examples should be presented. As a matter of fact a study of particular facts should lead the children themselves to frame general rules. The rules of arithmetic, of, grammar, of physical geography and almost of all sciences are based on the principle of proceeding from particular instances to general rules.

Proceed from indefinite to definite. Ideas of children in the initial stages are indefinite, incoherent and very vague. These ideas are to be made definite, clear, precise, and systematic. Effective teaching necessitates that every word and idea presented should stand out clearly in the child's mind as a picture. For classifying ideas, adequate use must be made of actual objects, diagrams and pictures. Every possible effort should be made to make the children interested in the lesson.

Proceed from empirical to relational. Observation and experience are the basis of empirical knowledge. Rational knowledge implies a bit of abstraction and argumentative approach. The general feeling is that the child first of all experiences knowledge in his day to day life and after that he feels the rational basis. For instance, plane geometry makes better sense when taught in the context of everyday life instead of it in the format of a highly abstract theory. It is always better to begin with what the children see, feel and experience than arguing and generalising.

Proceed from psychological to logical. Logical approach is concerned with the arrangement of the subject matter. Psychological approach looks at the child's interests, needs, mental make up and subject logically. When we treat a subject logically, we re usually thinking of it from our own point of view and not from the point of view of the child. In psychological approach, we proceed from the concrete to the abstract, from the simple to the complex and from known to unknown. We start reading by teaching the child to read a whole sentence, as for him, the unit is the sentence, not the word or the letter as it is for the adult. This is psychological approach. In a drawing lesson a child has little sense in lines and curves. Logically we start with simple lines and curves but psychologically we start with drawing a whole animal.

Proceed from whole to parts. Whole is more meaningful to the child than the parts of the whole. J.P. Guildford, E.B. Newman and May Seagoe conclude after their research that the 'whole' approach is generally better than 'part' learning because the material to be learnt 'makes sense' and its parts can be seen by the learner as interrelated. The learner sees a relationship between the central idea of the material to be learned. The 'whole' unit or passage for slow learners should be smaller than the 'whole' for the fast learners.

From near to far. A child learns well in the surroundings in which he resides. So he should be first acquainted with his immediate environment. Gradually he may be taught about things which are away from his immediate environment. In a geography lesson we start from the local geography and then take up tehsil, district, state, the country and the world gradually.

From analysis to synthesis. Analysis means breaking a problem into convenient parts and synthesis means grouping of these separated parts into one complete whole. A complex problem can be made simple and easy by dividing it into units.

From actual to representative. When actual objectives are shown to children, they learn easily and retain them in their minds for a long time. This is specially suitable for younger children. Representative objects in the form of pictures, models, etc., should be used for the grown ups.

Proceed inductively. This maxim includes almost all the maxims stated above. In the inductive approach, we start from particular examples and establish general rules through the active participation of the learners. In the deductive approach, we assume a definition, a general rule or formula and apply it to particular examples. An example will make this distinction very clear. 'The farmers in India are very poor' is a general statement in the deductive type of reasoning. The inductive will follow thus: Ram is a farmer. He is very poor. Shyam is a farmer. He is very poor. Krishan is a farmer. He is very poor. In this way from several such examples it will be evident that farmers are poor. Thus, we derive generalisations. Both of the approaches i.e. the deductive and inductive have their own importance. However in general, inductive approach is considered a better one.

In the ultimate analysis it must be observed that the maxims are meant to be our servants and not masters. Moreover, by and large all are interrelated. It is also to be kept in view that children differ in their aptitudes, capacities, interests, mental and physical make-lip. Different maxims suit different situations and different children. It is, therefore, essential that a judicious use should be made of each maxim.

Exercise

1. Explain programmed learning. How does it differ from traditional teaching?
2. State the meaning, characteristics, merits and limitations of programmed learning.
3. Name the major styles of programming. Discuss their features and limitations.

4. What is programmed learning? Does it replace the teacher? Outline the role of the teacher in programmed learning.
5. "Programmed instruction, in spite of its important place in teaching-learning, is still in its infancy in 'India'? Explain. Suggest measures for its popularisation.
6. What are the various steps in programming? Prepare a programme on any topic.
7. "I teach children, not subjects." Explain this statement in the context of child-centred education.
8. Explain any five principles of teaching.
9. Elucidate the role of the teacher in the child-centred education.
10. State the significance of any four maxims of teaching.
11. Explain fully what is meant by the maxims' Proceed from the known to the unknown,' from 'simple to complex' and from 'concrete to abstract.' Illustrate their values and limitations.

7

METHODS OF TEACHING-1

PROBLEM SOLVING METHOD

The basic purpose of educations is to enable the child to adapt himself to life in society which is full of problems. To be successful, one must be adequately equipped with proper reasoning and reflecting power. Not only life in society, there are problems and puzzling situations which are a normal feature of a child's everyday life in school also. These problems grow in complexity as he grows older and older. Therefore, it is very important that problem solving must be encouraged in school life.

Children are curious by nature. They want to find out answers of several questions which sometimes are baffling even to adults. Nevertheless they must be helped to satisfy their curiosity as far as possible by providing answers to their questions. This implies that we must teach them how to think and reflect that they are able to apply this to a vast number of varied problem situations.

Problem solving ability enables the child to find appropriate solutions of problems which confront him.

Problem solving is an instructional method or technique whereby the teacher and pupils attempt in a conscious, planned and purposeful effort to arrive at some explanation or solution to some educationally significant difficulty. It is a planned attack upon a difficulty or perplexity for the purpose of finding a solution. Yoakam Simpson define it as, "A problem occurs in a situation in which a felt difficulty to act is realized. It is a difficulty that is clearly present and recognised by the thinker. It may be a purely mental difficulty or it may be physical and involve the manipulation of data. The individuals recognise it as a challenge."

Dewey explains problem solving as, "Whenever-no matter how slight and common place in character—perplexes and challenges the mind so that it makes a belief at all uncertain there is a genuine problem. The problem fixes the end of thought and the end controls the process of thinking."

According to Gates, "a problem exists for an individual when he has a definite goal he cannot reach by the behaviour pattern which he already has available."

Wesley thinks that, "The problem method may become a seminar method."

Problem solving is not merely a method of teaching. It is more a method of organisation of subject matter in such a way that it can be dealt with through the study of problems. However, this concept of problem solving does not seem to be suitable at the schools stage.

Problem solving involves reflective thinking which according to Deway is, "active, persistent and careful consideration of any belief or supposed form of knowledge in the light of the grounds that support it and further conclusions to which it tends, constitutes reflective thinking." Deway classifies thought processes into four types, beginning with the most rudimentary phases of mental activity and extending to the most complex forms of intellectual behaviour." At its first level, it is just idle fancy or day-dreaming when anything may fit across the mind without continuity or particular organisation or sequence. The second level or phase of thinking is reflected in imaginative stories and incidents. These stories and incidents have continuity and organisation as well but are not accepted as facts or truth. The third type of thinking is illustrated in our beliefs, prejudices and superstitions which are accepted and held by individuals uncritically or without rational analysis. The fourth and the highest level of thinking is reflective thinking.

Bossing has stated the essentials of reflective thinking in terms of the following abilities:-

1. Ability to sense the presence of a perplexing problem.
2. Ability to recognise clearly the nature of the problem.
3. Ability to hold the problem in mind as it is studied and not to get side-tracked or lose enthusiasm.
4. Ability and readiness to venture a bold guess or hypothesis by way of a solution.
5. Ability to finally formulate a possible hypothesis or solutions to the problem.
6. Ability to examine and evaluate critically the proposed solution or solutions of problems.
7. Ability and readiness to cast aside the hypothesis which has not been found valid. This needs courage and objectivety.
8. Ability to maintain an attitude of suspended judgement until all facts are gathered, weighted, sifted and evaluated.
9. Ability and readiness to recheck conclusions and to test their validity. This is known as the process of verification in deductive reasoning; one of the procedures in problem-solving.

Following are the essential features of the problem:

1. The problem should be meaningful, interesting and worthwhile for children.
2. It should have correlation with life.
3. It should have some correlation with other subjects if possible.
4. It should arise out of the real needs of the students.
5. The children must possess some background of the problem which they are going to discuss.

6. The problem should be clearly defined.
7. The solution of the problem should be found out by the students themselves working under the guidance and supervision of the teacher.

The steps of problem solving are as given below.

Formation and Appreciation of the Problem. The nature of the problem should be made very clear to the students. They must also feel the necessity of finding out a solution for the problem.

Collection of Relevant Data and Information. The students should be stimulated to collect data in a-systematic manner. Full cooperation of the students should be secured. They may be invited to make suggestions as to how they could collect the relevant data. The teacher may suggest many points to them. He may ask them to read extra books. He may also ask them to organise a few educational trips to gather the relevant information.

Organisation of Data. The students should be asked to sift the relevant material from the superficial one and put it in a scientific way.

Drawing of Conclusions. Discussions should be arranged collectively and individually with each pupil. Panton suggests that the teacher's aim should be to secure that, as far as possible, the essential thinking is done by pupils themselves and that their educative process produces the particular solution, formulation of generalizations at stake. "Care should be taken that judgements are made only when sufficient data is collected."

Testing Conclusions. No conclusion should be accepted without being properly verified. The correctness of the conclusions must be proved. The students must be taught to be critical, to examine the "truths" which they "discover" to see "whether they fit all the known data." We should have our minds free from every bias in the process of problem-solving.

Valentine Davis quotes Prof. Pasher who suggests the following points in problem-solving:

1. Get them (the students) to define the problem clearly.

2. Aid them to keep the problem in mind.
3. Get them to make many suggestions by encouraging them; (*a*) to analyse the situation in parts, (*b*) to recall previously known similar cases and general rules that apply, (*c*) to guess courageously and formulate guesses clearly.
4. Get them time to evaluate each suggestion carefully by encouraging them: (*a*) to maintain a state of doubt or suspended conclusion, (*b*) to criticise the suggestion by appeal to know facts, minister experiments, and scientific treatises.
5. Get them to organise the material by proceeding: (*a*) to build an outline on the board, (*b*) to use diagrams and graphs, (*c*) to formulate concise statements of the net outcome of the discussion.

It has been stated that for the success of the problem-solving teaching technique we need "a teacher who has the ability to see problems clearly, the power of analyses with a keen discernment and the faculty to synthesize and draw conclusions with an uncanny accuracy."

Procedures in Problem-Solving. There are two procedures in problem-solving and they are (*i*) the Inductive, and (*ii*) the Deductive.

Schorling describes the role of the teacher in problem solving as, "The teacher should set up an atmosphere of freedom in the class for proper problem-solving. This involves proper physical conditions and informality of procedure and mutual respect for personality."

Merits of Problem-solving.

Following are the merits of problem solving:

1. It helps in stimulating thinking.
2. It develops reasoning power.
3. It helps to improve knowledge.
4. It helps in developing good study habits.
5. It affords opportunities for participation in social activities. Problems are solved with the joint efforts of many students.

The students learn to appreciate the different points of view and thus become tolerant.

6. The students learn to be self-dependent.
7. Discussions help to develop the power of expression of the students.
8. The method provides opportunities to the teachers to know in detail their pupils. They learn which students are shy in nature and which are very active and accordingly they assist the students.
9. Students learn facts which are meaningful and which have been discovered by their own efforts.
10. It helps in the maintenance of discipline. The students remain busy in finding out the answers to their own problem.
11. Knowledge is easily assimilated as it is the result of a purposeful activity.
12. Learning becomes more interesting in place of a dread.
13. It gives the power of critical judgement.
14. It helps to verify an opinion.
15. It satisfies curiosity.
16. It helps to learn how to act in a new situation.

Demerits

The demerits are given below:

1. Generally speaking problem-solving involves mental activity only. There is less of bodily activity.
2. Small children do not possess sufficient background information and therefore they fail to participate in discussions.
3. There is a lack of suitable reference and source books for children.
4. It involves a lot of time and the teachers find it difficult to cover the prescribed syllabus.
5. Problem method needs very capable teachers to provide effective guidance to students.

6. There is the danger that the problem method may lead to the selection of trivial topics and in some instances to those that generate more feeling and emotion than thought.

Two general approaches to problem-solving are termed as inductive and deductive and both are complimentary and supplementary.

The Inductive Method. The inductive method is a method of development. In the inductive method, the child is led to discover truth for himself. The various processes in the inductive method are: (*i*) Observation of the given material: (*ii*) Discrimination and analysis noting differences and similarities, (*iii*) Classification, (*iv*) Abstraction and generalization, and (*v*) Application or verification.

In the inductive method, the pupils are led from particular instances to general conclusion. Concrete examples are given and with their help students are helped to arrive at certain conclusions or principles. In the teaching of science including geography, mathematics and languages, this method is very helpful. The students by examining a number of examples in science, conclude that heat expands and cold contracts.

In a geometry lesson the students by measuring the angles of a triangle come to the conclusion that their sum is equal to two right angles.

In a geography lesson the students by examining the heights of the places located at high places conclude that temperature decreases as height increases. The students may examine the heights and temperatures of places like Shimla, Nainital, Dalhousie, Darjeeling, etc.

In a lesson in economics, the students by examining a number of cases, may conclude that agriculturists in India are in debt. The process runs like this. Ram is in debt. Sham is in debt. Krishna is in debt, and so on. Ram is an agriculturist. Sham in an agriculturist. Krishna is an agriculturist, and so on. From this, it will be concluded that all these persons are agriculturists and are in debt. In a language lesson, the teacher while teaching preposition may give examples, like 'Ram is in the room.' 'The cat is under the table'. 'The book is on the table' and may lead the students to find out the definition of 'preposition'. We find that a crow is black; we find another crow also black; still another crow black, and so on and say that all crows are black. This method is more useful in lesson where rules, definitions, generalisations, laws and casual connections between facts are to be established.

Merits

Following are the merits of the inductive method:

1. Knowledge is self-acquired and is soon transformed into 'wisdom.' 'General truths in order to be learned must be earned' is a famous saying and the inductive method is true to it.
2. It promotes mental activity on the part of the pupils and makes them active participants in the learning teaching process.
3. It makes the lesson interesting by providing challenging situations to the students.
4. The method affords opportunities to the students to be self-dependent and develops self-confidence.
5. The student's curiosity is well-kept up till the end when generalisations are arrived at.
6. This method is very natural because the knowledge in possession of man has been acquired in this way from the practical side of experience.'
7. The child learns how to tackle problems. He not only acquires more facts but also learn the way of acquiring facts which proves him useful for practical life.
8. The method is based on sound psychological principles. Learning by doing is the basis of this method.

Demerits

Following are the demerits of inductive method:

1. There is every possibility that the students may draw conclusions very hastily and these may be based on insufficient data and, therefore, may be wrong.

2. The method is very slow and lengthy.
3. It is not very helpful in the case of small children.
4. It is not suitable in the teaching of subjects in which there is more stress on the teaching of facts. It is not possible for us to experience facts in history and in so many other subjects.
5. The inductive method is not a complete method in itself. It has been said, "Induction does not prove but only provides the material to prove, it only discovers." When we have discovered a principle, we have to apply it again on some concrete instances for its verification. Therefore, we need deductive method to ensure the value of inductive process.

This method is the other way round. In the deductive method rules, generalisations and principles are provided to the students and then they are asked to verify them with the help of particular examples. The students are told that places situated at these altifudes are cold and then particular examples are taken to prove it. Such examples can be multiplied.

Merits

The merits of the deductive method are as below:

1. The teacher's work is simplified. He gives general principles and the students verify them.
2. This method is very economical. It saves time and energy both of the students and the teachers. Many principles for the discovery of which mankind has taken a lot of pains can be told to the students easily.
3. It is very suitable for small children who cannot discover truths for themselves. They get ready-made material.

Demerits

These are as follows:

1. Knowledge is not self-acquired and, therefore, not assimilated properly.
2. The child is deprived of the pleasure of self-activity and self-effort as ready-made formulae, principles and rules are given to him.

3. It encourages memorisation of facts which are soon forgotten and, therefore, knowledge is rendered useless.
4. This method is unnatural and unpsychological for the students who do not possess ability to appreciate abstract ideas in the absence of concrete examples.
5. It fails to develop motivation and interest in the learning as the truths are not of much value to them.
6. It fails to develop self-confidence and initiative in the students.

Comparison of Inductive and Deductive Methods

Inductive	*Deductive*
1. First particular cases are dealt with and then definitions, principles and rules are derived from them.	1. First general definitions, principles and rules are stated and particular cases are taken as examples to prove them.
2. It leads to new knowledge.	2. It does not lead to new knowledge.
3. It is a method of discovery and, therefore, it is a method of teaching.	3. It is method of verification and explanations and, therefore, it is a method of instruction.
4. The children acquire first-hand information and knowledge by actual observation.	4. The child gets ready-made information and makes use of information acquired by others.
5. This method is rather slow.	5. This method is comparatively quick.
6. This method provides training to the child to depend upon himself and he develops self-confidence and initiative.	6. This method encourages dependence upon others as it is based on borrowing from others.
7. It is an upward process of thought and leads to principles.	7. It is a downward process of thought and leads to more comprehension.
8. This method is full of activity.	8. This method provides comparatively less scope for activity.

The Combination. According to I. E. Miller, induction is the making of the tools of thought and deduction is the using of tools. Both supplement each other and are not opposite things. Both are wanted for the discovery of truth as both legs are wanted for walking.

The only method for the teacher is the method by which minds add to its knowledge.

Inductive should be followed by deduction and deduction by induction. Our approach should be inductive-cum-deductive.

Balanced Use. It is aptly observed by I. E. Miller that induction is the making of the tools of thought and deduction is the using of tools. Both supplement each other and are not opposite things. Both are wanted for the discovery of truth as both legs are wanted for walking. Induction should be followed by deduction and deduction by induction. In fact, the only method for the teacher is the method which helps in providing appropriate knowledge, skills and attitudes among the students.

PROJECT METHOD

School is a community in 'miniature' and the project method aims at providing community life activities on a small-scale in the school. The Project Method is the outcome of the pragmatic educational philosophy of John Dewey, the noted American philosopher-cum-educator. The pragmatic educational philosophy lays great stress on providing different kinds of rich experiences to children. The method was developed and given a concrete shape by William Head Kilpatrick of the University of Columbia. It is a revolt against the traditional environment of the school which is usually marked by listlessness and passivity and which lacks active involvement of the students. At its best, the project approach is characterized by high level of student activity, enthusiasm, interest and commitment. The Project Method is one of the modern methods of teaching in which school, the curriculum and the contents of studies are considered from the child's point of view, his needs and interests in the context of real life situations-activities in the school are closely connected with the child's daily life and needs. In the traditional environment much of the subject-matter taught and many habits formed in schools do not conform to desirable social life and the project method aims at rectifying this deficiency.

The Project Method is the expression of the widespread dissatisfaction against the bookish, encyclopedic method which makes children passive and in which children are drilled and spoon-fed with information which mostly is unconnected with real life situations. The modern educators speak in no uncertain term about disconnected facts, disconnected subjects and pigeon-hole time tables, "Ignore these," they say, "Give the class a real life project to bite at and watch the result."

Following definitions of the project method throw a good deal of light on its meaning and significance.

Ballard. A project is a bit of real life that has been imported into the school.

Burton. The problem is a project which resets in doing. The motor element is not what makes the activity a project, but the problem solving of a practical nature accompanying the activity.

Charters, W.W. In the topical orgnisation principles are learned first while in the project the problems are proposed which demand in the solution the development of principles by the learner as needed.

Good. A project is a significant, practical unit of activity having educational value and aimed at one or more définite goals of understanding; involves investigating and solution of problems and frequently the use and manipulation of physical materials, planned and carried to completion by pupil and teachers in a nature 'real life' manner.

Kilpatrick, William. A project is a whole-hearted purposeful activity proceeding in a social environment.

Parker. A project is a unit of activity in which pupils are made responsible for planning and purposing.

Snedden. A project is a unit of educative work in which the most prominent feature is some form of positive and concrete achievement.

Stevenson. A project is a problematic act carried to completion in its natural selling.

Tomas and Ling define project as "a voluntary undertaking which involves constructive effort or thought and ventures into subjective results."

The above mentioned definitions bring out the following characteristics of a project.

(1) A project is a purposeful activity.

(2) A project is a real-life activity.

(3) A project is an activity in a natural setting.

(4) A project is a problem-centred activity.

(5) A project is an activity in a social setting.

(6) A project is a whole-heasted activity.

(7) A project is an activity which results in concrete and positive achievement.

(8) A project is a cooperative activity.

(9) A project is an activity which provides an integrated view of a subject.

(10) A project is an activity through which solution of a problem is found out by the pupils themselves.

(11) A project is a new way of looking at the child.

(12) A project is a new way of teaching the child to live.

(13) A project seeks to encourage individuals to understand life in its unity.

(14) A project provides a lot of freedom to the child.

The Principle of Purpose. Knowledge of purpose is a great stimulus which motivates the child to realize his goal. The child must have an ideal. Why is he doing certain things? Purpose motivates learning. Interest cannot be aroused by aimless and meaningless activities.

The Principle of Activity. Children are active by nature. They love activity. The instincts of curiosity, construction, pugnacity and herd make them active by nature. Therefore, such opportunities should be provided to them that make them active and learn things by doing. Physical as well as mental activities are to be provided to them. They are to be allowed to 'do' and to 'live through doing'.

The Principle of Experience. Experience is the best teacher. What is real must be experienced. The children learn new facts and information through experience.

The Principle of Social Experience. The child is a social being and we have to prepare him for social life. Training for a corporate life must be given to his childhood. In the Project Method, the child works in groups.

The Principle of Reality. Life is real and education to be meaningful must be real. The child who is to live in a life of reality must be trained as such through his education. The Project Method is a method of educating the child and, therefore, it must also be real. Real life situations are presented in the life of the school.

The Principle of Freedom. The desire for an activity must be spontaneous and not forced by the teacher. The child should be free from imposition, restrictions or obstructions so that he may express himself fully and freely. He must be given the freedom to choose an activity, to do an activity according to his interests, needs and capacities. The Project Method follows this principle.

The Principle of Utility. Knowledge will be worthwhile only when it is useful and practical. The traditional system of instruction simply stressed formal and vital information for its own sake and was of little utility. The Project Method develops various attitudes and values which are of great significance from the practical point of view.

Different Types of Projects. Now W. H. Kilpatrick mentions four types of projects:

1. 'The Producer Type', in which the emphasis is directed towards the actual construction of a material object or article.
2. 'The Consumer Type'. Where the objectives is to obtain either direct or vicarious experience, such as reading and learning stories, listening to a musical delectation etc.
3. 'The Problem Type,' in which the chief purpose is to solve a problem involving the intellectual processes, such as determining the density of a certain liquid.
4. The Drill Type,' where the objectives is to attain a certain degree of skill in a reaction—as learning a vocabulary.

Timely. Projects should be related directly to the lesson and vocational interest. Projects should suit the particular mental and chronological ages of the students.

Environmental and seasonal factors should also be taken into consideration. It is a well-known fact that there are definite relationships between the seasons of the year and current community interests and those of pupils. Therefore, projects should be timely.

Usefulness. Practical aim of the project should not be lost sight of. It must fulfil a long-standing need. The learning experiences in a project must be capable of being applied in life.

Interesting. Projects should be interesting to the students. They must make an appeal to the emotional needs, hungers or drives of the students.

Challenging. Projects should neither be too simple and easy nor too long and difficult. They should be challenging. It is an admitted fact that the youth wants to do tasks which are challenging in nature.

Economical. The projects should be economical. They should not unnecessarily tax the energy and pocket of the students. There should be optimum use of the time.

Rich in Experiences. Many experiences of the sociable nature should be provided in a project. The project-selected should be capable of correlating different subjects and practical activities of life.

Co-operativeness. The students should be allowed to think and plan independently as well as co-operatively. The projects should be executed in such a way as the students are kept active both physically as well as mentally.

Among the most important steps involved in a project are : (1) Providing a situation (2) Choosing and purposing (3) Planning (4) Executing (5) Recording and (6) Evaluating.

Providing a Situation. Stevenson taught the uses of the electric bell to high school students by the project method. It so happened that the school bell developed some defect and it is common knowledge that the school bell is a great regulatory element of school work. The occasion was utilised by Stevenson in providing a situation—overwhelming the bell system in the school. So the project on this problem was taken up by the class. The teacher for the use of the bell provided a real situation for taking up the project. Innumerable situations could be provided to the students to take up a project.

Choosing and Purposing. Purposing is very important. It is the centre round which a project moves. The project selected must be such as to satisfy a definite need or purpose. This purpose, as far as possible, must be acceptable to all the students of a class. Dr. Kilpatrick remarks, "The part of the pupil and the part of the teacher in most of the school work depends largely on who does the purposing. It is practically the whole thing." The students themselves should choose the project. The teacher should not be in a hurry to choose the project. Better results and better satisfaction can be had only through self-choice. Many situations should be provided to children. These situations should be discussed and the teacher should give useful suggestions. Decision should always be democratic. The teacher should merely guide and not thrust his opinion. The children must tell that the project is of their own choice.

The following points may be considered in the selection of a project:

1. Does it have a definite educational value?
2. Is it challenging?
3. Does it require a reasonable amount of effort?
4. Is it adapted to the ability, interests and activities of the students?
5. Is the cost of the material required in the execution of the project within reach?
6. Are the materials required locally available?
7. Is the time sufficient for the execution of the project?
8. Is it selected by consensus of the students?
9. Does it provide definite goals and purposeful activity?

Planning. Careful planning leads to better results. To drive the optimum benefit out of a project, it must be ensured that pupils play an important part in planning the project. Of course, in the very beginning the teacher should impress upon the students to take into consideration even the minutest detail. Different proposals coming from the students should be discussed. Thereafter the plan may be finalised. It must be stressed that the teacher must be ready with some proposals regarding the plan beforehand so that it may be possible for him to help the students in the best possible manner.

Executing the Plan. This step is the longest of all and requires a lot of work. The whole project is to be executed through the cooperative efforts of all students. The various activities of the project should be divided according to the individual interests and abilities of the different children in the class. This is the stage at which the students perform many activities and learn various useful experiences. The children keep themselves busy in collecting information, reading and writing in various languages, keeping accounts, calculating prices, looking up maps, collecting specimens of different things, measuring length and area, visiting markets, museums and zoos, visiting field and crops, seeking help from others and the like. The teacher should give sufficient guidance to the students. He should not dictate them.

Recording. A complete record of all activities connected with the project must be maintained. The project book should be well maintained. All the details in the various steps should be noted down. The project book should give a comprehensive picture of the project as a whole. It should give the procedure of providing a situation and of choosing the project, duties assignment, difficulties felt and experience gained, etc.

Evaluating. The entire work of the project is to be reviewed after its completion. Lessons must be learnt from the mistakes committed. This step provides an opportunity to the students to criticise constructively their own work. Self-criticism is a valuable form of training. At the same time the students should review the ideas, principles, facts, etc., which they have learnt from the project.

Merits

Based on the Laws of Learning. It is in accordance with the following psychological laws of learning. (*a*) *The law of readiness.* According to this law, we learn most when our minds are ready to receive. The Project Method prepares the mind of the students by providing them with suitable situation. (*b*) *The law of exercise.* Learning to be effective must be practised. The Project Method affords many opportunities to the students to learn by doing. (*c*) *The law of effect.* This law states that if learning is to be effective and fruitful, it must be accompanied by satisfaction and happiness. The students derive immense pleasure when they manipulate their own activities.

Related with Life. Learning becomes practical and intimately related with life when meaningful and purposeful activities are provided to the students. The children get opportunities to acquaint themselves with the real problems of life. The students learn the practical usefulness of different subjects of the curriculum.

Correlation with Other Subjects. The Project Method gives unity to the curriculum. The water-tight treatment of the various subjects which is commonly found in our schools gives way to an integrated programme. Subjects do not remain isolated. Learning comes as a by-product of purposeful activity.

Training for a Democratic Way of Life. The method provides sufficient opportunities to the students to work co-operatively for a common purpose. Decisions are arrived at democratically. The students have a say in the activities they choose, plan and execute.

Training in Citizenship. This method imparts training to the student to inculcate in them primary virtues like tolerance, independence, open-mindedness, resourcefulness, etc.

Inculcating Dignity of Labour. Dignity of labour is engendered through the Project Method. The students have to perform their activities with their own hands and thus they develop a taste for all kinds of work. They learn that there is nobleness in working and doing things with their own hands.

Problem-Solving. It discourages cramming and memory work. It stresses problem-solving. It helps in developing the thinking and reasoning powers of the students.

Providing a Source of Happiness for the Backward Students. The Project Method provides a great relief to the backward children by providing them opportunities of participation in practical situation. Such children as are incapable of thinking abstract things easily keep themselves busy in concrete and practical situations.

Providing Freedom. The students work with great enthusiasm for the completion of their self-chosen project. They do not feel tired as there is a good deal of variety in their work and atmosphere is full of freedom.

Solving the Problem of Indiscipline. As the children remain busy with their self-chosen work they do not get opportunities to think of anti-social acts.

Satisfying Effort. Students get the joy and take pride in the finished product of their labours.

Durable Learning. Whatever the students learn, stays with them for a longer time.

Natural Way of Learning. Project Method is a natural and playful way of learning.

Neglect of Intellectual Work. There is a widespread misconception that the Project Method glorifies hand work at the cost of intellectual work. The critics argue that the children are kept busy in model-making and the like.

Haphazard and Unconnected Teaching. Projects, many a time, do not keep the examination and curriculum in view. It is not possible to deal with all the subjects in a single project. There are many topics which cannot be taught through this method.

Upsetting of the Time-Table. In a project method it is not possible to fôllow a rigid time-table. It upsets the routine work of the school.

Neglect of Drill Work. This method neglects practise and the development of skill in various subjects. The students do not get adequate drill in arithmetic, reading, spelling, drawing etc.

Difficulty in Getting Suitable Text-Books. Preparation of books suitable for the Project Method is by no means an easy task.

Artificial Correlation. Sometimes teachers show over-enthusiasm in stretching the projects upon which the class is working beyond its natural limits and try to connect those topics which have remote connections with the project in hand.

Unsuitable for the Shirkers and Shy. Some students who are not included to take responsibility may remain in the background and do every little work.

Too Much Reliance on Young Children. It is not wise to depend too much on the choice of the children.

Lack of Competent Teachers. For the successful working of this method, very learned, efficient and resourceful teachers are needed. The method imposes heavy burden and responsibility upon the teachers.

Unsuitable for Transfers. A child reading in an ordinary school finds it very difficult to adapt himself to a school that follows Project Method and vice versa.

Costly. Sometimes the execution of the project requires materials which are very costly and beyond the reach of ordinary schools.

Difficult to Cover Courses. It is extremely difficult to cover the prescribed course.

Lack of Suitable Learning Material. It is generally observed that school libraries are not suitably equipped to provide opportunities to prepare material.

Lack of Accommodation and Equipment. Adequate buildings and equipments are not readily available in our schools.

Incomplete Mastery. Project approach often results in an incomplete mastery of the tools of learning which are essential means to child's education in the later years.

Too Ambitious Project. Projects may be too ambitious and beyond the pupils' capacity to accomplish.

Unsuitable to the Overall System of Education. The Project Method does not fit in the scheme of higher education.

A Project Method should not be considered in isolation. It should be accepted as one of the important methods of teaching and not the only and the executive method of teaching. It is definitely a supplementary method in the normal school. The project to be successful must be based on a definite procedure. The first and the main responsibility of the teacher is to provide those situations to the students wherein they should fell a spontaneous urge to solve some of their practical problems. The teacher must be on the lookout of discovering their interests, tastes, aptitudes and needs. There are different methods of providing situations. As far as possible, problems or situations which are provided to the students should be social ones. These provide better social training and give more satisfaction.

The teacher may converse with the class on different topics of interest to them. Pictures of different scenes may be shown to them. Surveys of the surrounding conditions may be undertaken. The projects for study and work may arise out of the festivals like

Diwali or Dussehra. The teacher is to tap all resources to provide worthwhile situations.

Most of the educators are of the view that the projects should be selected by the students themselves. They think that this will stimulate pupil purposing and that they will be more interested in their work if they have share in determining what they are to make.

Others who think that teachers should selecte the projects argue that this method will ensure that the students undertake only those projects which are within their reach. Students are immature and they require adequate guidance to select their projects.

However, the safer course would be to arrive at a compromise. According to this, the 'planning' and 'doing' should be under the guidance of the teachers. There should be no hard and fast rules in the selection of the project.

The relation of the teacher with his students is closer in the Project Method than in the ordinary class teaching. The teacher is like a friend, an elder brother who works together with the students and helps them to gain rich experiences. He must stimulate the shy students to put in their best. He must help the students to help themselves. He must see that the project is carried on in a democratic way. He must read intensively as well as extensively. He should have adequate patience, skill, knowledge, tact and sincerity.

PAGEANT ON THE LIFE OF LORD BUDDHA

History. The social, religious and political conditions of Indians at that time, sources of information regarding the life of Buddha.

Geography. Different places connected with the life of Buddha, preparation of maps showing these places.

Languages. Study of books which throw light on the life of Buddha, writing of the various details of project.

Religion. Evils of untouchability, love for all, truth and non-violence, teachings of Buddha.

Civics. Co-operative spirit to make the project a success.

Drawing. Preparation of stage, making lighting arrangement.

Art. Designing and decorative work in the project.

Moral Training. Learning lessons of piety, simplicity, etc., from the life of Lord Buddha.

VILLAGE SURVEY

History. History of the village, if any, relics and mountains, dwellings of primitive man—caves, huts, houses through different ages and at different places.

Geography. Occupation of the people, agricultural yield per acre, village handicarfts, rural indebtedness, co-operative societies.

Civics. Working of the Village Panchayat, co-operative store, educational facilities.

General Science. Health and sanitation of the village, water facilities, causes of diseases, village dispensary, ventilation, etc.

Arithmetic. Estimate of the cost of the village drainage system, calculation of the per capita income of the villager, measurement of land holding, calculation of different items in the family budgets, total area of the village land, area sown and cultivated, calculating agricultural produce per acre.

Language. Description of the various details of the survey.

Art Work. Preparation of charts depicting conditions of an ideal village.

Social Work. Dignity of labour.

MONTESSORI METHOD

The Montessori method derives its name from Maria Montessori (1870-1952), the originator of this method. Maria Montessori was an Italian doctor who later on became one of the greatest educationists of the world. Her entry into the medical profession has an interesting story behind it. In those days, doors of medical colleges were practically closed for women. Montessori had a keen desire to become a doctor. So she thought of a trick. She signed herself 'M. Montessori' when she applied for admission. The authorities could never imagine that a lady could apply in this way. They admitted her thinking to be a man. She became the first Italian lady to get the Doctor of Medicine. This speaks of her imaginative mind and her sharp intellect. While working as a Professor of Anthropology, she got interested in the education of the children. Initially she worked with mentally deficient children. Later on she became the supervisor of schools. Children between the age of 3 and 7 whose parents were mostly out of work attended these schools. The first of these schools was opened in 1907 by her and was named 'Children's House.' Here she developed a new method of educating children. This method was based on sense training. In 1922, she was appointed as Inspectress of Infant Schools by the Government of Italy. She began to impart training to teachers in the new method discovered by her, side by side her job. Teachers from other countries of Europe, including England received training.

Her running away from Italy. Mussolini, known as a Fascist Dictator came to power in Italy. He wanted to educate children for war. Montessori who was an ardent supporter of child's freedom, could not work under such a regime. She was obliged to run away from Italy and went to Holland where she founded a school.

Montessori's visit to India. Montessori came to India in 1939, and stayed here upto 1946. She spent most of her time at Madras and Ootacamund and promoted her views on early childhood. Apart from opening several nursery schools, she trained a large number of teachers for nursery schools. She again visited India in 1948 and spent about 3 years. Maria Montessori delivered the followeing twelve talks on child training from the Madras Station of All India Radio, during June 1 to 12, 1948.

(1) The Social Question of the Child. (2) The New Born Babe. (3) Incarnation. (4) Sensitive Periods. (5) Further Examination of

Sensitive Periods. (6) Order. (7) The Inner Order. (8) Intelligence. (9) Deviations. (10) Training. (11) The Naughty Child. (12) How to Solve the Conflict between the Adult and the Child.

Publications of Madam Montessori :

1. *The Discovery of the Child*
2. *Education for a New World*
3. *To Educate the Human Potential*
4. *The Secret of Childhood*
5. *The Child, Peace, Education*
6. *Reconstruction in Education*
7. *The Absorbent Maid*
8. *What You Should Know about Your Child?*
9. *Child Training*
10. *The Montessori Method*

Education as Development. According to Montessori. "Child is a body which grows and a soul which develops—these two forms— physical and psychic, have one eternal front, life itself." It follows then that "We must neither mar nor stifle the mysterious powers which lie within these two forms of growth, but we must await from them the manifestation which we know will succeed one another."

Development from Within. Montessori believes that education of a child is from within. She states, "If any educational act is to be efficacious, it will be only that which tends to help towards the complete unfolding of the child's individuality."

Principle of Individual Development. In the words of John Adams, Dr. Montessori "has rung the death knell of class teaching." She believes that every child is peculiar to himself and he progresses at his own speed and rate and collective methods of teaching crush his individuality. She treats each child as a separate individual and recommends that he should be helped and guided in a manner that helps him in his proper growth and development. The teacher is concerned with his mental as well as his physiological development.

Principle of Self-Education or Auto-Education. Montessori has shifted the emphasis from teaching to learning. She believes that self-education or auto-education is the only true education. She advocates that the child should remain undisturbed by adult interference. She has devised the Didactic Apparatus which attracts the attention of the children, keeps them busy spontaneously, leads, them to learn the powers of movements, reading, writing and arithmetic, etc.

The Doctrine of Freedom or Liberty. The doctrine is the outcome of the concept of education as development. Her belief is that there should be no hindrance or interference in the way of child's growth and development. She believes that the freedom is the birth right of every individual and she advocates the spontaneous development of the child through full liberty. She does not believe in putting restraints as she thinks that these may 'mar or stifle the innate powers of the child.' She says, 'The school must permit the free, nature manifestations of the child if he is to be studied in a scientific manner."

No Material Rewards and Punishements. According to her, they are incentives unnatural or forced effort and the development that comes with their help will also be unnatural. She writes, " The jockey offers a piece of sugar to his horse that he may respond to the signs given by the reins, and yet neither of these runs so superbly as the free horse of the plains."

Principles of Sense Training. Montessori asserts that our senses are the gateways of knowledge and therefore on their training and development depends the acquisition of knowledge throughout life. She pointed out that the senses are very active between the ages of 3 and 7 and that a lot of learning takes place during this period. She advocates that the sensory training is the key to intellectual development.

Principle of Motor Efficiency or Muscular Training. She has also attached importance to muscular training as a part of the early education of children. She believed that muscular training facilitates other activities like writing, drawing, speaking etc. She takes muscular activity as purely physiological in character. She stresses that running, walking, etc., all depend on muscular training.

The Teacher as the Directress. She replaces the word 'teacher by the word 'directress' as she thinks that the function of the teacher is to direct and not to teach. Her motto should be, "I must diminish to let you grow."

No Place for Fairy Tales. She would like to banish fairy stories from the curriculum of young children since these tend to confuse children and to hinder them in the process of adjusting themselves to the real world.

The following will explain the method of sensory training :

Purpose	*Apparatus*
1. For perception of size	1. Series of wooden cylinders varying in height only, in diameter only or in both dimensions; Blocks varying regularly in size and rods of regularly varying lengths.
2. For perception of colour	2. Pink cubes, brown prisms, green and alternately red and blue rods and coloured tablets, etc.
3. For perception of form	3. Geometrical insets in metal, wood, a chest of drawers containing plane insets, series of cards on which are pasted geometrical forms in paper.
4. For discrimination in 'Weight'	4. Tablets of wood similar in size but different in weight.
5. For discrimination in 'Touch'	5. Rectangular tablet with rough and smooth surface etc.
6. For discrimination in 'Sound'	6. Cylindrical boxes containing different substances. Musical bells, Small Wooden discs for the notes.

Scientific Basis of Development and Education. She states, "If a new and scientific pedagogy is to arise from the study of the individual, such study must occupy itself with the observation of free children."

The Montessori Method of teaching may be divided into four parts as given below :

1. Sensory training
2. Training in practical life activities.
3. Motor training.
4. Language and arithmetic teaching.

Sensory Training. Madam Montessori gives much importance to sensory training as she regards senses as the gateways of knowledge. Different kinds of materials are used to develop sensory training of children.

Method employed has three stages :

(i) Association of the sensory percept with the name, "This is red."

(ii) Recognition of the object, "Give me the red."

(iii) Recalling the name of the object, "What is this"?

Training in Practical Life. According to Dr. Montessori exercises are called "exercises in practical life" because in the Children's House real everyday life is carried on in which all house work is entrusted to the little ones, who execute with devotion and accuracy their domestic duties, becoming singularly calm and dignified. The students are required to sweep their rooms, dust and clean the furniture and arrange it as they like. They learn dressing and undressing and washing themselves. They are expected to hang up their clothes tidily. They lay their tables. The children take turns in various household duties and learn by imitation to conquer their difficulties in the process. "Enthusiasm and delight, fellow feeling and mutual aid are characteristics of the children learning the jobs." The students learn how to wash their hands. They learn how to use wash stands with small pitchers and basins. Children learn how to use their own soap and towels. They learn how to comb their hair, cut their nails and brush their teeth. The main purpose is to give children training in self-reliance and liberty and also to be independent.

Motor Education. These practical life exercises are considered to be very helpful for motor education. Muscular education is imparted in connection with the movements of walking, sitting and holding objects. The care of child's own body, managing the household affairs, gardening and manual work and rhythmetic movements provide motor education. Children also learn how to walk in straight lines and to balance them properly.

Didactic Apparatus for Teaching Language and Arithmetic. Madam Montessori is of the opinion that muscular skill in children is very easily developed and, therefore, the teaching of writing should precede the teaching of reading. According to her, writing is a purely mechanical activity and reading partly intellectual.

(a) Teaching of writing. There are three factors involved in writing.

(i) Movements which help in reproducing the forms of letters.

(ii) Manipulation of the pen.

(iii) The phonetic analysis of words in writing to dictation.

The letters of the alphabet are cut in sand paper and pasted on card-boards. The students are asked to pass their fingers on them. The students learn to establish the visual muscular images of the letters. At the same time, the phonetic sounds are also taught in three stages—association, recognition and recall. There are certain exercises through which the students are taught the handling of the pen.

(b) Teaching of reading. Montessori is not in favour of reading the sentence aloud. The child is handed over a card on which the names of the familiar objects are written and pasted. The child is asked to translate the writing slowly into sounds and then he is

asked to read faster. After some practice the child learns the correct pronunciation of the word. Then the child is asked to attach the cards with the objects lying there.

(c) Teaching of number. A `long stair' is used in the teaching of numbers. It consists of a set of the rods varying in length from 1 to 10 decimetres. It is divided into parts painted red and blue alternately. The child learns first to arrange the rods of size and then he counts the red and blue divisions and names the rods as one, two, three, etc. The signs of the numbrs are cut in sand paper and the same procedure of three stages—association, recognition and recall is followed.

The Didactic Apparatus for teaching language and arithmetic consists of the following:

- *(a)* Two sloping desks and various iron insets.
- *(b)* Cards on which are pasted sand paper letters.
- *(c)* Two sets of alphabets of coloured cardboard and of different sizes.
- *(d)* A series of cards on which are pasted sandpaper figures (1, 2, 3, etc.)
- *(e)* A series of large cards for the enumeration of numbers above ten.
- *(f)* Two boxes with small sticks for counting.
- *(g)* Drawings.
- *(h)* Frames for lacing, buttoning, etc. which are used for motor education of the hand.

Children's House' is the name given to a school by Dr. Montessori. This House provides all the requirements of a good `Family House'. As a metter of fact, it has all the qualities of a school, a workshop and a home. There are many rooms in the Children's House. The main room of the building is a study room. Smaller rooms—common room, lunch room, rest rooms, room for mutual work, a gymnasium, a lavatory or a children's bath room—are attached to this main room. The rooms are well equipped according to the needs of the children and spirit of the Montessori Method. The tables, chairs, etc, are specially made for children. They facilitate movement from one place to another. So far different shapes and long row cupboards are also provided. The children keep their Didactic Apparatus in the cupboard and their things in a little drawer. The black-boards are fixed in the walls on which the children draw or paste pictures of different kinds, according to their own interests. The students are provided with flowers, toys, pictures, indoor games, etc. The lunch room contains low tables, chairs, spoons, knives, tumblers, etc.

The children are provided with their own little shelf in the drawing room where they keep their soap and towel for washing. There is a small garden also which is looked after by the students themselves. Shelters are provided in the garden so that they can enjoy the open air, can play and work there, may take rest or sleep. They may have their lunch there if they do so please.

Paedometer to measure height and also the weighing machine are also there in the Children's House to keep a record of the heights and weights of the students.

Discipline. Discipline comes by an indirect route, by developing activity in spontaneous work. Every individual is expected to learn how to control himself by his own efforts and through calm, silent activity which is directed towards no external aim but is meant to keep alive that inner flame on which our life depends. Montessori writes, ``In truth, the `good' are those who move forward towards the goodness which has been built up by their own efforts." Such discipline can never be attained by way of commands, by sermons, by any of the disciplinary methods universally known.

Teacher as gardener. She thinks that a teacher should care for the child like a gardener who cares for the plant so that the natural growth of the child is properly guided and aided in the process of unfolding itself.

Knowledge of each child. The teacher should have an intimate knowledge of the mind and character of each individual. He should keep the physiological records of each child's development : his weight, height and other measurements.

The directress and not the teacher. Dr. Montessori has replaced the word 'teacher' by the word 'directress' and she thinks that the primary duty of the person in authority is to direct and not to teach. She insists that the directress should have an extensive knowledge of psychology and laboratory technique.

Doctor-cum-scientist-cum-missionary. In the words of Montessori, the Directress should be partly doctor, partly scientist and completely religious. Like a doctor she should avoid scolding or suppressing the patient in order to avoid worst situations. Like a scientist she should wait patiently for the results and should conduct experiments with her material. Like a religious lady she should be there to serve the child.

Faith in the personality of the child. She should allow the child to grow according to his own inner law. Her business is to provide for suitable environments. She should provide children with suitable opportunities to think for themselves.

Moral qualities. Virtues and not words are the main qualifications of the Directress." She must acquire moral alertness, patience; love and humility. She must banish anger which is a great sin and which prevents from understanding the child. The soul of the child, which is pure and very sensitive, requires her most delicate care. Her motto should be "I must diminish to let you grow."

Merits

The principles and practices of teaching advocated by Dr. Montessori almost revolutionized the traditional notions. Madam Montessori's profound love and affection, keen sensitiveness, artistic imagination and exceptional sympathy for children have given a new touch to various aspects of education. In fact, she has ushered in a new era in child education and especially of small children at the nursery stage. The chief merits of the Montessori method are :

Reverence for Small Children. To Madam Montessori "The child was God." Her school was the temple and duty of the temple was the recognition of the essence of childhood. She further writes, ``Today there stands forth one urgent need—the reform of methods in education and instruction, and he who struggles towards this end is struggling for the regeneration of man."

Scientific Bases of the Method. The method is based upon scientific grounds. Madam Montessori was a scientist and she applied scientific principles based on experience and observation and not upon prejudices.

Individual Teaching. Individualism is the key-note of the Monetessori method. Her method is a reaction against collective teaching. As observed by John Adams, Dr. Montessori. ``has rung the death knell of class teaching."

Freedom for Children. She ranks among the forefront educators who want to give education in an atmosphere of complete freedom. In her method discipline is that of self-control and self-directed activity.

Sense Training. The Montessori method aims at educating the children through the sense training. It is based upon the maxims `proceed from concrete to abstract', from 'general to abstract.'

Unique Method of Reading and Writing. Special importance to the learning of writing has been provided in the method. She takes into consideration the muscular movements in the process of writing. Properly graded and correlated exercised for reading and writing are provided.

Learning Through Living. She has provided practical exercises in her school which enable children to learn good habits of cleanliness and order. The students learn the lesson of dignity of labour and self-help by attending to their needs themselves. Many practical lessons are provided.

Training in Social Life. Though her method is individualistic in nature, yet it is full of social values. The social value of serving at the table and lunching together and cleaning plates, etc., is inculcated beyond doubt. The students perform many other activities cooperatively.

Demerits

Mechanical and Artificial Nature of Didactic Apparatus. Too much importance has been given to the Didactic Apparatus. The critics argue that the apparatus handcuffs both the teacher and the pupil. The pupil is expected to do different types of exercises with the help of the apparatus and the teacher also has to teach through the Didactic Apparatus with the result that the free expression of the children is limited and so the work of the teacher. The apparatus is unreal and unnatural.

More Emphasis on Biological Aspects and Less on Psychological. The teacher in this system takes special care in keeping records of the height, skull, and limbs of each individual child. She hardly observes temperament and other emotional traits.

Transfer of Training. The idea of sense training in the Montessori method is based on the old theory of `formal training of the senses.' She feels that by training particular faculties through particular senses it will be possible to get advantage of that training in other life situations through transfer of training to the desired field. Modern psychology disapproves of this idea.

Neglect of the Training of Imagination. There is no place for fairy tales in the Montessori system. Fairy tales used in a proper way form part of the literacy training of children and help in the development of imagination.

Lack of Suitable Teachers. The successful working of the Montessori system depends upon teachers who posses extensive knowledge of child psychology and acquisition of laboratory procedure. It is not possible to find such teachers in sufficient number.

Little Scope for Projects and Correlation. The present tendency is to teach all subjects together in the form of projects. Learning by doing is the key-note of the present methods of teaching. In the Montessori method the children have to depend upon the mechanical apparatus.

Comparison

Froebel's Kindergarten	Montessori Method
1. *Based on philosophical background.* The educational principles of the kindergarten are based on the philosophy of Froebel who was a philosopher and who became interested in education afterwards. To under-stand the method one has to understand his philosophy.	1. *Based on scientific background.* The Montessori Method is the outcome of the efforts of a doctor and scientist. Therefore, it has a scientific foundation. Its principles are clear-cut.
2. *Scope for development of Imagination.* For the development of imagination. Froebel recommends story telling.	2. *No Scope for fairy tales.* In the Montessori Method there is no place for fairy tales. Realities of life are given more importance.
3. *More scope for social development.* The children are encouraged to work in groups. Same things and same subjects are taught to them together.	3. *Comparatively less scope for social development.* There is too much stress on the development of the individual child and less on social development.
4. *Class-room teaching.* Class-room instruction forms an important part of instruction. A fixed time-table is followed.	4. *Individual learning.* Montessori is individualistic out and out. There is no set time-table. Students ar free to learn according to their taste.
5. *Sense training through gifts.* In the Kindergarten there is a set of gifts to be presented to the child in a set order and each child is provided with an information with the gift.	5. *Sense training through the Didactic Apparatus.* There is the sensory apparatus for the development of sense which is entirely different from that of the Kindergarten.

contd.

Froebel's Kindergarten	Montessori Method
6. *Emphasis on Play-way.* The Froebelian system puts more stress on play activities. All lessons are accompanied by songs, gestures and movements.	6. *Self-corrective apparatus* is provided to the child and this apparatus is to be used in a specific way and it affords little opportunities for play.
7. *Importance of manual activities.* There is much scope for activities like gardening, nature study, clay modelling, etc., in this system.	7. *Stress on daily-life activities.* Besides manual activities, dusting, cleaning, washing, sweeping, etc., the students learn how to take care of themselves.
8. *The teacher as leader.* The teacher is like a gardener who looks after the young human plant. He is a leader who guides their songs and movements.	8. *The teacher as a directress.* The function of the directress is to provide apparatus and work like a spectator and watch from a distance.
9. *Easily applicable.* This method can be made use of even without the apparatus. We do not require any elaborate material to equip a school to run on Kindergarten lines.	9. *Apparatus is indispensable.* An elaborate and costly apparatus is required to set up a school on Montessori lines. No school can be set up without the apparatus.
10. *Not a detailed system.* It lacks a suitable system for the teaching of three R's.	10. *Detailed System.* A detailed system of teaching three R's, *i.e.*, reading writing and arithmetic has been formulated.
11. *Training of teachers.* Froebelian method of training has not become so popular.	11. *Definite system of teacher training.* Madam Montessori evolved an elaborate system of training of teachers.

Very Expensive. It requires a lot of money to set up a school on the lines as suggested by Dr. Montessori. It is very doubtful if we could spare huge sums on such schools.

Recognition of the Importance of Nursery Education. Froebel as well as Montessori have given us a method of educating the infant. They have brought about a revolutionary change in the concept of education at the pre-school age.

Education as Development from Within. Both the educators regard education as the development of the inner nature of the child. They point out that the function of the educator is to draw the inner out.

Congenial Environment. Both the educators stress the importance of providing a congenial environment in which the growth of inner nature of the child should take place in a suitable manner.

Reverence and Affection for the Child. Froebel as well as Montessori have greatly stressed that there should be an environment of love and affection for the child; his personality should be recognised and even worshipped.

Stress on Sense Training. Froebel as well as Madam Montessori have devised apparatus for the training of senses of the child.

Role of the Teacher. The teachers in both the methods play the role of a guide.

Exercise

1. Explain the problem method. State its merits and limitations.
2. Describe the various steps in teaching through problem solving.
3. How does a problem method differ from lecturing or telling method? How can we derive the best results from the problem method?
4. State the values claimed for problem-solving as a teaching-

learning procedure. To what extent the realization of these values depends upon the teacher?

5. "Induction is the making of the tools of thought and deduction is the using of tools." Explain this statement.
6. Compare the inductive and deductive method of teaching. "Two general approaches to problem-solving are termed as inductive and deductive and both are complimentary and supplementary." Elucidate this statement.
7. "The conception of projects, or concrete units of work is at the bottom of a revolt against the tyranny of the textbook." Discuss.
8. Define a project. What are the stages in the Project Method? Evaluate its merits and limitations.
9. "To be truly educative a project must afford genuinely spontaneous and purposeful activity." Explain.
10. "In the Project Method, knowledge is assimilated through experience." Elucidate.
11. How can the Project Method be adopted to teach normal teaching? State the role of the teacher in following this method.
12. "Montessori deserves the credit of sounding the death-knell of class teaching." Discuss.
13. What is the importance of the `Didactic Apparatus' in the Montessori method?
14. Compare the Kindergarten Method and the Montessori method.
15. Evaluate the Montessori method. State the role of the teacher in this method.

8

METHODS OF TEACHING-2

KINDERGARTEN METHOD

Friedrich Wilhelm August Froebel (1782-1852) popularly known as Froebel who was a German educator founded the Kindergarten Method. Kindergarten is a German word which means the 'children's garden, i.e. a place where young human plants are cultivated. Froebel regarded school as a garden, the teacher as a gardener and the children as plants. The teacher like a gardener carefully tends the children under his care and helps them to grow. Before becoming a teacher at the age of 23, Froebel had worked as an apprentice to a forester, a farer, a clerk, a surveyor, private secretary, a book keeper and a student of architecture.

Son of a village clergyman. Froebel was born in 1782 in South Germany. The sad memories of his early childhood as well as his youth made him very eager in promoting the happiness of children. Having lost his mother when he was just nine months old, he was brought up by a strict father and an indifferent step mother. Rejected at home by his step-mother, scorned at school for his stupidity and repressed child and seemed to be out of control for sometime. However, at his tolerant and liberal uncle's place in Switzerland, Froebel first tasted affection, freedom and trust. Froebel served for sometime in military also.

Froebel spent a few years at the University of Jena, University of Gottingen and University of Berlin. He was greatly influenced by the idealistic philosophy of Fichte (1762-1884) and Schelling (1785-1854) great German philosophers. Froebel worked for three years at Pestalozzi's (1746-1827) school at Yuerdum.

The year 1816 was a turning point in the life of Froebel. For in this year he established a small school at Griesheim. The school was meant for the education of small children between the age of 3 and 7. In 1827, the school was transferred to Blankenbug, near Keithan.

The school attracted world-wide attention for its novel approach to methods of teaching. The school was named "Kindergarten'—a German word which means the children's garden. As already stated Froebel regarded the school as a garden and the teacher as a gardener.

Froebel gave many lectures in different towns in Germany and started regular courses of instruction and training for teachers at Blakenburg and other towns and villages. The great aim and purpose of his life is summed up in his famous saying ``Come, let us live for our children.'

Sad End. Froebel spent his entire life for the cause of child education. The German Government did not approve of his method of teaching and prevented him from establishing any school. This was a great shock for the great educator and he could not survive it. Froebel died in 1852 in agony, misery and poverty. His grave is marked by a slab with a cube, a cylinder and a sphere on it—his gifts representing carefully graded materials for educating the children.

Publications of Froebel. Froebel's important publications are 1. *Education of Man.* 2. *Pedagogy of Kindergarten.* 3. *Education by Development* 4. *Mother Play Stet Nursery Songs.*

Froebel's philosophy of education derives its inspiration from the following principles:

1. The law of unity or interconnectedness. The unity of universe is three-fold in nature. (a) Unity of substance; (b) Unity of origin (c) Unity of purpose.

2. The principle of continuous development from within.
3. The principle of self activity.
4. The principle of development of individuality through social institutions.

Functions of Education. The functions of education, according to Froebel, may be summed up as "Education should lead and guide man to clearness, concerning himself and in himself to peace with nature, and to unity with God. It should lift him to knowledge of himself, to mankind to a knowledge of God and of nature, and to the pure and holy life."

Why Stresson the Education of the Pre-School Child. One might rightly ask why Froebel, with his comprehensive training in so many fields of knowledge and his philosophical interest, finally concentrated his efforts particularly on the education of the pre-school child. There are two reasons for it. One is psychological. Froebel reveals an astounding insight into the importance of the early experiences of childhood for the future development of the personality. This anticipation of modern analytical psychology, which he shares with Pestalozzi and Herbart, led him naturally to emphasize the importance of pre-school education. The other reason is of sociological nature. Froebel lived in the period of the Napoleonic wars, with all their destructive influences, upon which followed the early period of capitalism and a series of social revolutions. He saw that in all these crises nobody was so imperilled as the children.

Froebel's educational principles grew out of his idealism and these can be summed up as under :

1. The child must be educated in accordance with the laws of his development.
2. Education should enable the child to realize unity in diversity.
3. Directed self-activity through social participation should be the basis of all education.
4. Froebel envisaged the problems of education in the sociological background. "His kindergarten or school was a little world where responsibility was shared by

all, individual rights respected by all, brotherly sympathy developed by all, and voluntary cooperation practised by all," observed Hughes.

5. Froebel developed both the theory and practice of play in education.
6. Froebel combined play and work.
7. Froebel recognised that head, hand and soul are developed in an integrated way through play-way activities.
8. Froebel advocated that education should be in accordance with the nature of the child.
9. Froebel introduced manual instruction in the school curriculum.
10. Froebel stressed upon religious education.
11. Froebel considered childhood as the most important stage of the development of man and humanity.

Meaning of Kindergarten. Froebel discovered much similarity between a child and a plant. He believed that the process of growth and development of the child and the plant is the same. The plant grows from within according to the seed that is within. In the same way the child grows from within. He unfolds the tendencies and impulses from within. The teacher in the school is like a gardener who looks after the little human plants and waters them to grow to beauty and perfection. Froebel, therefore, named his school as kindergarten. Kindergarten is a German word which implies a children's garden. Froebel conceived the school as a garden, the teacher as the gardener and the students as tender plants.

Objects of the Kindergarten. In the words of Froebel the object of a Kindergarten is "to give the children employment in agreement with their whole nature, to strengthen their bodies, to exercise their senses, to engage their awakening mind and through their senses to make them acquainted with nature and their fellow creatures. It is specially to guide them about the heart and the affections, and to lead them to the original ground of all life, to unity with themselves."

Free Self-Activity. Education should provide for free self-activity and self-determination on the part of man, he being created for freedom in the image of God.

Education Through Doing. "Plastic-material-representation in life and through doing, united with throught and speech, is by far more developing and cultivating than the mere verbal representation of ideas.

Education Through Play. 'Play is the purest, most spiritual activity of man—it gives, therefore, joy, freedom, contentment, inner and outer rest, peace with the world. It holds the source of all that is good!

Study of Nature. Froebel wants to study nature 'as life—the plants development—the animal as acting—the organ as functioning.'

'Drawing Out' as the Objective of Teaching. 'The object in teaching is to bring more and more out rather than to put more and more in."

Teaching-Learning a Double Side Process. 'All true education be simultaneously double sided—giving and taking, uniting and dividing, prescribing and following, between educator and pupil."

Religious Education. 'Religious instruction quickens, confirms and explains the feeling that man's own spiritual self, his soul, his mind and spirit, have their being and origin in God and proceed from God.

Discipline Through Love. Froebel believed "Control over the child was to be exercised through a knowledge of his interest and by the expression of love and sympathy."

Self Activity. Froebel believed that the growth of the child is directed by inner force in the child. "Education," said Froebel, should provide for "free self-activity and self-determination on the part of man—the being created for freedom in the image of God." He regarded self-activity as a process by which the individual realised his own nature and builds up his own world and then unites and harmonises the two. An Inspector reported about this self-activity, "Self-activity of the mind is the first law of this institution, the kind of instruction given here does not make the young mind a strong box into which, as early as possible kinds of coins of the most different values and coinage, such as are now current in the world that are stuffed, but slowly, continuously, gradually and always inwardly that is according to a connection found in nature of the human mind, the instruction steadily goes on without any ticks, from the simple to the complex, from the concrete to the abstract, so well adapted to the child and his needs that he goes as easily to his learning as to his play." The following points should be noted regarding activity :

(i) It should not be vague.

(ii) It should be a sublimated or controlled activity.

(iii) Social atmosphere is essential in order to secure meaningful activities.

(iv) Self-activity may take the form either of work or of play.

Play. According to Froebel, "Play is the purest, most spiritual activity of man at this stage. ... It gives, therefore, joy, freedom, contentment, inner and rest, peace with the world. It holds the source of all that is good." Froebel recognised that play needs to be organised and controlled on definite materials so that it may not degenerate into aimless play "instead of preparing for those tasks of life for which it is destined." There should be rational conscious guidance. Conseuently, Froebel has given seven gifts to children to play with.

Songs, Gestures and Construction. Froebel saw an organic relationship between songs, gestures and construction. He regarded these as three coordinate forms of expression in the child. What is to be leant by the pupils is first expressed in a song, then it is dramatised or expressed in gesture or movement and lastly illustrated through some constructive work such as paper or clay. Thus, a balanced development of the mind, the speech organs and the hand is aimed at. These three activities provide exercise to the senses, limbs and muscles of the child.

Selection of Songs. He has given songs in his book. *Mother and Nursery Songs.* These are fifty play songs. The idea of the introduction of songs is to enable the child to use his sense, limbs and muscles and also to familiarise him with the surroundings.

The child begins to use language through these songs. Each song is accompanied by a game such as 'Hide and Seek'. The selection of the song is determined by the teacher in accordance with the development of the child. There are three parts in a song.

(i) A motto for the guidance of mother or teacher.

(ii) A verse accompanied by music.

(iii) a picture illustrating the song.

The song for drill is :

Let us have a drill to-day,
March along grand array,
And whoever steps the best
Shall be captain over the rest,
And lead us on our way.

Gifts and Occupations. We have already stressed the place of activity and play. To provide activities, Froebel devised suitable materials known as gifts. These have been carefully graded. They possess all the novelty of play things. The order of the gift is devised in such a way as it leads the child from the activities and thought of one stage to another. The first gift consists of six coloured balls contained in a box. The balls are of different colours. The child is to roll them about in play. The occupattion consists in rolling them. The balls are intended to give the students an idea of colour, materials, motion and direction. The rhymes accompanying the rolling of the ball are :

Oh, see the pretty ball
So round so soft and small
The ball is round and rolls each way,
The ball is nice for baby's play.

Second gift consists of a sphere, a cube and cylinder made of hard wood. These are contained in a box. The child plays with them and notices the difference between the stability of the cube and the mobility of the sphere. He learns that the cylinder is both movable and stable and it harmonises the qualities of both.

Third gift, often called 'the first building box' has a large cube divided into eight smaller equal cubes from which the child can build up a number of artistic forms such as benches, steps, doors and bridges, etc. Through these cubes, the child can also gain elementary knowledge of addition and substraction.

Gift 4 is composed of large cubes divided into eight oblong prisms in each of which the length is twice. The breadth is twice the thickness. This is helpful to the child in constructing different types of buildings and patterns when combined with the third gift.

Gift 5 is very much similar to gift 3. It consists of a large cube divided into twenty-seven small cubes, three of which are again divided diagonally into halves and three into quarters. With these, the child can construct several beautiful forms and patterns by combining the third and fourth gift. Gift 5 is very helpful in teaching form and numbers to children.

Gift 6 is again very much similar to gift 4. It consists of a large cube divided into eighteeen whole and nine small oblong blocks. Children can form several designs from this gift. It is also very useful in teaching numbers.

Gift 7 comprises a set of square and triangular tablets made of fine wood in two colours. It provides help in many exercises in geomêtrical form and mosaic work.

There are several other gifts which can be used in occupations (activities) such as basket making, drawing, embroidery, mat-making, modellingperforating, paper-cutting, and threading of beads etc.

The Place of Teacher. The teacher is not to remain passive. The teacher has to suggest the idea of occupation when gifts are offered to children. He is also required to demonstrate certain activities to them. He also sings a song with a view to help the child to form appropriate ideas.

While presenting a cube, the teacher sings a cube song, e.g.
Fight corners, and twelve edges see,
And faces six, belong to me;
One face behind, and one before,
One top, one bottom, that makes four.
One at the right, at left side one,
And that counts six, if rightly done.

While presenting a sphere, the teacher sings the songs of the sphere, e.g.

(1) The Ball is such a pretty thing,
About it I do love to sing.
So round it is, and light and soft,
I hold it in my hands full oft.

(2) It is made of wool, and do you know
That on a sheep the wool did grow?
Until some men fleece did take,
Warm clothes and pretty ball to make.

Discipline. A teacher has important responsibilities to perform. He has to inculcate sympathetically values like love, sympathy, humility, cooperation and obedience to elders. He has to avoid external restraint and bodily punishment. The child should be made to realize that discipline depends upon his love for order, goodwill and mutual understanding. Froebel stressed that women should be trained for training children at this stage.

Curriculum. The divisions of the curriculum are :

(i) Manual work,
(ii) Religion and religious instruction.
(iii) Natural science and mathematics.
(iv) Language
(v) Arts and objects of arts.

Merits

1. Froebel laid emphasis on pre-school or nursery education.
2. He stressed the importance of play in the early education.
3. He broadened the concept and scope of the school as an essential social institution. He regarded school as a miniature society where children get training in important things of life. They learn the virtues of co-operation, sympathy, fellow-feeling, responsibility etc.
4. Froebel stressed the necessity of the study of child's nature, his instincts and impulses.

5. The gift and occupations of the Kindergarten give a new method of teaching.
6. The inclusion of productive work in the school makes children productive workers.
7. There is sufficient scope for activity in a Kindergarten.
8. Various gifts provide sensory training.
9. The inclusion of nature study in the curriculum helps to develop love for nature and world in the mind of the students.

Demerits

1. Froebel expects too much of the child. It is not possible for the child to be able to understand abstract ideas of organic unity while playing with gifts.
2. In the Kindergarten, too much stress has been laid on the development from within. The importance of the environment has not been fully recognised.
3. Songs as given by him are out of date. These cannot be used in every school.
4. The gifts to Froebel are formal in nature. The order of presentation of gifts is arbitrary. They do not serve much purpose of sense training.
5. The kindergarten of Froebel does not provide for the study of the individual child.
6. There is little of correlation in the teaching of various subjects.
7. It is not possible to accept his excessive emphasis on play in education as it is likely to detract the child from serious learning.
8. Philosophy on which Froebel based his method is very complicated. It is very difficult for children to understand his symbolism.
9. It is very difficult to follow the principle of organic unity.

Froebel invited us to live for our children and love them. The school for young children are no more jails and the children are no more passive learners. There is no doubt that all the tendencies in the modern educational thought and practice find their roots in Froebel's conceptions. He helped to make the society conscious of education for very young children. The chief areas in which he influenced the modern education are as under :

Emphasis on Pre-Primary or Pre-Basic Education. The present educator fully recognises the importance of the education in the early years. Today we find a large number of schools catering to the needs of such children. Froebel had also realised that until the education of nursery was reformed, nothing solid and worthy could be achieved.

New Conception of School. Hughes says, "His kindergarten school was a little world where responsibility was shared by all, individual rights respected by all, brotherly sympathy developed and voluntary co-operation practised by all." His school was a society in miniatue.

The present tendency in education is to regard school as a society in miniature. Dewey also regarded the school as a social institution. The present school is being regarded as a co-operative institution.

Respect for the Child' Individuality. Froebel lived for children, worked for children and died for children. He had profound love and sympathy for children.

Stress on the Study of the Child. Froebel stressed the need for the study of the nature of the child, his instincts and impulses. Modern education is very particular to see that adequate scope is provided for the free play of the impulses and instincts of children.

Education Through Play. Froebel believed that play is the highest phase of self-development. He introduced play-way in the activities of the school. Today we find that the principle of play-way has been accepted by every educator. We teach children through songs, movements, gestures, dramatisation, hand-work etc.

Sense Training. Froebel introduced gifts for the training of the senses of children; with the help of these gifts he wanted to give the idea of shape, form, colour, size and number. In every modern school those activities are introduced that help in the training of senses. Audio-visual aids form an integral part of the present system of education.

Nature Study in Education. Froebel was the first educator to make self-activity as the basis of education. 'Learning by doing' is the slogan of the day. The present school has become a place of activity and joy for children. We provide activities to students so that they may satisfy their instincts of construction, manipulation, curiosity and acquisition.

Nature Study in Education. For Froebel nature study was a means of bringing the child nearer to God. He advocated a syllabus of nature study to enable the child to understand the world in which he lived and to develop habits of careful observation. This idea has taken such a strong hold today that we do not regard any school worthy of name if it does not provide for nature study.

Women Teachers at the Nursery Stage. It will not be wrong to say that it is due to the influence of Froebel that we find a trend to entrust the education at the pre-primary or pre-basic stage to women teachers who are considered to be more suited for this task of instruction at this stage.

Concluding Remarks. Froebel's gifts and songs can be adopted/adapted to local conditions. Likewise locally available material can be provided so that it could be made as inexpensive as possible. There is no doubt that kindergarten method as founded by Froebel is, by far the" most original, attractive and inspirational" method for infant development. On account of this, this method is now used in all the progressive schools of the world.

PROGRESSIVE AND DYNAMIC METHODS

The effect of recent developments in educational philosophy and educational psychology upon the methods of teaching has been revolutionary. The central place in the school, in theory at least, has been given to the student. Any process that is not based upon the 'student-activity' is not in accord with recent educational theories. The present century has been termed as 'The Century of the Child'. Rousseau considers that' child' is a 'hero' in 'the drama of education' and as such he must play the dominant role.

The origin of modern methodology may be traced to *'Great Didactic'* of Johann Amos Comenius who lived in the seventeenth century. Comenius believed that all instruction should be carefully graded and arranged in a natural, order. He advocated that the teacher, in his methods, should appeal through sense perception to the understanding of the child. He set forth his principles in his *'Great Didactic'*. The work of Comenius, however, like that of other educators of his time was buried beneath the sea of religious controversy and bigotry of his age.

'Emile' of Rousseau in the second half of the eighteenth century laid the foundations of the methodology and became the inspiration of forward looking and progressive educators. Comenius provided some ideas, Rousseau improved and enlarged and others worked upon them and put them into practice. In his chief educational work 'Emile', Rousseau begins with his principle "Everything is good as it comes from the hands of the luthor of nature; but everything degenerates in the hands of man." He points out that there are three great teachers, "nature, man and things."

Johann Heinrich Pestalozzi attempted to "psychologise instruction." He declared that the basis of all education was a drawing out process and not a pouring in process, that the basis of all education lay in the nature of the child and that methods of instruction must be sought and constructed to that end.

Wilhelm August Froebel and Johann Friedrich Herbart, disciples and followers of Pestalozzi developed elaborate systems of education. The work of Froebel dealt largely with the Kindergarten stage. Herbart gave his famous 'Herbartian Steps' which cast a flood of light on existing methods. Herbartian steps became the stimulators of various other movements in the field of education. Herbart condemned the rote method and stressed comprehension and association. The concept that the outcome of education was not the strengthening of the mental faculties but rather the building up of an "appreciative mass" of ideas was very revolutionary. Herbartian theory and practice became popular in Germany between 1865 and 1885. Teachers and students from many lands studied at Jena, a centre of Herbartian teaching. By

1890, these ideas were brought to America where they received an almost universal acceptance.

The period of Herbartian influence, on the whole, was a transitional one. It prepared the way for newer and better concepts of education. By 1910, Herbartian as a system of education was quite generally criticised. Herbartianism stressed the teacher and the formal procedure of teachings; the new theories of educational philosophy emphasised the pupils. Emphasis during recent years has been on individual instruction in the classroom but the socialisation of the individual is not to be neglected. Almost all modern methods and procedures can be used to promote both. It is believed that socialisation can be used in connection with individual development. Through his own activities intermingled with the activities of the group, The pupil can learn and develop. Education must begin with the child and must be adapted to the needs and requirements of the child as he grows. Only in this manner, according to this philosophy, can the individual be made socially efficient.

In the words of Herbart Ward and Frank Roscoe, "While it is true that good method is not merely a collection of artifices or mechanical devices and that every teacher must devise his own method, it is important to remember that good method can result only from the constant observation of certain broad principles. These include orderly procedure in teaching, an arrangement of the subject-matter which will avoid waste of time and of energy and a distribution of emphasis which will secure the greatest cooperation from the pupils and maintain their active interest."

The Secondary Education Commission (1952-53) has emphasised the need for right methods of teaching in these words, "Every teacher and educationist of experience knows that even the best curriculum and the most perfect syllabus remain dead unless quickened into life by the right methods of teaching and the right kind of teachers. Sometimes even an unsatisfactory and unimaginative syllabus can be made interesting and significant by the gifted teacher who does not focus his mind on the subject-matter to be taught or the information to be imparted but on his students—their interests and aptitudes, their reactions and response. He judges the success of his lesson not by the amount of matter covered but by the understanding the appreciation and the efficiency achieved by the students."

Likewise the Education Commission (1964-66) has stated, "In a modern society where the rate of change and of the growth of knowledge is very rapid, the educational system must be elastic and dynamic. It must give freedom to its basic units-the individual pupil in a school, the individual teacher among his colleagues, and the individual school (or cluster of schools) within the system of move in a direction or at a pace which is different from that of other similar units within the system without being unduly hampered by the structure of the system as a whole." Progressive methods of teaching provides suitable opportunities for 'learning by doing,' for 'observation,' for 'experimentation' and for 'cooperation'.

The word method is often used very loosely. It has been supposed to involve a body of fixed and stereo-typed modes of procedures each applicable to its appropriate subject as a kind of ritual to be observed by all teachers, and in all circumstances. In this sense method has been rightly scorned and is now becoming discredited. In the words of Herbart Ward and Frank Rose, "While it is true that good method is not merely a collection of artifies or mechanical devices and that every teacher must devise his own method, it is important to remember that good method can result only from the constant observation of certain broad principles. These include orderly procedure in teaching, an arrangement of subject matter which will avoid waste of time and energy and a redistribution of emphasis which will secure the greatest cooperation from the pupils and maintain their active interest." A method is not merely a device adopted for communication certain items of information to students and exclusively the concern of the teacher who is supposed to be at the 'giving end'. A method must link up the teacher and his pupils into an organic relationship with constant mutual interaction.

1. They should aim at developing 'love for work'.
2. They should aim at inculcating the desire to do work with the highest maximum of efficiency which one is capable of. The motto before the teachers and the students should be "Everything that is worth doing at all is worth doing well."

3. They should develop the capacity for clear thinking.
4. They should provide adequate opportunities for participation in freely accepted projects and activities in which cooperation and discipline are constantly in demand.
5. They should expand the student's interest. As recommended by the Secondary Education Commission 1952-53. "We Would urge all schools to provide in the time table, at least one free period everyday in which students pursue their favourite hobbies and creative activities individually or in groups, preferably under the guidance of some interested teacher."
6. They should aim at providing opportunities to pupils to apply practically the knowledge and skill acquired by them.
7. Their aim should be to transform schools into 'work schools' and 'activity schools'.
8. They should aim at the quickening of interest and training efficient techniques of learning and study.
9. They should be adapted to the 3 A's—age, ability and aptitude of the students.

The new teaching recognises the right of the pupil to do things in his own way, within reasonable limits.
-Adains

Observation more than books, experience rather than person, are the prime educators.

-Alcott

The first principle of true teaching is that nothing can be taught.

The teacher is a helper and a guide. His business is to suggest and not to impose.

-Aurobindo, Sri

The method of teaching which approaches most likely to the method of investigation, is incomparably the best.

-Burke

Teaching is the stimulation, guidance, direction and encouragement of learning.

-Burton

In a real sense, a teacher may be compared like a conjurer who surprises his audience by keeping the balls in the air at once. The teacher has to encourage forty minds to think of the same subject during a given time. Minds that have different previous knowledge, different interests, and work at different rates. And as the conjurer must be aware of each of the balls so must the teacher be aware of each of the students, now giving a word of special help to one, now asking the question that will make another try to think out a difficulty.

-Catty, N

Effectiveness in learning lies not in reading and listening but in action, performance and experience.

-Cladwell Cook

Impression must be ensured by expression and what has to be done must be learnt by doing

-Coomenius

(a) Where there is experience, there is the living being.

(b) Action must precede knowledge.

(c) Education is by experience.

(d) The teacher is a guide and director, he steers the boat but the energy that propels it must come from those who are learning.

(e) The sole direct path to securing improvements in the methods of instruction and learning consists in catering upon the conditions which exact, promote and test thinking.

-Dewey

To awaken interest and kindle enthusiasm is the sure way to teach easily and successfully.

-Edwards, Tyran

(a) The object of teaching is to bring more and more out rather than to put more and more in.

(b) Play is the highest phase of child-development-Play is the purest, most spiritual activity of man at this stage (childhood).

(c) To learn a thing in life through doing is much more developing cultivation and strengthening than to learn it merely through the verbal communication of ideas.

-Froebel

(a) In my scheme of things the hand will handle tools before it draws or traces the writing. The eyes will read the pictures of letters and words as they will know other things in life, ears will catch the names and the meanings of things and sentences. The whole training will be natural, responsive, and, therefore, the quickest and the cheapest in the land.

(b) The superstition that no education is possible without a teacher is an obstacle in the path of an educational progress. A man's real teacher is himself. A diligent person can easily acquire knowledge about many things by himself and obtain the assistance of a teacher when it is needed.

(c) Pupils should know to discriminate between what should be received and what rejected. It is the duty of the teacher to teach his pupils discrimination.

(d) When our children are admitted to schools, they need no slate and pencil and books, but simple village tools which they can handle freely and remuneratively. This means a revolution in educational methods.

(e) I want the whole process of education to be imparted through some handicraft or industry.

(f) The core of my suggestion is that handicraft are to be taught not merely for production work but for developing the intellect of the pupils.

(g) I do not want to teach the village children only handicraft. I want to teach through handicraft all the subjects like History, Geography, Arithmetic, Science, Language, Painting etc.

-Gandhiji

(a) The main principle which psychology tends to the theory, of education as its starting point, is the need that all communication of new knowledge should be a development of previous knowledge.

(b) Interest arises from interesting objects and occupations. Many sided interest originates in the wealth of these. To create and develop this interest is the task of instruction which carries on and completes the preparation begun by intercourse and experience.

(c) Interest means self-activity. But not all self-activity, only the right degree of the right kind is desirable, else lively children might well be left to themselves. There would be no need of educating or controlling them. It is the purpose of instruction to give the right direction to their thoughts and impulses, to incline these toward the morally good and true.

-Herbart

I care not what subject is taught if only it is taught well.

-Huxley

I keep six honest serving men,

They taught me all I know.

Their names are What, and Where and When,

And How and Why and Who. *Kipling, Rudyard*

A tutor should not be continually thundering,, instruction into the ears of his pupil, as if he were pouring it through a funnel, but induce him to think to distinguish and to find out things for himself; sometimes opening the way, at other times leaving it for him to open; and so accommodate his precepts to the capacity of this pupil.

-Montaigne.

We have burried the tedious and stupid ABC primer side by side with the useless copy books.

-Maria, Montessori.

Nature invented play as a device for using that energy to prepare him for serious business of life.

-Num, T.P.

Modern teaching sets no limits to the kinds of experiences which may be employed, and imposes no restrictions upon the ways in which these are to be conducted.

-Panton, J.H.

(a) Our unpsychological schools are essentially only artificial stifling machines for destroying all the results of the power and experience that nature herself brings to life.

(b) When I now look back and ask myself: What have I specially done for the very being of education? I find I have fixed the highest, supreme principle of instruction in the recognition of sense impression as the absolute foundation of all knowledge.

(c) All the beneficent powers of man are due to neither art nor chance, but to nature, and that education should be in accordance with the courses laid down by nature.

(d) Nature develops all the powers of humanity by exercising them, they increase with use.

–Pestalozzi

(a) Do not give your pupil any sort of verbal lesson, for he is to be taught only by experience.

(b) Nature wills that children should be 'children' before they are men... Childhood has ways of seeing, thinking, feeling peculiar to itself, nothing is more absurd than to wish to substitute ours in their place.

(c) I wish some discreet person would give us a treatise on the art of observing children-an art which would be of immense value to us, but of which fathers and schoolmasters have not as yet learnt the very first rudiment.

(d) The highest function of the teacher consists not so much in imparting knowledge as on stimulating the pupil in its love and pursuit.

(e) To know how to suggest is the art of teaching.

(f) Children are restless and then curious. Instead of making the child stick to his books, I keep him busy in workshop, his hands will work to the profit of his mind.

-Rosseau

(a) Teach the pupil not only to answer questions but also to question answers.

(b) Education does not mean teaching pupils what they do not know. It means teaching them to behave as they do not behave. It is not teaching youth the shapes of letters and the tricks of numbers and then leaving them to turn their arithmetic to roguery and their literature to lust. It means, on the contrary, training them into the perfect exercise and kingly continence of their bodies and souls.

-Ruskin

(a) The object of teaching by the heuristic method is not so much to teach facts ... as to teach how knowledge of facts may be obtained, of how they can be systematised and of how they may be used. Pupils who are taught in this way learn to be observant, exact and to think for themselves.

(b) The guidance of the teacher is mainly a matter of giving the right kind of stimulus to help him to learn the right things in the right ways.

(c) It (teaching) is also the encouraging and training of the emotional life. This is an aspect of teaching which is very commonly neglected at least in practice. But our teaching will be only one sided and distorted unless we take into account the necessity for helping the child to develop a stable emotional life.

(d) To teach we must use experience already gained as a starting point for our work.

–Ryburn

The sector of successful teaching is to teach accurately, thoroughly, and earnestly; this will impart interest to instructions and awaken attention to them. All sciences, in their nature of connections, are replete with interest, if teachers properly, illustrate and impress their truths in a pleasing, earnest manner.

—Simmons, C

Children should be told as little as possible and induced to discover as much as possible

-Spencer

To the child, the environment will provide an ever ready background for its spontaneous activity.

-Tagore

And other's follies teach us not,

Not much their wisdom teaches:

And most, or sterling worth, is what
Our own experience teaches. —*Tennnyson*

Teaching means skilful questioning to force the mind to see, to arrange, to act.

(a) No one was ever really taught by another, each of us has to teach himself.

(b) You cannot teach a child more than you can grow a plant. The plant develops its own nature. The child also teaches itself.

(c) All knowledge, therefore, secular or spiritual, is in the human mind. In many cases it is not discovered, but remains covered, and when the covering is being slowly taken off we say, "We are learning" and the advance of knowledge is made by the advance of this process of uncovering. The man from whom this veil is being lifted is the more knowing man, the man upon whom it lies thick is ignorant, and the man from whom it has entirely gone is all-knowing omniscient.

(d) From the lowest man to the highest yogi, all have to use the same method to attain knowledge. The chemist who works in his laboratory concentrates all the powers of his mind, brings them into one focus, and throws them on the elements: the elements stand analysed, and thus his knowledge comes. The astronomer concentrates the powers of his mind and brings them into one focus; and he throws them on to objects through his telescope and stars and systems roll forward and give up their secrets to him. So it is in every case: with the professor in his chair, the student with his book, with every man who is working to know.

-*Vivekananda, Swami*

TRADITIONAL METHOD

1. They are dominated by 'verbalism' the delusion that if a student is able to memorise or repeat certain words, or phrases, he has grasped the facts or the ideas that they are meant to convey.

2. They seldom relate teaching to life.
3. There is no determined attempt to develop expression in speech and writing.
4. They do not provide enough suitable opportunities to students for self-activity.
5. They lack motivation and fail to arouse real interest.
6. The teachers rely upon dictating notes and the children memorise them at home for passing examinations and tests.
7. Practical and productive work does not find a prominent place.
8. "Chalk and talk" dominate.
9. Methods are usually devoid of correlating and integrating various subjects and experiences.
10. They do not train the students in the 'art of study'.
11. They do not suit different levels of intelligence.
12. They encourage learning from 'notes' and summaries rather than textbooks.
13. They do not make adequate use of audiovisual aids.

Characteristics

1. The methods of teaching in schools should aim not merely at the imparting of knowledge in an efficient manner, but also at inculcating desirable values and proper attitudes and habits of work in the students.
2. They should, in particular, endeavour to create in the students a genuine attachment to work and a desire to do it as efficiently, honestly and thoroughly as possible.
3. The emphasis in teaching should shift from verbalism and memorisation to learning through purposeful, concrete and realistic situations, and, for this purpose, the principle of *'Activity Method'* and *'Project Method'* should be assimilated in school practice.
4. Teaching methods should provide opportunities for students to learn actively and to apply practically the knowledge that they have acquired in the class-room. 'Expression work' of different kinds must, therefore, form part of the programme in every school subject.

5. In the teaching of all subjects special stress should be placed on clear thinking and clear expression both in speech and writing.
6. Teaching methods should aim less at imparting the maximum quantum of knowledge possible and more on training students in the techniques of study and methods of acquiring knowledge through personal effort and initiative.
7. A well-thought-out attempt should be made to adopt methods of instruction to the needs of individual students as much as possible so that dull, average and bright students may all have a chance to progress at their own pace.
8. Students should be given adequate opportunity to work in groups and to carry out group projects and activities so as to develop in them the qualities necessary for group life and cooperative work.

Feeling of reform in the air. The individual teacher is most likely to try bold changes in teaching practice if there is a feeling of reform in the air and if he sees his small contribution as part of a major social revolution.

Eagerness of the inspectorate. The experimenting teacher must have much more than the passive acquiescence of the school inspectors. He must feel that officers of the Education Department are personally eager to see experimentation and that they are willing, within reasonable limits, to accept a proportion of failures as part of the price.

The Inspectors are the key figures in any reform of class-room practice. They are Authority, present and obvious. They should be consulted from the beginning, should know that their criticisms and suggestions carry weight, and should be made to feel that the proposed changes are, in some measure, their reforms. A school system can be no more elastic or dynamic than the Inspectors will let it be. Which is why the in-service education of inspecting officers assumes great significance.

General support of the profession to experimentation. The sympathy and support of headmasters and senior teachers must be won quite early in the programme if they are not to dampen all youthful ardour to experiment and explore. They may not want to break new ground themselves. But if they do not feel they are, being bypassed and that the new system is not being foisted on them, they can become its patrons, if not its practitioners. There is also much to be gained by winning the approval of teachers' organisations to any movement that increases flexibility in the school system. Individuals will experiment more readily if they feel that experimentation has the general support of the profession.

Team work and a sense of security. Anything that breaks down the isolation of the teacher increases his sense of assurance and makes it easier for him to adventure. The strengthening, of the teacher's sense of inner security is a purpose common to all the methods advocated to increase the elasticity or dynamism in a school system. It is the basis of all real reform in teaching practice. There are occupations where a mass advance can be achieved by the invention of new equipment and the issuing of instructions for its use. No worthwhile advance is possible in teaching method unless the individual teacher understands what he is doing and feels secure enough to take the first new steps beyond the bounds of established practice. It is easier for a teacher to do so in a small group than when he is working alone. The success of 'team teaching' in introducing new teaching techniques into some American schools is based on the fact that it is not the individual but the team that is responsible for the planning and execution of new methods. It is our belief that the proposed organisation of a school complex in which the teacher works in a cooperative group is more likely to help flexibility than the present system of isolation.

Mastery of the subject-matter. Nothing reduces a teacher's sense of security or his willingness to take advantage of freedom so seriously as does his ignorance of the subject-matter he has to teach. If he is only a few lessons ahead of his class he dare take no risks, and finds safety in the old routine of rote memorising. Increasing the teacher's level of general education is, in general, the surest way of ensuring that some of them will adopt livelier and more meaningful methods of teaching.

Provision for a good library and teaching-learning material. Obviously elasticity or dynamism will be increased if there is a reasonable provision of books, teaching materials, and services that will enable some children to undertake part of their work alone or in groups. There is a limit to what can be expected of the most imaginative teacher if all he has is a bare room, a blackboard, a standard text-book, and sixty pupils. The most pressing needs for a teacher who wants to branch out on new methods are, therefore, a good supply of books and paper, and particularly at the lower levels of school education, some simple tools and materials for making equipment. As the proper use of a well-equipped school library is absolutely essential for the efficient working of every educational institution and for encouraging literacy and cultural interests in students every secondary school should have such a library; class libraries and subject libraries should also be utilised for this purpose. Trained librarians, who have a love for books and an understanding of students' interest, should be posted in all secondary schools and all teachers should be given some training in the basic principles of library work, in the training colleges as well as through refresher courses. Where there are no separate public libraries, the school libraries should, so far as possible, make their facilities available to the local public and all public libraries should have a special section for children and adolescents.

Role of teacher's training institutes. When in doubt, teachers will teach in the way they were taught themselves and not in the way they were told to teach. So, if a school system is to become more flexible and teaching methods more lively and varied, it is essential that these qualities be established very early in the practice, as well as in the theory, of at least some of the teacher training institutions at both the primary and the secondary level should become centres for devising, testing, and adapting methods and materials to be used in the schools.

Demonstration and experimental schools. In order to popularise progressive teaching methods and facilitate their introduction, "Experimental" and "Demonstration" schools should be established and given special encouragement where they exist, so that they may try out new methods freely without being fettered by too many departmental restrictions.

Cooperation of the parents. A teacher or an institution will be able to introduce innovations more easily if the parents of the pupils know enough about their purpose so as not to have any fear that they will interfere with their children's chances at the final examination. A strong and respected headmaster or teacher can probably best win over the parents by his own efforts; but in most cases, it will be necessary for the Department to help in convincing parents that changes in methods are desirable and officially approved.

Inspirational methods. These methods are primarily based on high activity on the part of the teacher.

Expository methods. In these methods cognitive emphasis is very high, while student activity and emphasis on experience is low. One good example of expository method is the lecture method in which the main emphasis is on imparting cognitive information to the learners.

Natural learning methods. The main rationale of these methods is that learning takes place in a natural way and planning for learning is not necessary. Learners are left on their own, with free and unplanned activity. Thus, the emphasis on learning activity is high, whereas it is low on planned experience and on cognitive inputs.

Individualized methods. These methods are quite well known mainly through the popularity of programmed instruction. The main characteristic of these methods is the guided search encouraged by the instructor or the teacher. In addition to programmed instruction, self-study, computer-oriented instruction, case method and prescribed experiments in science are other examples of individualized learning in which the main emphasis is for each learner to learn at his own pace.

Encounter methods. Carl Rogers had popularised the term encounter,' although several other terms are used like T-group, sensitivity training, interpersonal confrontation and so on. In these methods the main emphasis is on experience and learner activity. Since the emphasis is on providing experience through confrontation or through encounter, and not through cognitive understanding, these methods are effective for change in basic behavioural patterns and developing new ways of looking at things. Role play also involves some amount of encounter.

Discovery methods. These methods are high on all the dimensions: learner activity, experience and experimentation by the learner, and cognitive understanding. Simulations primarily come under the category as also self-generated experiments in science. The main emphasis of methods in this category is on problem-solving and providing necessary framework to the learner, so that while solving the problem the learner is also able to learn the rationale and logic of what he has done.

Group methods. Project method and socialised classroom method come linder this category.

Methods are also classified as under:

In this classification, a few devices of teaching are also included as some writers term these devices as methods of teaching. In fact, there is no clear-cut distinction between the term methods and devices.

1. Assignment Method
2. Dalton Plan
3. Discussion Method
4. Laboratory Method
5. Lecture Method
6. Montessori Method
7. Observation Method
8. Play-way Method/Approach
9. Questioning
10. Problem Method
11. Project Method
12. Review Method
13. Socialsed Classroom Recitation Method
14. Source Method

15. Story Telling Method
16. Supervised Study Method
17. Text Book Method

Meaning and Significance. Teaching and learning in the outdoors implies teaching and learning outside the four walls of the classroom. It may also imply teaching and learning outside the school premises i.e. from natural surroundings and from various community resources. This approach to education is based on the well-established principle of 'learning by doing.'

The principal premises underlying the implication of outdoor education for all subjects and at all levels are:

That which can be learnt inside the classroom should be supplemented by outdoor learning.

That which can be learnt in the outdoors through direct experience is more durable and effective.

That people and things are seen in their true relationships in the outdoor learning.

That school is not the only place of teaching-learning.

That the hidden curriculum outside the school should be taken note of.

Over the years, educator-philosophers like Comenius (1592-1670), Rousseau (1782-1852), Pestalozzi (1746-1827), Herbart (1746-1841), Froebel (1782-1852), Spencer (1820-1903), Dewey (1859-1952), Tagore (1861-1941) and Gandhiji (1869-1948) have pointed out the need for reinforcing abstract learning with concrete experiences. Going back to the Vedic and Epic periods, we find that Ashrams, mostly located at pleasing surroundings in the countryside/forests were the most important places of teaching-learning.

Lord Chesterfield (1694-1773) in a letter to his son away at school, aptly advised him, "The knowledge of the world can only be acquired in the world and not in a closet. Books will never teach you but they will suggest many things to your observation."

Gandhiji observed, "it is gross superstition to suppose that knowledge can be obtained only by going to schools and colleges.

The world produced brilliant students before schools and colleges came into being."

Outdoor education aims at enriching, vitalizing and complementing content areas of the school curriculum by means of first hand observation and direct experience outside the classroom. By expending the classroom into the out of doors, a setting can be provided for bringing deeper insight, greater understanding and real meaning to those areas of knowledge which, ordinarily, are merely read and sometimes discussed and seldom experienced.

Justification for outdoor education also lies in the fact that concepts necessary for everyday living are more readily developed through first hand learning.

Scope of Outdoor Learning. There is a lot of scope for learning outdoor. The outdoor activities for learning begin with the trees in the school yard, shrubbery, grass and playground. Of course, here learning experiences are available from **a** few minutes to one hour or more. Learning experiences of longer duration may be conducted at a nearby park, bird sanctuary, city museum and zoo, etc.

In Andhra Pradesh, a teacher teaching second grade may take her class in a tobacco farm. Here, over a period of two hours, the children observe how tobacco is cultivated, picked and cared for marketing. Outdoor education is here agricultural and industrial education.

In Assam, a group of high school students learns the skill involved in archery during their physical education periods.

In Delhi, a sixth grade class may start the school year with one week of camping. Students fish, swim, hike, cook over an open fire and sleep under the stars. The students learn several things including training in citizenship.

During snowfall, students can learn where and how do insects and animals spend the winter! What constellations are visible in the night sky. Scope for learning is very vast. Outdoor Learning Activities Related to School Curriculum.

Arithmetic

Measuring: a board foot, age of tree through ring count, dimensions of buildings, etc.

Estimating: Time of the day, height of tree etc.

Averaging: Temperature readings, barometric readings, operating bank, a store etc.

Languages

Writing letters to friends and relatives, keeping field notes, using the library for supplementary information, labeling specimens, newspaper reading etc.

Social Studies

Looking for old relics, visiting local spots of historical interest, putting on a pageant about a local historical event, witnessing the proceedings of the village panchayat, etc.

Natural Sciences

Taking nature hikes, learning to recognize bird and animal sounds, using microscope and hand-lense for closer scrutiny of parts, studying and collecting rocks, fossils and soils, visiting a quarry, conducting soil experiments, night study of major constellations, recording phases of moon, making weather observations, visiting game and forest reserves, etc.

Health, Physical Education and Recreation

Practising outdoor safety, carrying out service projects, skating, skiing, playing games, etc.

Arts, Crafts and Music

Clay work, making simple camp furniture, taking photographs, collecting weeds, grasses, feathers, etc.

To achieve the maximum benefit from outdoor learning programmes, it is very important that they are properly planned and implemented. The teachers and the students should work out the plan jointly. Every outdoor programme must be a result of careful thinking. The teachers and others associated with the programme would do well to obtain adequate information well in advance regarding the places to be visited so that they are able to provide suitable replies to the queries of the students.

The fact that outdoor programmes are arranged for educational-cum-recreational purposes should not be lost sight of. Learning and laughing should go hand in hand.

The appointment of group teachers facilitates work to a considerable extent.

The importance of maintaining discipline in outdoor work can hardly be ignored. Of course, students may be given reasonable amount of freedom for observing and mutual exchange of ideas.

The outdoor teaching-learning programme extends back to the regular classroom before it can be said that the project is completed. Following are the important activities involved in follow-up:

1. Classifying and identifying all collections and specimens brought back
2. Learning more about these specimens from books and other sources
3. Preparing exhibits and sharing materials and learning with others
4. Returning borrowed equipment to others
5. Writing 'thanks you' letters
6. Evaluating the outcomes of the outdoor programme
7. Preparing notes on the outdoor programme

Exercise

1. Describe the working of the kindergarten method and explain the concept of play, gifts, songs and occupations.
2. Evaluate the contribution of Froebel to the methodology of teaching.
3. "The dominant idea in the kindergarten is natural but directed self activity focused upon education, ends." Discuss.
4. Bring out the salient features of the kindergarten method. How can we make the best use of this method in our schools?
5. Why did Froebel stress the importance of education of the pre-school child? Briefly describe the role of the teacher in the kindergarten method.
6. "Children should be told as little as possible and induced to discover as much as possible." Explain this statement.

7. "Effectiveness' in learning lies not in reading and listening but in action, performance and experience." In the light of this statement, bring out clearly the significance of modern methods of teaching.
8. "To know how to suggest is the art of teaching." Elucidate this statement.
9. How do modern methods of teaching differ from the traditional ones?
10. List the chief characteristics of dynamic methods of teaching. How can dynamic methods be popularised?
11. Suggest measures for encouraging teachers to use dynamic methods of teaching.
12. "Learning and teaching are not confined to classroom." Explain this statement and suggest revenues for outdoor learning and teaching.

9

THE TECHNIQUES

Most of the teaching methods or strategies and techniques have been developed for secondary level to achieve the lower objectives of learning. At college and university level- teaching, lecture method is most commonly used which does not encourage the higher learning. Our teaching confines' to memory level from primary level to university level.

The purpose of higher learning is to develop the abilities of criticism, appreciation, to respect the ideas and feelings of others, to present own views and seek clarification. The learner' should be able to present his own views on a theme. The potentialities can only be developed by employing higher techniques of teaching and instruction at college and university level. The following are the main techniques which are- used for higher learning:

1. Conference Technique,
2. Seminar technique,
3. Symposium Technique,
4. Workshop Technique, and
5. Panel Discussion.

The details of these techniques have been provided in the present chapter.

CONFERENCE TECHNIQUE

In the area of higher teaching-learning, the conference is one of the most important technique. It is used to create higher learning situations by using appropriate instructional technique. The higher cognitive and affective objectives of education are achieved by employing the conference technique.

The conference technique is a meeting of large or small group of people. The participants make up a close-knit group which considers certain problems in normal and serious fashion. A conference of Non-Align Movement (NAM) was organized in 1983 to consider the measures of International Peace. The specific problems of International Peace was discussed by representative of hundred countries of NAM.

During 1920 the technique was encouraged and it was used to discuss the major problems of social sciences, behavioural sciences, and anthropology.

The conferences were organized during 1930 to discuss the problems of interdisciplinary nature. An inter-disciplinary approach of research was introduced as the result of these conferences.

During 1940, the conferences were organized to discuss the contemporary problems in different areas. The new direction was given for research activities as the result of this technique. The new concepts were evaluated and determine their utility in our situation. During 1950, subjects of conference were encouraged.

The conference technique has acquired important place in different areas to discuss and solve the problems: Social, Political, Health, Religious education.

It is becoming increasingly true as conference and workshop tend to involve ever wider cross-section of educators.. These new kinds of technique provide rich experiences upon which to build this type of programme and techniques.

Meaning and Definition : It is a meeting of large group, organized to discuss current problems and its specifics to provide a workable solution.

"A conference is a meeting of individuals called together to engage 'in discussion with the aim of accomplishing a limited task within restricted time."

Generally conferences are organized by an organization. An organization has permanent members and life members. Every organization forms executive committee, which consists of president, vice president, secretary, joint-secretary, treasurer and three members. The conferences are organized every year, known as Annual Conference on current topic or problem of the area. The members of the organization and some experts of the field are invited by secretary and provided by the president.

Now-a-days conferences are organized subject-wise by the associations of the subject concerned on the current problem of the area. Most of the conferences are organized on research problems. Some conferences are organized at national, international and regional level to discuss the social, religious, political and educational problems. Some, conferences are organized to discuss human problems, scientific problems, ,technological problems and new innovations.

The Objectives : The conferences are organized to study the specific problems of nations, society, religion, science and education. The objectives of conferences are usually broad to develop cognitive and affective aspects. The objectives are determined by the organization. For examples—Teacher-education Association and All India Educational Technology Association. The purpose of these organizations are different. The objectives of a conferences are formulated by the organization relating to current problems of the field, but the following are the general objectives of the conferences.

Cognitive Objectives : the conference technique has the focus to achieve the following cognitive objectives:

— To develop analysis, synthesis and evaluation or creative abilities of the participants.

— To develop reasoning and critical abilities.

— To develop the abilities of 'expressing his own feeling and observations.

— To make sensitive towards the problems of the area.

— To develop the abilities to study in depth the facts, concepts and problems.

Affective Objectives : By using the, conference technique, the following affective objectives are to be achieved:

— To develop the tendency to study a fact or concept in broader perspective.

— To develop the tendency of emotional balance.

— To respect and tolerate anti.-ideas and criticism of others.

— To develop the feelings of cooperation and freedom of thoughts.

By participating the conferences behavioural skills and good cultural manners are developed among the participants. They are trained to present and define the ideas. They learn how to put questions and how to answer the question and how clarification is sought.

The Procedure : A conference consist of twenty or thirty participants to thousands participants in one meeting. The conference are organized periodically or annually. In the conference of the meeting members of the organization and experts of related fields are invited. A meeting of the organization is organized by the president and secretory or local organizing secretary. The topic of the conference is broad in nature mid related to current problems of the area. The papers are invited on different aspects of the topic from the participants. The cyclostyled copies are prepared of each paper. The programme of the conference dates, days, time and place is finalized before hand and communicated to the participants accordingly. Generally programme is sent along the notice organizing the conference. A conference is organised in three stages:

First Stage : At the first stage the beginning of the meeting of a conference the participants are registered according to the schedule. The inauguration is done by chief guest and key note of the conference is given by the president. The activities of the conference are organized under direction of the president. The large group is divided into small groups to discuss the different aspects of the problem or theme of the conference. A convener of each small group is appointed by the president of the conference. These groups meet in different rooms to discuss specific aspect.

Second Stage : At the second stage group activities are organised. The convener of the group organizes and conducts group discussion. The schedule of the group is designed by the convener. The papers are presented on theme of work assigned to the group. The members of the group place their points of view on the theme. The papers are followed by group discussion. A record is prepared for the papers and group discussion. The convener organizes the ideas presented by the members. Generally group activities are conducted more than one day if the conference schedule is more than three days. The convener prepares a report of his group discussion on the presented papers' ideas and points of views of the members of the group.

Third Stage : At the third stage all the groups assemble in conference hall where it is inaugurated. It is known as valedictory function of the conferences, it is presided by president of the organization. A chief guest is also invited at this stage. The conveners of the groups present their reports on the sub-task assigned to them. The members of conference are provide to react and comment on the reports of the conveners. The relevant ideas and practical suggestions are given place in the report. The reports of the conveners yield the outcomes of the conference. A schedule for next meeting is prepared at this stage, If the period of executive members is over, then new executive committee is formed by electing the office bearers. The results of conference are published in news papers. At the end vote of thanks is given for the participants for making the conference successful.

Generally a report is published stating the objectives, theme, discussions and outcomes of the conference to disseminate the knowledge to other persons work in the same area and to implement some practical suggestions to improve and modify the present situation.

The Advantages : It is technique of higher learning to achieve the highest objectives of cognitive and affective domains. This technique is used to generate learning situations to develop the abilities of problem solving, analysis, synthesis, criticising and evaluating.

Participants usually have great interest in the -area being discussed. They generally attend the conference meeting because of their own desire to do so not because they are required a delegated to attend their local organization as are members at institute.

Some specific characteristics are enumerated as follows:

1. Democratic tradition and values are developed among the participants.
2. A topic of common interest is discussed in the meeting of the conference.
3. It increases the interest and faith in the meeting of the conference.
4. It develops the habit of independent study and to think independently on a theme.
5. Ability of problem-solving is developed among participants.
6. Capacity of tolerance or anti-ideas of others is also developed.
7. Ability of expressing ideas and feelings is developed by attending a conference.
8. Good manners for asking questions, seeking clarification, presenting own point of view and defending others ideas are developed.

The Limitations : A conference technique suffers from the following, limitations—

1. It is hard to predict about attendance. Advance arrangements must be made for conference facilities and housing accommodation.

2. An evaluation of the conference outcome is often difficult to determine unless participant observer or recorders are asked to critique the section.
3. Generally the nature of topic is broad, hence discussion is confined to specific issues.
4. Group discussion is generally dominated by the good speakers or those who talk too much and do not give opportunities to take part in the discussion.

SEMINAR TECHNIQUE

Teaching is continum from conditioning to indoctrination. It is organized from memory level to reflective level. Our teaching is confined upto memory level even at college and university level. At the most teaching can be organized at but understanding level, instructional situations should be organized in such way so that teaching may be done at reflective level. Higher objectives of cognitive and reflective domains are achieved by creating such conditions of learning. As the development of higher cognitive mid affective abilities is essential at the higher stage of education. Several instructional techniques have been evolved with human interaction as underlying pedagogical principles viz. a discussion, seminar, debate, panel discussion, buzz-session, role-planning, brain storming, etc. Description here is however confined to the seminar technique.

A seminar, as an instructional technique, involves generating a situation for group to have guided interaction among themselves on a theme which is generally presented to the group by one or more members. The person who presents the theme should have studied the theme thoroughly before hand. This would mean selection of relevant material at its organization. The collected material is put in the form of paper which is circulated among the participants in advance or before the paper reading. It provides the structure of the theme, to facilities its communication.

Thus, seminar is an instructional technique of higher learning which involves paper reading on a theme and followed by the group discussion to clarify the complex aspects of the theme.

The Objectives : This technique is employed to realize the higher objectives of cognitive and affective domains which have been enumerated as follows:

Cognitive Objectives : This technique creates learning situations so that the following higher cognitive objectives may be realized:

1. To develop the higher cognitive abilities, analysis, synthesis and evaluation as compared to the situations involving human interaction.
2. To develop the ability of responding in this manner would involve higher cognitive actions: valuing, organizing and characterization of quick comprehension of the situation examination, if and against the knowledge he possesses and construction of his reaction to the situation.
3. To develop the ability to seek clarification and defend the ideas of others effectively.

Affective Objectives : The following higher aspect of affective domain are developed by employing the instructional technique:

1. To develop the feeling of tolerance the opposite ideas of others.
2. To develop the feelings of co-operation with other colleagues and respect the ideas and feeling of others.
3. To develop emotional stability among the participants of the seminar.
4. To acquire good manners of putting questions and answering the questions of others effectively.

The human interaction under this technique develops good manners and skills among the participants.

Various Roles : In organizing a seminar the following roles are performed:

(1) Organizer or Instructor (2) President or Chairman or Convener of the seminar (3) Speakers of the day (4) Participants and (5) Observers.

Role of the Organizer: It is the responsibility of an organizer to plan and prepare the whole programme of the seminar. He decides the topic or theme of the seminar and assigns the different aspects of theme to different persons who have to play the role of speakers. The date, time and place are decided by him. Generally he also suggests the name of convener of the seminar. He prepares total schedule of the seminar.

Role of President: The participants propose the name of president. In suggesting the name of chairman, it should be taken into consideration that the person must be well acquainted with the theme of the seminar. He must know his rights and duties as chairman of a seminar. Virtually the seminar's activities are conducted by the conveners. He directs the whole programme. He encourage the participants to take part in discussion. He keeps the discussion on the theme of seminar.

In certain situations he also takes part in the discussion; he provides the opportunities to each participant. At the end he has to summarize the discussion and may present his viewpoint on the theme. He has to give thanks to the speakers, participants guests and observers.

Role of Speakers: The organizer assigns the topics to the speakers. They prepare the topics thoroughly and cyclostyle copies of the papers are prepared and these are distributed among the participants before the commencement of the seminar, so that participants should also prepare themselves on the theme. It encourages the discussion to last long. The speakers should be ready to defend the questions. The speakers should have the tolerance of anti-ideas or criticism of others.

Role of Participants : The participants of the seminar should be well acquainted with the theme. They should appreciate the performances of the speakers. They should be able to seek clarification and put questions. They should place their own ideas regarding the theme on the basis of their experiences. They should address the president for seeking clarification. They should not put question directly to the speakers. There are 25 to 40 participants in the seminar.

Role of observers : Some guests and observers are also invited and allowed to observe the activities of the seminar. They should be allowed at the end to discussion and present their observations by permission of the chairman.

The Procedure : Seminar as an instructional technique and involves creating a situation for a group to have guided interaction among themselves on a theme which is generally presented to the group by one or more members, The person who presents the theme should have studies the theme thoroughly before hand. This would mean selection of relevant material and its organization. Generally, this organized material put in the from of a paper which is circulated among members in advance. The paper helps structure the theme, facilitates its communication, and focuses the scope for discussion. After the theme is presented, it is discussed by the group. During the discussion participants may (i) seek clarifications of the theme presented, (ii) make observations in the light of their knowledge and experience regarding the theme, and (iii) raise issues relating to the theme for further analysis and evaluation.

Proceedings of a seminar are guided by a chairman who may be knowledgeable about the theme. The chairman's role would be to keep the discussion on track, stimulate maximum participation and consolidate at appropriate stages the view points expressed. Seminar as an instructional technique seek to provide maximally for interaction among the members. This means that sufficient time should be allowed for the discussion session if this necessiates cutting down the time for presentation. It could be done since the main purpose of the presentation is to initiate the discussion.

The interaction in a seminar can be linked to the field of forces in machines. Different view points or opinions expressed will represent forces in varied directions. However, unlike physical forces which when acting in opposite direction, at times, result is zero, the different viewpoints or even opposite opinions will not results in neutrality but will induce further thinking among participants. It is this stimulation for further thinking that should be reckoned with significance as the net instructional value of the seminar. When there is an agreement of ideas among individual members, these may be considered as forces acting in the same direction and thereby having a reinforcing affect on the individual's view on the theme. In either cases the individual is benefited as he is either led to further analysis and evaluation of his viewpoints, or helped in validating and thus strengthening them.

The Advantages : From the above analysis of the basic mechanism of interaction in seminar, it may be said that seminar as an instructional technique, has the potential to develop several abilities in students.

(1) Due to the process stimulation of thinking brought about through interaction, different higher cognitive abilities like analytical and critical thinking synthesing and evaluating the ideas will tend to be developed.

(2) Apart from these cognitive abilities certain effect attributes like tolerance for other's views openness to ideas co-operation with others, emotional stability and respect for other's feeling will be inculcated among the participants during the course of such sessions.

(3) These effects attribute to represent the norms of behaviour for the group in the seminar situations. Moreover, these norms are the same as these of a democratic society. Deliberate efforts to adhere to these norms would of necessity be made during the course of seminar discussions. The adherence to these group norms would gradually inculcate the affect attributes in the participants.

(4) Concomitant effect of seminar as instructional technique will be the development of better learning habits. While preparing for presentation and participating in the discussion, learners will get induced to pursue independent study, engage in post-seminar discussions covering the themes discussed as well as related ones, develop critical outlook to any ideas thereby leading the learner to self-initiated learning which will be more permanent in nature.

(5) As can be seen from the above, seminar has great instructional value as it makes the instruction learner-centred and provides for-learning through enquiry which is based on a very natural characteristic of inquisitiveness in humans.

(6) This natural way of learning through seminar established an important place for this technique at all level of instruction. From practice, however, one may notice that it is mainly confined to higher education.

Essentials of a Seminar—A situation seems to have to arise mainly from the presumptions that the technique demands maturity in terms of language, social and emotional make-up and the facility to deal with abstractions. Since the students at lower levels of education do not possess maturity to this extent. It is generally considered that seminar is less feasible to be adopted as an instructional technique at these levels. Such a demarcation of feasibility regarding the use of seminar stems from the rigid notion about the nature of themes to be discussed therein. It is generally considered that the seminar should have an abstract theme to be presented and discussed. Although there is noting against the suitability-of such themes for seminars confining seminars only to cover there is more of historicity of the technique rather than its demands about the nature of the themes. In fact the value of seminar should be seen in terms of the basic mechanism of the involvement of learners. Here the learners are expected to present to others their ideas or experiences who would react to them in the light of their own experiences. And, it is this interaction on the ideas or experience however, high or low, concrete or abstract, they may be in nature, that should be aimed at through this technique. Seeing seminar in this perspective, it may be quite feasible to utilize this technique effectively even at lower levels of instruction. At these levels the themes for seminar could be even simple and concrete experiences which could be narrated to follow children who in turn could discuss them in the light of their own. Interaction on such themes also would involve behaviours like question making observations, evaluating the theme by comparing it with their own experiences.

Various Types : The said mechanism is employed in conducting a seminar but seminars are organized at different levels. On the basis of levels of organization, the seminars are of four types- (1) Mini-Seminar, (2) Main Seminar, (3) National Seminar, and (4) International Seminar.

Mini Seminar : A seminar organized to discuss a topic in class is known as mini-seminar. The purpose of the mini-seminar is to train the students for organizing the seminar and play different roles. It is a stimulated situation for the students. In an institution such seminars should be organized before the Main seminar.

Major Seminar : Such seminars are organized at departmental level or institutional, level on a major theme. All the students and staff members take part in such seminars. These seminars are orgranized weekly or monthly in departments. Generally specific themes are selected for main seminar.

National Seminar : A national seminar is organized by an association or organization at national level. The experts are invited on the theme of the seminar. The secretary of the seminar prepares the schedule, theme, time, dates, days and venue. Generally NCERT organizes such seminars at national level, on the theme:

Education Technology, Population Education, Trends of Education, Distance-Education, Non-formal education, Quality central of educational research in India.

International Seminar: Generally such seminars are organized by UNESCO and other international organization. The topic or theme of seminar is very broad, e.g., students unrest or activisms, Innovations in teacher-education and Examination reform. A nation can also organize such seminars on International theme.

The Limitations : A seminar technique has the following limitations:

1. A seminar can not be organized on all the content of a subject matter. Some topics are highly structured. A theme of a seminar should be such on which discussion may be held.

2. This technique cannot be used for all levels of education. It can be used for higher level of education. The members of seminar should have social and emotional maturity. Thus, it can not be used for lower level of education.
3. When a seminar is being organized, the persons who speak too much, dominate the discussion of the seminar and do not provide opportunities to others to take part in the discussion. It means that the discussion confines only few persons rather than whole group.
4. During discussion, groups are formed in two ideas anti-ideas and provide on the theme. As a result they try to win over the other. The purpose of the seminar is not served. The chairman should discourage this type activities.
5. It the two groups already exist among the participants. The generally try to oppose even for the-contractive or relevant ideas of the opposite group. The opposition is done for the sake of opposition. The instructional situations of 'such discussion is not conducive for leaning.

SYMPOSIUM TECHNIQUE

Symposium technique is also one of the techniques of higher learning. It is also an instructional technique which is used to achieve higher cognitive and affective objectives.

Meaning and Definition : The word 'symposium' has serval, dictionary meanings. Firstly, Plato has used this term for 'good dialogue' to present the views towards God. Another meaning of the term is the intellectual recreation of enjoyment.

The recent meaning of the term is a meeting of persons to discuss a problem or theme. The view on a theme are presented in a sequence. The specific aspect of a theme is presented by an expert of the theme. The definition of the term symposium is as follows—

"The symposium technique serves as an excellent device for informing an audience, crystalizing opinion and generally preparing the listeners for arriving at a decision, policy, value, judgement or wider standing."

The main purpose of the symposium is to provide understanding to the students or listener on a theme or a problem specifically to develop certain values and feelings.

The Objectives : The following are main objectives of the symposium technique:

1. To identify and understand two various aspects of theme and problems.
2. To develop the ability to decision and judgement regard a problem.
3. To develop the values and feeling regarding a problem.
4. To enable the listeners to form policies regarding a theme or problem.

The Mechanism : The symposium is a type of discussion, in which two or more speakers talk from ten to twenty minutes, develop individual approaches or solutions to a problem or present aspects of a policy, process, or programme. The speeches are followed by questions or comments from the audience, as in the panel-forum. The speeches may be persuasive, argumentative, informative or evocative. Each 'speech proceeds without interruption. The chairman of the symposium introduces the topic, suggests something of its importance, sometimes indicates the general approaches., The symposium forum serves an excellent device for informing an audience, crystallising opinion; and in general preparing the listeners for arriving at a decision policy, value, judgement or understanding.

Since there is no need for symposium interaction other than careful listening (unless the symposium members are to discuss the topic after the delivery of the speeches) all members of the performing group can sit in a straight line behind a table or an adjoining chairs, with the chairman in the middle or to one side of the speakers. Or if the symposium is to present two conflicting points of view, the seating arrangement can separate the speakers on the platform in order to indicate difference in opinion or in order to preserve peace.

The Precautions : We suggest three conditions in the use of the symposium technique:

Firstly, The moderator should be sure to prepare the speakers or see that they are prepared. They should know the rules of procedure, sequence of speaking, and way in which the forum will be conducted; and they should be aware of the ideas and back ground of the other performers. Like panelist, they might benefit from a brief -warm-up.

Secondly, the chairman or whosoever is responsible for preparing the agenda, should not attempt to stack the cards by omitting or ignoring vital phases of the problem as he selects or delegates his speakers. It is not good to face up to an inadvertent misinterpretation or commission. To distort or omit an important point of view deliberately is to invite disaster.

Thirdly, the chairman in all the forum situations must plan very carefully for the questioning period that follows the prepared speeches, unless he wishes to risk boredom.

The Scope : The symposium technique is used to realise the higher cognitive and affective objectives. The following are the main topics on which symposium technique is used:

1. Use of television for education.
2. Scope of distance education in our education.
3. Use of essay and objective type tests.
4. Semester system in education.
5. Causes of students unrest.
6. Quality control of educational research.
7. Use of micro teaching in teacher-education.
8. Use of team teaching in schools.
9. Use of action research in classroom teaching.
10. Scope of education technology in our education.

The nature of the topic should be such that the audience should be interested in the theme.

The Characteristics : The symposium technique has the following main characteristics :

1. It provides the broad understanding of a topic or a problem.
2. The opportunity is provided to the listeners to take decision about the problem.
3. It is used for higher classes to specific themes and problems.
4. It develops the feeling of cooperation and adjustment.
5. The objectives as synthesis and evaluation (creativity) are achieved by employing the symposium technique.

The Limitations : This technique suffers from the following limitations:

1. The chairman has no control over the speakers as they have full freedom to prepare the theme for discussion. The can present any aspect of the theme or problem.
2. There is a probability of repetition of the conduct because every speaker prepares theme as a whole. The different aspects of theme are not prepared separately. It creates difficulty of understanding to the listeners.
3. The different aspects are presented simultaneously. Therefore the listeners are not able to understand the theme correctly.
4. The listeners remain passive in -the symposium because they are not given opportunities to seek clarification and put questions.
5. The discussion and presentation of theme is not summarized at the end. The participants take decision according to their own. Hence mature persons can make use of this technique.
6. This technique is employed to achieve the higher objectives of cognitive domain but affective objectives are not emphasized properly.

WORKSHOP TECHNIQUE

Education process has two aspects : theoretical and practical. The instructional techniques are used to develop the theoretical aspects of the students. The conference and seminars are organized for achieving higher cognitive and affective objectives. The psychomotor aspect is developed through training. Teaching is a continum from conditioning to indoctrination and training is also inclusive in it. The new innovations and practices of education are introduced by organizing workshop in which persons are trained to use new practices in their teaching learning process. The workshops are organized to develop the psychomotor aspects of the learner regarding practices of new innovations in area of education. Under this technique participants have to do some practical work to produce instructional, teaching and testing material.

The Definition : Workshop is defined as assembled group of ten to twenty five persons who share a common interest or problem. They meet together to improve their individual and skill of a subject through intensive study, research, practice and discussion.

Source of Workshop Technique : The word workshop has been borrowed from engineering. There are usually workshops in the engineering. In these workshops persons have to do some task with their hands to produce something, e.g., Railway workshop, Roadways workshop, etc. Under these workshops railway engines are repaired and manufactured. Similarly, workshop are organized in education to prepare questions on the subjects in Question Bank workshops. The participants of the workshop prepare questions of their subjects. The participants are given knowledge and training for preparing questions in the workshop. The word workshop has been borrowed form technology.

The Objectives : The workshops are organized to realize the following objectives cognitive and psychomotor.

Cognitive Objectives : The workshops are organized to achieve the following cognitive objectives:

1. To solve the problems of teaching profession.

2. To provide the philosophical and sociological background for instructional and teaching situation.
3. To identify the educational objectives in the present context.
4. To develop an understanding regarding the use of a theme and problem.

Psychomotor Objectives : The following objectives are achieved by this technique:

1. To develop the proficiency for planning and organizing teaching and instructional activities.
2. To develop the skills to perform a task independently.
3. To determine and use of teaching strategies effectively.
4. To train the persons for using different approaches of teaching.

The workshop technique is used to seek, explore and identify the solutions to a problem; to permit the extensive study of a situation its background and its social and philosophical implication.

It is used for in-service teacher for giving awareness and training of new practice in education.

It provides an opportunity to prepare specific professional, vocational or community, service functions. A high degree of individual participation is encouraged. It permits group determination of goal and method.

The Procedure : Generally workshops are organized for three to ten days duration. The period of workshop may be 40 days, it dependents on the nature of task assigned to the workshop. It is organized in three stages:

First Stage : Presentation of the theme of providing awareness.

Second Stage : Practice the approach for its applicability,

Third Stage : Evaluate the material prepared by the participants and follow-up programme.

First Stage : The resource-persons or experts are invited to provide the awareness and understanding of the topic. This stage is like a seminar type. The paper reading is also alone to discuss the different aspects of the theme. The trainee or participants are given opportunities to seek clarification. The experts provides the suitable illustration and step for using it in classroom teaching or education. This stage continues first two days of the schedule.

Second Stage : In the first stage theoretical background is provided to the participants. In the second stage the group is divided into small groups, e.g., a workshop for lesson planning or writing, objectives in behavioural terms a Questions Bank workshop. The group formed on the basis of subjects (Hindi, Science, Maths, Social Studies). A resource-persons or expert provide, guidance and supervision their work of each trainee of his group. Every participant has to work individually and independently. Every trainee has to complete his task within the given period. At the end they meet in their groups and discuss and present their task to be completed.

Third Stage : At this stage all groups meet at one place and present their reports of work done at second stage.. The participants are given opportunities to comment and given suggestions for further improvement. The experts also provide suggestions on different aspects of the reports and formalities are observed at the end of the workshop.

Follow-up : A follow-up programme is an important part of a good workshop. The trainees have to go back to their institutions. They are asked to continue their task and examine the workability and usability in their institutions. The effectiveness of a workshop is ascertained by a follow-up programme. The participants are invited to meet again and present their experiences regarding applicability of the topic or new practices. They may give some practical suggestions in this context. A report is also prepared of workshop.

The Scope : The workshop technique is used mainly in the following areas of education:

1. New format of lesson-planning.

2. Writing objectives in behavioural terms.
3. Preparing objective type tests which are objective centred.
4. Action research projects for classroom problems.
5. Preparing instructional material or teaching model.
6. Workshop for micro-teaching.
7. Workshop for international analysis technique.
8. Workshop for task construction.
9. Workshop for prepare research synopsis or proposals.
10. Workshop for non-formal education.
11. Workshop for designing programme for teacher-education or any level.

Various Roles : In organizing a workshop the following four roles are to be performed:

1. Organizer of the workshop.
2. Convener or Chairman in first stage.
3. Experts and Resource persons.
4. Participants or Trainees.

Organizer of the Workshop Technique: Whole programme and schedule is prepared by the organizer. He has to arrange for boarding and lodging facilities for participants as well as the experts. The date, days, venue of workshop are decided by him. The workshops are also organized by certain institutions like NCERT.

Convener in First Stage: At first stage of the workshop theoretical aspects are discussed by the experts on the theme of the workshop. Therefore, a convener is nominated or invited who is well acquainted with the theme of the workshop. He has to conduct work of this stage and he has to observe the formalities and key-note of the workshop.

Experts or Resource Persons : In organizing a workshop, resource-persons play an important role in providing theoretical and practical aspects of the theme. They provide guidance to participants at every stage and train them to perform the task effectively.

Role of Participants or Trainees : The participants should be keen or interested in the theme of the workshop. At the first stage, they have to acquire understanding of the theme and at second stage, they have to practice and perform the task with great interest and seek proper guidance from the experts. They should try to carry the concept to their classroom to evaluate its workability in actual situation. They may suggest some modification in using the concept in classroom. The effectiveness of any workshop technique depends upon the involvement of the participants in the task.

The Advantages : A workshop is an instruction of situation which is used for the following purposes:

1. It is used to realize the higher cognitive and psycho-motor objectives.
2. It is a technique which can be effectively used for developing understanding and proficiency for the approaches and practices in education.
3. It is used for developing and improving professional efficiency.
4. The teaching proficiencies can be developed by using the workshop technique for in-service teachers.
5. It provides the opportunities and situations to develop the individual capacities of a teacher.
6. It develops the feeling cooperation and group work.
7. It provides the situation to study the vocational problems.
8. The new practices and innovations are introduced to in-service teachers.

The Limitations : It suffers from, the following limitations:

1. The workshops in education are seminar-cum-workshop on any theme or problem.

2. The in-service teachers do not take interest to understand and use the new practices in their classroom.
3. The workshops can not be organized for large group so that large number of persons are not trained.
4. The teachers do not take interest in practical work or to do something in productive form.
5. The effectiveness of a workshop technique depends on the follow up programme. Generally follow-up programmes are not organized in workshop technique.

It requires a lot of time form participants and staff. A large number of staff members are needed to handle participation. It demands special facilities or materials. Participants must be willing to work both independently and co-operatively.

PANEL DISCUSSION TECHNIQUE

All techniques of higher learning require the discussion among the participants. The discussion provides equal opportunities in the instructional situation to every participant.

The discussion technique of learning is based on the modern theory of organization. The assumption of this theory is that every member of the organization has the capacity to initiate and solve the problem and bring certain attitude and value to the organization. Thus, interactional technique is the most appropriate in democratic way of life.

The Origin : This technique at first was used by Herry A. Ober Street in 1929. He organized a discussion for small group to definite period for the audience. At the end of the discussion audience had also participated. The important questions were put by the audiences on the topic. The experts tried and answer the questions and certain points were clarified, which were not included in the discussion.

Generally this type of panel discussion are organized on television and radio. The current topics are considered for such programme.

The Objectives : The following are the main objectives of the technique:

1. To provide information and new facts.
2. To analyse the current problem from different angle.
3. To identify the values.
4. To organize for mental recreation.

It is used to find out the solution to current problems of important nature and provide full understanding of significant topic. It is an effective instructional technique which creates situation to facilitate higher cognitive learning.

Theoretical Basics : This technique is based on the following principles:

1. It observes the democratic principles of human behaviour. Equal opportunities are provided to every participant.
2. It encourages the active participation with originality and independently.
3. It involves the social and psychological principles of group work. Feeling cooperation and sympathy and to respect the ideas of others.
4. It is based on modern theory of organization.

The panel discussion organizes teaching at reflective level which is most thoughtful and employ independent thinking of the participants.

Various Types : The group discussion is organized in different forms for different levels, for different purpose and on different themes. It may be to two type:

(1) Public Panel Discussion, and

(2) Education Panel Discussion.

Public Panel Discussion : This type of panel discussions are organized for the common man's problems. Three type of objectives are achieved by these type of discussion:

(a) To provide factual information regarding current problems.

(b) To determine the social value.

(c) To recreate the common men.

The public panel discussions are organized in Television programme. The current problems: educated unemployment, Annual budget, Increase in prices of things, jobs delinking with degrees.

Education Panel Discussion: It is used in educational institutions to provide factual and conceptual knowledge and clarification of certain theories and principles. Sometimes these are organized to find out the solution to certain problems.

The following three objectives are achieved by the education technique:

(a) To provide factual information and conceptual knowledge.

(b) To give awareness of theories and principles.

(c) To provide solution to certain problems.

This type of panel discussions are very useful but they are not used in any institution even at higher level. The conferences, seminar, symposium and workshops are commonly organized. These techniques provide the situation for group discussion but of different types. The situation of panel discussion is usually autocratic where as other technique have democratic situations of group discussion.

The Procedure : A panel discussion consists of four types of persons. It means four roles are played in organizing panel discussion :

1. Instructor, 2. Moderator, 3. Panelists, and 4. Audience.

Instructor : In the panel discussionmost important role is of instructor. It is the responsibility of instructor, how, where and when panel discussion will be organized. The schedule of panel discussion is prepared by him. Sometimes he has to plan rehearsal of discussion.

Moderator : In the discussion moderator has to do significant job. He has to keep the discussion on theme and encourage the interaction among the members. He has to summarize and highlight the discussion more often. The moderator must have the mastery on the theme or problem of the discussion.

Panelist : There are four to ten panelists in the discussion. The members of the panel sit in semi-circle before the audience. The moderator sits in the middle of the panelists. The panelists must have the mastery on the theme of the discussion.

Audience : After the panel discussion, audience are allowed to put question and seek clarification. They can present their point of view and their experiences regarding the theme or problem. The panelists attempt to answer the question.

At the end of the discussion, moderator summarises the discussion and presents his point of view. He expresses thanks to panelists and audience.

The Use : This instructional technique has following advantages:

1. This technique encourages social learning.
2. The higher cognitive and affective objectives are achieved.
3. It is used to develop the ability of problem solving and logical thinking.
4. It develops the interests and right type of attitude towards the problem.
5. It develops the capacity to respect others ideas and feelings and ability of tolerance.
6. It provides the opportunities of assimilation of theme and content.

The following topics may be taken for this purpose:

(a) Education as an instrument of social change.

(b) Student-teaching in teacher-education programme.

(c) Population Education.

(d) Scope of Educational Technology in our country.

(e) Adult-education.

(f) Delinking jobs to degrees.

(g) 'Examination reform'.

(h) Environmental Education.

The Characteristics : The following are the main characteristics of panel discussion technique:

1. It is used at college and university level to organize teaching, at reflective level.
2. It develops the ability of problem solving.
3. It provides the opportunity to understand nature problem or theme of the discussion.
4. It develops ability of presentation of theme and giving their point of view logically.
5. It develops the right type of attitude mid ability to tolerate anti ideas of others.
6. It develops the ability of creative thinking and criticising the theme.
7. It develops the manners of putting questions and answering questions.

The Limitations : The following are the limitations of this technique:

1. There are chances to deviate from theme at the time of discussion, hence the purpose of the panel discussion is not achieved.
2. Some members dominate the discussion and do not provide the opportunities to participate others in discussion.
3. There is possibility to split the group into sub-groups, i.e. for and against the theme. It does not maintain the conducive situation of learning.
4. If panelists belong to different groups. It may not create appropriate learning situation.

Suggestions for Organizing Discussion : The following suggestions should be taken into consideration to organize an effective panel discussion:

1. There should be rehearsals before the actual panel discussion.
2. The moderator should be matured person and have the full understanding of theme or problem. He should have control over the situation.
3. The seating arrangement for panelists and audience should be such that everyone should be at equal distance. They can observe each other.
4. The moderator should encourage the discussion on the points which may lead to constructive aspect of the problem. He should encourage the constructive discussion among panelists and audience.

Origin. Play-way approach to teaching is based on the philosophical thought of Caldwell Cook. According to him, "good work is more often the result of spontaneous effort and free interest than of compulsion and forced application." This means that teaching should characterise the elements of 'spontaneous effort' and 'free interest' Since these two characteristics are inherent in play, this approach or method of teaching is called playway. Having discovered the unwillingness and distaste of his pupils for lessons in English literature, he employed a method by means of which the boys showed a keen interest in the subject. The Shakesperean plays, meanings of which were generally memorised without any interest and understanding came to be treated like real plays when 'dramatised' by the pupils. An open-air theatre was organised in the school. Literature now acquired a new meaning for them and lessons acquired the spirit of play. Similarly, activities were planned for grammar and composition lessons. The pupils participated eagerly in the lesson and were allowed to express their ideas freely. Thus, the English period was welcomed with joy. Gradually the scope of play-way became enlarged and it began to be applied to the teaching of other subjects. The play-way approach aims at introducing the elements of freedom, interest, realism and spontaneity into the entire school work.

Definition and meaning. With a view to have a comprehensive understanding of the play-way, it is felt appropriate to consider the definitions of play and the key words understanding this concept.

Crow and Crow observe, "play can be defined as the activity in which a person engages when he is free to do what he wants."

Dewey defines play as, "Activities not necessarily performed for the sake of any result beyond themselves."

Froebel noted, "Play is the purest, most spiritual activity of man at this stage (Childhood). It gives therefore, joy, freedom, contentment, inner rest and peace with the world."

Good defines play as, "Any pleasurable activity carried on for its sake, without reference to the ulterior purpose of future satisfaction."

Gullicks writes, "Play is what we do when we are free to do what we will." Hurlock states, "play relates to any activity engaged in the enjoyment it gives, without consideration of the end results." Monetessori visualized play as "When a child plays it resembles the never ending activity of the flowering stem of the growing tree."

Nunn holds that "play is a profound manifestation of creative activities."

Ross regards play as "joyful, spontaneous, creative activity, in which man finds his fullest expression."

Ryburn writes, "Play is a way, a means which is used by the self when the different instinctive urges are trying to express themselves."

Stern regards play as "a kind of voluntary self-constrained activity."

Thomson looks upon play as "the impulse to carry out certain instinctive action."

Principles

(i) The play-way is based on the principle that learning takes place through doing.

(ii) It is based on the principle that learning takes place in an environment of freedom.

(iii) It is based on the principle that learning should be adapted to life situations and not to books.

(iv) It is based on the principle that the method should be suited to the needs and interests of the students.

(v) It is based on the principle that the child should be freed from authoritariansim.

(vi) It is based on the principle that the child should themselves take upon the responsibility of learning and progress in studies.

(vii) It is based on the principal that ample opportunity should be provided to children for self-expression.

Educative value. Play-way is important on account of the following :

(a) Play-way is a great motivating force. Play-way activities are based on the natural urges of the children. They put their heart and soul into work.

(b) Play-way kills drudgery and boredom. The students willingly undertake to do a piece of work.

(c) Doing and practice occupy the first place and telling the second and an unimportant place.

(d) The method is based on the laws of learning and it provides a great incentive to original creative work.

(e) Play-way provides opportunities for the sublimation of various instincts of children.

(f) Play-way assures maximum freedom for the child with the result that he develops originality, power of reasoning, imagination and insights.

(g) Play-way helps in sublimating the emotions of children. It provides suitable outlets which help in overcoming shyness, moodiness, timidity and sensitiveness.

(h) Play-way provides opportunities to the students to learn to cooperate, to take the lead and also to follow.

Materials. These include (1) Gifts of Froebel (2) Sand play (2) Water-play (4) Wooden toys (5) Rubber toys (6) Glass toys (7) Plastic toys (8) Pictures (9) Picture book puzzles (10) Cut-outs (11) Card board games (12) Doll and doll house (13) Play-ground games (14) Story telling (15) Dramatics (16) Art work (17) Excursions (18) Dancing (19) T.V. (2) Community work etc.

The application of the principles of play-way is found in all the progressive methods of education and other school activities in one way or the other.

Project Method. 'Purpose element' is used to secure the interests of the students. The play-spirit pervades throughout the various activities connected with the completion of the project. The students work in an atmosphere of reality, freedom and responsibility.

Kindergarten Method. Froebal's Kindergarten provides a lot of action for children. Doing, singing, acting and playing are its chief characteristics. Gifts are given to the students with the help of which they learn the idea of shape, colour, number and weight etc.

The Montessori Method. Didactic apparatus imparts training in various fields. With the aid of this apparatus children learn reading, writing and arithmetic. The children's Home provides an atmosphere of complete and unrestricted freedom. Children are kept active and playing while learning.

The Dalton Plan. The children are free from the tyranny of the time-table. They work according to their own rate and speed of learning. They are at liberty to move from room to room and laboratory to laboratory. A sense of self-help and responsibility is generated in the students. The students take a real pleasure in studies.

Gary System, Winnetke Plan, etc. All these methods are based on the play-way principles. School becomes the hub of activities in which children take keen interest.

The Heuristic Method. This method places the child in the position of a discoverer. Thus, he acquires and learns some of the most fundamental skills through his own effort. The child is always mentally active as he wants to satisfy his curiosity.

Basic System of Education. This is a revolt against the verbal and bookish system of education. Here too the child learns by doing and thus derives immense pleasure side by side.

School Life. The play principle should be at work in all aspects of school life. The work of the educator is to make more and more use of this technique. The following play-way activities may be mentioned :

(a) ***Self Government in Schools***—This is very helpful in sublimating the various instincts of children—self-assertion, gregariousness, self-submission and pugnacity. Students develop valuable social and civic virtues. They themselves frame their rules.

(b) ***The Boy-Scout and Girl Guide Movement***—This movement makes the life of children full of activity, competition and cooperation. Students learn valuable social, intellectual and civic lessons through camping and trecking etc.

(c) ***Dramatics***—Students prepare the stage, learn their parts and prepare costumes. They are working, but it is play.

(d) ***NCC, Excursions, School Celebrations, etc.***—All these are examples of play-way spirit.

Application of Play-Way to School Organisation and Administration. Lane Homer's school called 'The little Commonwealth' a reformatory school, A.S., Neill's Summer Hall School and Sri Aurobindo's Ashram Schools are the striking examples of the application of the play-way principle to the entire administration and organisation of a school. Children studying in these schools are provided complete freedom to manage the affairs of the school according to rules of their own making. Children study and work at different occupations according to their own interests.

Play-Way spirit can be utilised in many practical ways in the teaching of different subjects.

Languages and Mother Tongue. Dramatics, magazines and games are the different ways of introducing the spirit of play-way in the teaching of the mother tongue and other languages. Mock interviews, mock parliament, debates and panel discussions provide play-way means of training in oral expression in languages.

Mathematics. Running a school shop is the best way of teaching mathematics in a play-way spirit. Homely and practical examples should be selected. Surveys provide many opportunities.

History. The teaching of history provides a great scope for introducing the spirit of play-way. The school library should contain a good collection of books on history, Biographies, letters, historical atlases, historical albums and memoirs, etc. Historical plays should be staged. Visits to picture galleries and museums create an environment of reality. A pageant on the life of Lord Buddha may be prepared. Scenes from the lives of great freedom fighters of India may be depicted. Historical poems may be narrated. Debates on historical events can be made a popular form of activity in schools.

Geography. The use of films and slides is very helpful in providing a clear and vivid picture of the lives of remote and distant areas. Visits to canals, dams and rivers give vivid glimpses.

Nature-Study. Specimens of leaves, flowers, plants feathers may be collected by children. Opportunities for observing natural phenomena may be provided to the students.

Science. Illustrative scientific journals and books should be made available in the school library. Books on the lives of great scientists and discoverers should find a prominent place. Scientific hobbies should be encouraged. Science clubs may be organised effectively. Experiment work should be taken up in abundance.

Moral and Social Training. Various co-curricular activities like self-government, student parliament, scouting, cooperative store, cleanliness campaigns in the school and the community, etc., provide useful training in moral and social values.

Dramatic Play. Dramatic play is basically an exercise of the imagination, at the same time, it can also be a valuable learning experience. To a young child, a doll is not just a doll. It is like a real person. A toy telephone can be used to call and talk with someone.

Games. Games may be simple games, guessing games or more lively games such as musical chairs. Several types of inexpensive education games are available in the market.

Watching the Television. Television programmes can be educational-cum-recreational. Conducting of quiz programmes on a variety of topics is very helpful in enriching the experiences of students.

Projects. Projects provide immense scope for doing and learning.'

Celebration of Days. Literacy Day, Girl Child Day, Aged Day, Prohibition Day, Cleanliness Day, Republic Day, etc, are full of providing rich educational experiences.

Educational Tours and Excursions. All these if properly planned and executed are full of educational potentials.

It is wrong to regard play-way as soft pedagogy. It is in the words of Smith and Harrison, "an all absorbing activity in which initiative, forethought, control and skill can be exercised in full measure." Emphasis on play does not mean absence of serious work. On the other hand, introductions of the play-way spirit in work reduces drudgery. Play-way is an approach to do a difficult and boring task in an interesting way.

Play-way puts heavy demands on the teacher. It requires a lot of imagination and a real effort on the part of the teachers as well as students. A teacher has to plan and execute activities, teaching points and projects very carefully and skilfully. Thus, play-way is by no means a softy pedagogy. As observed by Griffith, "Play is the child's characteristic mode of behaviour and any system of education which hampers this natural direction for the expanding of energy endangers the health-mental and physical of the child." Indeed play-way has a unique place in dynamic and progressive teaching.

Exercise

1. What are the chief characteristics of play? State the advantages of using play-way in education. Do you agree that the play-way in leads to soft pedagogy?

2. The term play-way has been applied to certain methods of teaching. Explain and bring out the importance of the application of the principles of play-way in different subjects.
3. "Whenever you want a child to do heartily must be contrived and conducted as play" (Caldwell Cook). Elucidate this statement with reference to play-way method of teaching. Select any topic in any subject and suggest the games and activities through which the topic may be taught.
4. Enumerate the objectives and steps of conference technique. Describe its main characteristics.
5. Define the term conference and enumerate the various roles in organizing conference technique.
6. What do you understand by Seminar Technique? Describe its objectives and procedure of seminar technique. , ,
7. Differentiate between conference and seminar techniques and illustrate the answer with example.
8. Point out the origin of workshop technique and describe the mechanism of workshop technique.
9. A workshop technique is usually organized as seminar-cum-workshop technique'. Discuss the statement.
10. Describe the symposium forum or technique. Enumerate its objectives and procedure of organizing symposium forum.
11. Distinguish between seminar and symposium technique with reference to objectives, procedure, roles and uses.

10

PRACTICAL TEACHING

A debate is an intellectual programme in which two or more students holding opposite views on a particular topic present arguments. They are provided opportunities to rebut the opposite side. Equal time is allotted to each debator to present his views. In the class debates, usually the teacher concerned presides and a student is asked to conduct the proceedings. He is called a moderator. After the debators have debated, other students in the class may be asked to put questions to the debators or they may engage in a brief discussion with them, with a view to get significant results, the teacher is expected to provide guidance to the debators before arriving at some decision regarding performance of individual and group.

BY WAY OF DEMONSTRATION

Demonstration implies the presentation of a pre-arranged series of events or equipment to a group of students for their observation. This is accompanied by explanatory remarks. This device is most commonly used in science and fine arts. It can also be used in giving information, knowledge and training. Some of the important guidances for a successful demonstration are given below:

1. Plan all the activities relating to demonstration in great detail.

2. Ensure that all the equipment, illustrations and other relevant materials are procured in time and kept ready before the demonstration begins.
3. Break down the demonstration into suitable steps so that it can be easily understood by the students.
4. Proceed with the demonstration slowly so that all the students may grasp the details.
5. Wherever possible, involve students in demonstration.
6. Ascertain after every step whether the students have grasped the meaning, contents and explanation. Repeat if they have not followed it.
7. Give suitable verbal explanations for heightening the interest of the students.
8. Encourage students to analyse, record and tabulate the results of their observation.
9. Make an assignment based on the demonstration

Merits of demonstration. Demonstration enables the students to acquire knowledge in the first hand form. It brings about a close relationship between theory and practice. It helps in fixing facts and principles. It fosters creative thinking.

BY WAY OF DESCRIPTION

Description and narration are quite similar terms and there is not much difference between these two terms. Description demands a more effective use of the language than needed in narration. We usually describe a 'thing' or an 'object' and do not use the word 'narrate' to portray a thing. We describe events. We also narrate events. According to the dictionary meaning "to describe" is "to set forth, define, depict or portray in words" and 'description' is defined as "the act of representing a thing by words" account of the properties or appearance of something."

Description is needed in most of the lessons of all subjects and especially science, geography and history.

The following point should be kept in view while using this device in teaching :—

1. As far as possible, the teacher should try to see the object before describing it. A history teacher will not be able to present a vivid picture of the Red Fort until he sees it.
2. It may be borne in mind that without forming a clear visual image of the object or event in mind, it is not possible to describe an object or event or place in an effective manner.
3. Language employed should be very clear and simple.
4. It is preferable to give first a broad general view of the whole object and then field in the details.
5. Too many details at a time should be avoided for those may baffle the students imagination.
6. Key points should be stressed and repeated.
7. A definite order may follow in giving description.
8. Verbal description should be supplemented with diagrams, modes and pictures, etc.
9. The use of homely illustrations such as metaphors and similar helps to provide a vivid account of an object.
10. The aim of the description should be made very clear to the students in the very beginning of the lesson.

BY WAY OF DISCUSSION

Meaning and significance of discussion method. This method has been used in the teaching-learning process since times immemorial. It was widely used at the famous Nalanda University. The Greek scholars in their works used to discuss various problems and issues with their disciples. Discussion has been described as a thoughtful consideration of the relationships involved in a topic or problem under study. It is concerned with the analysis, comparison, evaluation and conclusions of these relationships. It aims at uniting and integrating the work of the class. It is carried out by organising, outlining and relating, the facts studied. It encourages the students to direct their thinking process towards the solution of a problem and to use their experiences for a further clarification and consolidation of learning material. Discussion is to be distinguished from debate in which the participants seek to prove a point rather than to discover a truth. Debate may also be marked by uncontrolled exchange of verbalism. Discussion is very important in stimulating mental activity, developing fluency and ease in expression, clarity of ideas in thinking and training in the presentation of one's ideas and facts. An exchange of ideas and opinions offers valuable training to students in reflective thinking.

Discussion may be used for the following purposes:-

(i) For planning new work.

(ii) For making decision concerning future work.

(iii) For sharing information.

(iv) For obtaining and gaining respect for various points of view.

(v) For classifying ideas.

(vi) For inspiring interest.

(vii) For evaluating, progress.

Discussion may be formal or informal. Formal discussion is one which proceeds in a pre-determined mauner and according to set procedures. An informal discussion involves the free verbal interchange of the participants without being governed by pre-determined set of rules.

Essential parts or constituents of discussion. These are as under:

1. The leader—the teacher
2. The group—the students
3. The problem or the topic
4. The content—body of knowledge
5. Evaluation—change in ideas, attitudes etc.

Organisation of discussion. Following are the main techniques of organising discussion

1. Introducing a topic or a problem by the teacher by giving points or explanations to serve as the basis of discussion.
2. Calling upon a pupil by the teacher to give facts, describe a scene or situation, explain an incident, event or happening for getting the discussion started.

3. Preparing an outline of points cooperatively by the teacher and a few students which may become the starting point for discussion.
4. Asking the students to describe their own experiences connected with the subject, topic or problem and making them points for discussion.
5. Presenting detailed papers by the teacher and discussions thereon.
6. Presenting detailed papers by the students and discussing them in the class.
7. Showing special works and projects to the class and discussing them.
8. Showing some pictures, charts, diagrams or any audio-visual material and discussion about them.

Merits of discussion. Following are the merits of discussion:

1. It helps in clarifying issues.
2. It helps children in crystallising their thinking.
3. It helps students in discovering what they do not know and what they have overlooked.
4. It engenders more reflection. It is farther from rote learning.
5. It represents a type of pooled knowledge, ideas and feelings of several persons.
6. It develops team spirit.
7. It engenders toleration of views which are at variance.
8. It affords opportunities to the students to learn together, make suggestions, share responsibility, comprehend the topic, evaluate the findings and to summarise results.
9. It provides opportunities to the students to speak distinctly, stand and sit correctly, respect the ideas of others, share interests, ask pertinent questions and comprehend the problem before the group.
10. It helps the teacher in discovering talented students who have potential for becoming good leaders.

Limitations of discussions. Limitations of discussion are:

1. It is not suitable in all topics.
2. It is likely to be dominated by a few students.
3. It is likely to go off the track.
4. It may lead to unpleasant feelings.
5. It may create emotional tensions.
6. It may involve unnecessary arguments.

Directing group discussion. The teacher has to show immense patience and skill to ensure that discussion takes place on right lines and in the appropriate environment. Following points may be considered in this respect:

1. Students should be well acquainted with the significance of the topic, its nature and scope and causes why the class should discuss it.
2. Discussion should be confined to important aspects.
3. Students should be encouraged to participate in the discussion.
4. Ideas may be invited without pressure or embarrassment.
5. Explanations, where needed, should be provided.
6. Personality cult should be avoided.
7. Cooperation rather than competition should be encouraged.
8. Efforts should be made to develop team spirit.
9. Doubts, mistakes and wrong interpretation should be made clear by the teacher.
10. Facts and points should be evaluated.
11. Facts and points should be summarised.
12. Students should be guided to appreciate difference of opinion and views.
13. Goals of discussion should be kept in view.
14. Only a few students should not be allowed to dominate classroom discussion.
15. Shy students may be given training in discussion in small groups so that their hesitation is removed while participating in bigger groups.

BY WAY OF DRAMATISATION

Meaning. Dramatisation has been described as 'a synthetic art', involving the purposive coordination and control of the delicate organs of speech and muscles of the body combined with a sense of rhythm, with a view to free and intelligent expression of emotions and ideas.

Dramatic art affords innumerable opportunities for the correlation of a large number of subjects. In the preparation of their roles, the students indirectly and unconsciously improve their speech habits and language. A systematic study of historical events has to be made when pageants of the life of great persons are prepared i.e. pageant on the life of Buddha, Chandragupta, Vikramaditya, Gandhiji, etc. Children prepare costumes suiting different ages and thus come to know about the dresses of the people during different periods of history. Dramatics also add to the geographical knowledge of the students. Carpentry and other mechanical arts facilitate the work of construction of the stage. Dance and music add to the beauty of a drama.

Drama has its great social value. It is a cooperative enterprise and develops qualities of cooperation and social understanding. It helps in fostering *espirit de corps* among the students. In various school functions dramas form the chief items of the programme. For the honour of the school, every student works to the best of his capacity.

Dramatics afford the students many opportunities for training in team work. They are very helpful in providing the students with opportunities for the release of the inhibitions to which they are subjected by the conventions of society.

There are many activities in a drama and as such students of diverse aptitudes get chances to choose items for which they are best suited and satisfy their urges, e.g., self-expression through the various activities of a drama.

Conditions for success. A number of rehearsals bring grace and success to the play when it is staged. Pupils should prepare as much stage material as they can.

Children should be encouraged to write their own play. The usual participants in this activity should be given opportunities to play different roles. The same pupils as far as possible should, however, not be allowed to play the role of a villain.

Selection of Play

1. Plays chosen should depict the evils of the social customs.
2. A play should have a literary value also.
3. The students should be able to understand and appreciate the play.
4. It should also have entertainment value.
5. It should be free from objectional subject-matter
6. There should be no vulgarity in the play.

BY WAY OF EXPLANATION

The main objective of explanation is to enable the children to take an intelligent interest in the lesson, to grasp the purposes of what is being done and to develop their insight and understanding of how to do it.

According to Panton, "Explanation forms a kind of bridge between telling and revealing knowledge of the lesson, and it involves a number of other techniques as well as narration and description." Explanation implies making ideas, concepts, events and actions clear. Explanation is more difficult than making factual statements or reports. When a teacher is explaining, he uses verbs like 'how' and 'why' in relation to a concept or condition or an event. The key phrases used in explanation are : 'therefore,' 'in order to' etc. These phrases indicate the links of the lesson. These key words and phrases help in directing the process of explanation. The effectiveness of the skill of explanation is greatly influenced by factors like continuity, fluency and simplicity. Continuity has two components, namely, sequence and fluency of the ideas explained. Fluency of explanation depends upon the mastery of the subject matter of the teacher, his ability to communicate ideas clearly and coherently and his self confidence to manage the class. Simple language within the student's vocabulary leads to effective communication. As far as possible, simple sentences instead of complex sentences should be used. Where needed, explanation should be done with the aid of charts, diagrams tables models, etc.

Panton advises, "throughout the process of explanation, the teacher must keep in close touch with the minds of his pupils, suggesting lines of thought—questioning them, answering their question, setting them on practical work, examining the results obtained, discussing significant problems, etc."

For effective explanation, the following points must be kept in mind by the teacher:

1. The teacher must keep in mind some definite aim so as to give definitions to the lesson.
2. The theme should be divided into different sections and must have a logical sequence and definite arrangements.
3. Due consideration should be given to the ability of the students to understand and assimilate the subject matter.
4. Too much dependence on telling or lecturing on the part of the teacher is likely to confuse the children instead of making things clear to them.
5. Essential points should be written on the black-board.
6. Questions of different types should be asked from the students to ascertain whether they are following the teacher or not.
7. Illustration, both verbal and non-verbal should be made use of.
8. A summary of the main points be given at the end of the lesson.

BY WAY OF EXPOSITION

Exposition is more then explanation. To expose means to open, to exhibit, to display, to disclose, to uncover and to bring to light. Exposition means an act of explaining and making clear the subject matter. The objective of exposition is to enable the students to grasp the meaning of the subject matter presented to them in an intelligible manner. Effective teaching is based on clear exposition. Hurried exposition results in faulty assimilation of knowledge.

The following points may be kept in view in using the device of exposition in teaching:—

1. Children's way of looking at things should be considered in exposition.
2. Subject matter to be exposed should be arranged logically as well as psychologically.
3. The teacher should have proper pauses in his exposition.
4. The rate of exposition should be slow when the class is backward.
5. Repetition should be judiciously done so that the class may not feel boredom.
6. Proper use of the black-board should be made.
7. Actual objects, models, diagrams, sketches, etc., should be used in exposition.
8. Students should be encouraged to ask questions.
9. Verbal illustration such as comparison, examples, etc, should be used.
10. The aim of the lesson should be kept in view.

BY WAY OF ILLUSTRATION

Meaning and significance. In education the term illustration implies the use of those aids which make ideas clear to children and help them to acquire correct knowledge and understanding. They secure better attention and possess as 'fixing power.' They illuminate what is presented or taught to children. They help in elucidation. Illustrations are used at all stages of education.

Types of illustrations. Illustrations are usually categorised under two main categories:

Concrete, non-verbal natural or objective illustration. Under this head, we include subjects, apparatus, black-boards, charts, demonstrations, diagrams, films, garden, graphs, models, pictures, radio and television, etc.

Verbal Illustrations. These include analogies, anecdotes, comparison, dramatisation, similes and stories etc.

The relative importance of these two types of illustrations depends upon : (a) The nature of the topic (2) The stage of education (3) The level of pupil's development.

Non-verbal illustrations are more useful at the lower stages. Object or their solid models are also very valuable in the lower classes. Similar to the case with story telling. Diagrams, graphs and sketches should be used freely in the higher classes. A higher level of intelligence is required to understand verbal illustrations, such as analogies and similes. Therefore, these should be used at a higher stage. It may not always be possible to bring actual objects or their representations in the class. Under such situation, educational excursions may be planned. Verbal illustration must remain the most important means of arousing appropriate mental imagery for learning.

Merits of illustration. Following are the chief merits of illustrations :—

1. They help to provide clarity and vividness to the subject-matter.
2. They help to simplify explanations.
3. They make the instructions concrete.
4. They create curiosity and interest among the students.
5. They help to strengthen the retaining and recollecting power of the students.
6. They are valuable in developing the power of observation of the students.
7. They help in the formation of good learning habits.
8. They are a ready means of fixing the attention of the students.
9. They help in making learning without burden.
10. They train the senses to greater acuteness of perception.

Illustrations as means and not ends. Illustrations are good servants but bad masters. Their misuse or overuse is likely to spoil the lesson in hand. They should not be regarded merely as means of making a lesson interesting. Their educative value should be the primary factor of their use. It must be remembered that it is a wrong belief that a lesson cannot be made effective without concrete illustrations. Gradually the students must be trained to think in abstract terms.

Following points need to be noted in the use of illustrations:—

Interesting illustration. Illustrations should appeal to the students. It is well-known that bright colour and simple design appeal to students.

Simple but comprehensive illustrations. Illustrations should be so simple that they can be easily comprehended by the students and should need little comments and explanations as far as possible. Illustrations like diagrams and tables can be worked out in the presence of the students in the classroom itself while teaching.

Exact illustrations. They should be very accurate and exact. Defective illustrations are likely to distort learning.

Relevant to the topic. Illustrations should be related to the subject-matter in hand. Illustrations should not be used for the sake of using illustrations as essential instruments of teaching.

Subordinate to the topic. Illustrations should not be used in such a way as the students remember only the illustrative material and not the subject-matter.

Proper display of illustrations. Non-verbal illustrations should be properly displayed so that the entire class is able to see them clearly and easily. They should be kept for reasonable period before the students so that they may observe them carefully.

Not too many illustrations. Too many illustrations are likely to distract the attention of the students from real subject-matter. They should be used rationally.

Collection of illustrative material. Every skilful teacher will try to have his own collection of illustrative material from different sources, i.e., journals, magazines, picture-post-cards etc.

In the end, it may be stressed that a wise selection, timely presentation and an intelligent use of illustrative material will be a very valuable asset of every teacher.

BY WAY OF LECTURING

Significance of lecture method. It is the oldest teaching method given by philosophy of idealism. As used in education, the lecture method refers to the teaching procedure involved in the clarification of explanation to the student of some major idea. This method lays emphasis on the presentations of the content. Teacher is more active and students are passive but he uses questions answer to keep them attentive in the class. It is used to clarify matters, to expand content and motivate the students. By changing his voice, by impersonation characters, by shifting his position and by using simple devices, a teacher can deliver his lesson effectively. While delivering his lecture, a teacher can indicate by his facial expression, gestures and tones the exact shade of meaning that he wishes to convey.

According to James Michael Lee, "The lecture is a pedagogical method whereby the teacher formally delivers a carefully planned expository address on some particular topic or problem." It can be used:

1. To clarify matters
2. To review significant details of the lesson.
3. To expand contents.

Merits of the lecture method. Following are the merits of the lecture method :

1. It is economical as it needs no apparatus and no laboratory. A large number of students can be taught at a time.
2. It saves time and covers syllabus in a limited time.
3. It is very effective in giving factual information and in relating some of the thrilling anecdotes. The life stories of great adventures, experimenters, investigators and thinkers can become very interesting and valuable talks by a teacher.

4. Lecturing makes the work of the teacher very simple. He need not make elaborate arrangements.
5. A good lecture not only stimulates the students but also lingers long in their imagination. It motivates students to become good orators.
6. It provides better ground for clarification and for laying stress on significant ideas.
7. It brings a personal contact and touch to impress or influence the pupils.
8. It provides flexibility. As the teacher is in close and intimate contact with his pupils, he can adjust his technique in accordance with their abilities, aptitudes and interests.
9. It gives the students training in listening.
10. It gives the students training in taking notes rapidly.
11. It develops good audience habits.
12. It provides opportunities of correlating events and subjects.
13. It enables the linkage of previous knowledge with the new one.

Limitations. The limitations of this method are as follows:

1. There is very little scope for pupil activity.
2. It does not take into consideration individual differences.
3. Lecturing is against the principle of 'Learning by Doing.'
4. It spoon-feeds the students without developing their power of reasoning.
5. Speed of the lecture may be too fast for the learner to grasp the line of thought.
6. An average student may not be able to fix up his attention to a lecture of forty to forty-five minutes.
7. A lecturer is likely to cover more content without realising that little learning takes place.
8. A lecture may become monotonous to the students after a while. Very few teachers can keep the interest of the students upto the end.

Guidelines for the effective use of the lecture method. The following points should be kept in view in using this device of teaching :

1. Matter should be arranged in such a way as to leave a single clear impression on the minds of the students.
2. The teacher should have pauses in between the lesson so that the students may learn the new knowledge bit by bit.
3. The rate of exposition should be slow when the class is backward. The teacher should utilise different ways of presenting the same information.
4. There should be abundant repetition but it should be in a new way so that the class may not feel dullness.
5. Children's way of looking at things should be considered in exposition. Language used should be familiar and suitable.
6. The lesson should be divided into sections which have a logical sequence. This will enable the students to understand easily and will also train them in systematic thinking besides assisting them to put their own thoughts logically.
7. The rate of exposition and the size of the subject-matter are determined by the individual capacity of children and teacher's natural rate of speech.
8. Proper use of the black-board should be made.
9. Actual object, models, diagrams, sketches, etc., should be used.
10. The students should be encouraged to ask questions. This will enable them to get their doubts removed.
11. Verbal illustrations such as examples, comparisons, etc., should be used to enable the students to grasp the exposition.
12. Pictorial illustrations such as pictures, maps and charts should be freely used as these help in motivating the students.
13. The aim of the lesson should be kept in view and the students fully made conversant with the aim.

ROLE OF LIBRARY

Significance. The library is the 'hub' of the academic life of the school. In the words of Edmonson, "The modern school library is conceived as a genuine service unit. It supplies materials for developing and expanding interests. Through its reference tools, indexes, bibliographies and catalogues, the realm of knowledge may be explored. The library co-operates with other agencies of instruction in helping students learn to use books and libraries, to find information, and to study. By its bulletin exhibits, posters and atmosphere, the library teaches informally. By its introduction to books, it suggests the life-time use of reading to further any interest."

Functions. The functions of the school library may be summed up in the words of the Joint Committee of the School Library Association in Britain, "We seek in the library to make children familiar with the sight and use of a collection of books and to help them to grow to love and care for them, to provide material for child's own recreational reading and explorations, to supply additional reading material illustrating the subjects taught in class, to give opportunities for elementary instruction in the use of books and for carrying out group and individual projects, to give scope for the exercising of simple responsibilities and finally to prepare the way for the use of larger libraries including public library, in adult life."

Salient features. Tagore has given a very good description of a good library in these words: "My idea of a small library is one that keeps books on every subject, but only select books, not one of which is there merely as an offering of worship to number, but each one of which stands on its own merit; where the librarian is a true devotee, devoid of ulterior seeking, free from pride in the mere loading of shelves, capable of discriminate rejection. A library, in short, which makes just enough provision that can be placed before its guests for their delectation, with a librarian who has the qualities of a host, not a storekeeper."

A good library has the following salient features :—

1. Suitable books, dictionaries and encyclopedias etc.

2. Well-equipped and airy library room.
3. Adherence to library rules.
4. Proper cataloguing.
5. Trained and friendly library staff.
6. Suitable display of new arrivals.

Encouraging the students to use the school library

1. The librarian should give thorough instructions to the students in not only how to find out books and other material in the library but also how to make the best use of the material which the library contains.
2. The teachers should give occasional talks to pupils on the importance of extra-reading.
3. As far as possible the open shelf system should be introduced so that the students may have free access to books.
4. Students should be asked to maintain a diary in which they should enter date-wise the names of all the books they have read. They may also be asked to write brief quotations or extracts from the books that may appeal to them. They may also write short reviews and appreciation of these books.
5. Marks may be allotted for extra-reading and entered in the monthly progress report.
6. Library periods should be provided for each class in the time-table.
7. Book competitions should be arranged from time to time and questions on titles, authors and subject-matter may be set.
8. The library should be made the most attractive place in the school so that it may attract the students in large numbers.
9. The cooperation of the students should be sought in decorating the library in order to give them the feeling that the library belongs to them.

10. The librarian should behave very sympathetically with the students.
11. The school library should be kept open during the vacation and long holidays.
12. The beautiful picture-cuttings from newspapers and illustrations from current events and topics should be displayed on the library Bulletin Boards.
13. Books suiting different tastes and interests should be provided in large numbers.
14. The furniture should suit the needs of the students.
15. A catalogue of library books should be available in the library for ready reference.
16. Library day may be organised once a year to popularise the school library.
17. Completed projects of the students can be exhibited in the library.

We may sum up the discussion with a quotation from Tagore, "In order to bring a library into the fullest use, it is necessary that its contents should be clearly and specifically brought to notice, otherwise it is difficult for the ordinary man to find his way about them, and the library is left as a city of vast accommodation that lacks sufficient means of communication. Those who frequent libraries on some special quest of their own may manage to make a track for themselves by dint of the urgency of their particular pursuit. But the library itself should recognise its share of responsibility in the matter. Because it has the books, it is incumbent on the library to get them read, for then alone it is justified. It is not enough that it passively permits visitors; its invitation should be active. For, as the Sanskrit proverb tells us *tannashtamyannadiyate*, "that which is not given is wasted." These views are applicable to school libraries also.

OTHER MEANS

Narration is an indispensable device of communicating knowledge. According to Panton, I.H., "Narration is an art in itself which aims at presenting to the pupils, through the medium of speech, clear, vivid, interesting, ordered sequence of events, in such a way that their minds reconstruct these happenings and they live in imagination through the experiences recounted either as speculation or possibly as participators." The skill of narration enables the teacher to come very close to the hearts of the students and thereby to attract their undivided attention. The art of narration involves the use of pictorial word images, a certain dramatic element in delivery and the ability to conjure up one picture after another. To be a good narrator, a teacher should know the skilful use of language.

Some teachers are born narrators and they are very fortunate in this respect. However, the art of narration can be cultivated through the following measures:

1. By observing skilful narrators.
2. By listening to speeches of good orators.
3. By critically observing one's own performance with the help of tape recording and making use of this feed-back.
4. By studying the work of effective writers of children's literature.
5. By using appropriate beginning and concluding statements.
6. By explaining links in the form of suitable words and phrases.
7. By using proper gestures.
8. By using common metaphors and similes.
9. By story telling.

Some Don'ts in Narration.

1. Do not use irrelevant or vague statements.
2. Do not allow any missing link or break in the logical sequence of interrelated statements.
3. Do not use fumbling ideas.
4. Do not utter incomplete or half sentences.

Dictation has the following merits:

1. Lack of suitable textbooks and filling up this gap.

2. Pressure of work with the teacher and less time for preparing the lesson.
3. Short cut to finish the over-crowded subject-matter.
4. Short cut to pass the examination.
5. Lack of adequate power of expression of the teacher.

Methods of Dictating Notes

1. Detailed notes on important topics after discussing the topic in the class.
2. Notes in the question-answer form primarily from examination point of view–guess questions and their answers.
3. Explanatory notes and summaries on the black-boards.
4. Instead of dictating notes to the students, they should be encouraged to prepare their own notes.

Defects in the Method of Note Dictation

1. It does not provide training in developing critical approach.
2. Note dictation makes teaching synonymous with memorisation of facts communicated by the teacher.
3. Note dictation fails to develop proper insight into the subject.
4. Note dictation proves to be a great hindrance in developing the habit of consulting reference books and textbooks also.

It is rightly believed that observation under the careful guidance of a teacher proves very effective in the process of learning, and facts, skills and behaviour learnt are retained for a longer period. Observation or direct experience or visits to actual places, say, a monument, a fort, a field, a river, a temple, an institution etc., provide ample opportunities to students, for 'seeing', 'hearing', 'examining', 'gathering data' and 'asking' questions. Visits to hospitals, telephone exchanges, telegraph offices, study trips to airports, etc., show how people and goods are transported from one place to another. Pupils understand better the working of markets, cooperative stores and factories when they see their working and thus acquaint themselves with the processes of production, distribution, exchange and consumption. Such experiences are most conducive to learning. Concrete data on cultural, industrial, political and geographical facts and relationship being more 'tangible', 'visible' and 'describable' serve as a great motivating force for further enquiry in social sciences. Observation lends vitality to the subject-matter.

Techniques of observation method. Following techniques are adopted in the observation method :

1. Field Trips or Educational Excursions
2. Community Surveys.
3. Community Service Projects.

Meaning of source method of teaching. Source method implies the use of original material and original sources in the teaching of social studies. A source method provides first hand experiences and leads to better understanding of the subject. Sources may be divided into two categories :

(a) Primary Sources.

(b) Secondary Sources.

Use of sources method. It can be used at the following stages of the lesson :

Pre-lesson use of resources. Visit to actual sites of monuments, forts or museums may be arranged. The teacher can ask the students to read selected passages connected with the lesson before hand.

Mid-lesson use of resources. Extracts from original or secondary sources can be read during the course of the lesson. They create real situations, impart reality and vividness to the lesson and reinforce the impact of teaching.

Post-lesson use of resources. Pre-lesson use of resources can also become the post-lesson use of resources and vice-versa. Students may be given assignments which need the use of resources. They may be encouraged to pursue their interest in a particular topic, do some critical thinking and analysis and prepare their own account.

Merits of sources method. Following are the merits of sources method:

1. It develops a sense of reality and vividness.
2. It develops a sense of objectivity.
3. It provides a congenial and motivating environment.
4. It arouses curiosity among the students.
5. It develops elementary skills of collecting data, sifting the relevant and organising the same.
6. It provides opportunities for useful mental exercise—right thinking and imagining, comparing and analysing, drawing inferences etc.
7. It promotes interest in the study of the subject.
8. It initiates the students in research.
9. It provides functional knowledge. Even the slow and backward children feel interested when they see original sources. Their learning becomes functional because it is gained in the real context.
10. It supplements class-room lesson.

Limitations of the source method. Limitations are given as follows:

1. It is very difficult for the school teachers to have an easy access to original sources.
2. Utilisation of original sources is a very difficult task for the school students as they lack the requisite training.
3. The method is very complex and technical.
4. Contemporary authors and writers have given their own prejudices, preferences and limitations with the result that it becomes very difficult to sift fact from fiction. The students are, thus, lost in the maze of conflicting views about the same event or movement.
5. Source method of teaching is very expensive.
6. Source method of teaching is time consuming.

How to make source method effective. The students should be encouraged to study the resource books in the library.

Educational tours to places of importance may be arranged. The students may be asked to write their own impressions and inferences about the places they visit. Copies of important extracts from the relevant records may be pasted on the blackboard for the use of students.

Dr. Keatings thinks that original sources can be used for creating suitable environment in the lower form. Well planned, purposive and well directed efforts have to be made by the teacher in the use of this method. By suggesting the use of resource method, we do not aim at making our students research scholars. Use of the method in selected topics is likely to make learning more meaningful and read.

Story telling as an art. Story telling is one of the most important methods of teaching. It is an art which enables the teacher to come very close to the heart of the students and thereby he attracts their attention. Some teachers are born story tellers and they are very fortunate in this respect. This art of story telling aims at presenting to the pupils, through the medium of speech, clear vivid, interesting, ordered sequences of events, in such a way that their minds reconstruct these happenings and they live in imagination through the experiences recounted either as spectators or possibly as participators. Story telling enables the teacher to make lessons lively and interesting to the pupils. Stories of great personalities, reformers, writers, saints, discoverers and scientists, etc., must be told to the students. Story telling helps in enhancing the interests of the students in the subject. It goes a long way in firing the imagination of the students. Story telling can be relied upon by the teacher as the best companion for helping in developing in his pupils traits of character such as charity, piety, truthfulness and valour, etc.

The art of story telling can be cultivated by :

1. Observing skilful narrators.
2. Studying the work of successful story writers.
3. Practising story telling.
4. Critically evaluating one's own performance and bringing about necessary changes.

In telling a story the teacher should be guided by the following points :

1. Suitable stories for the age of the students should be selected. A story that appeals and interests the seven-year child will not suit the child of four years of age. Small children of 4 or 5 years are interested in stories of boys and girls. The child of 7 to 8 years takes interest in hearing stories of magic and wonder, stories of giants, adventure and romance. Students at the secondary stage take interest in stories of scientific discoveries.
2. The stories should be short and the plot easy.
3. The teachers must know the story well that he wants to narrate. If he stops in the middle, it will detract charm from the story.
4. Language employed in telling a story should be very simple and easy.
5. A story should be told and not read. The story loses a great deal of its interest for the children if it is read.
6. The teacher himself should like the story and take interest in story telling.
7. There should be plenty of action in the stories. Key sentences and phrases should be repeated as the children enjoy this repetition. The stories should be loaded with activities and experiences familiar to the children. R. Strang has observed, "Stories for young children. upto the age of six years, a child is most alive to moving things—engines, boats, horses and wagons, animals, boys and girls in action. Children lose interest when the action is interrupted by a long descriptive passage. In telling a story one can notice the drop in interest during descriptive and explanatory portions, and the flare-up of interest again when the actions resumed. Since the young child's own activities and experiences are the ones most interesting to him, the first stories should be about experiences familiar to children."

8. Conversation, if any, in the story should be given indirect speech and not indirect.
9. The methods of introducing and developing the story should be thought out before-hand.
10. The story should be told in a natural way and very vividly.
11. Humour makes the story more interesting and should not be neglected.
12. To make the story more realistic, the teacher may use pictures and draw diagrams on the blackboard.
13. The story should suggest and inspire the students to action.
14. Ryburn suggests that well-known and familiar stories can be made fresh if they are told as though one of the characters in the story were telling it. He writes, "The story of Ashoka and the Kalinga war could be told as if Ashoka, himself, were telling it."
15. The story must have some aim besides mere enjoyment. The teacher must keep in mind the aim while narrating a story. It is all the more better if the students too know the aim.

HABIT OF READING

1. From the very beginning of their school career, the children should be stimulated to create a taste for reading by telling stories and recitation of children's poems.
2. Bold-typed, illustrated and attractive books, charts and other material arouse their interest in reading.
3. Some credit for extra reading should be given to the students. This fact may be mentioned in their progress report.
4. In the Higher Secondary classes the students should be encouraged to use dictionary and reference books. Students should be asked off and on to write down the difficult words and their meanings from the textbooks as their home assignment.

5. In the regular class periods, it should be stressed that the students must be equipped with the necessary tools, *e.g.*, pencil, note-book, etc.
6. Declamation contests and debates should be organised from time to time so that the students may consult books or other materials for preparing themselves.
7. Essay competitions should be held.
8. The students should also be instructed to pay due attention to their postures when they study books.
9. Apart from central library, class-room libraries may be organised,
10. The students should be asked to prepare a notebook in which summary of the books read by them should be recorded.
11. The school library and reading room should be well equipped, tastefully furnished, well lighted and ventilated so that the students may be attracted and encouraged to take advantage of it. It should be spacious enough and should be located in a quiet place.
12. Books and periodicals should be easily accessible to the students—the open shelf system is recommended.
13. New arrivals should be suitably displayed to attract attention of students and teachers.
14. It is very desirable that class-libraries containing sufficient number of books on suitable topics be organised. Adequate library grant should be given for the purpose by the managements and the Government. Parents can also help in equipping the library by donating books, periodicals, etc.
15. The time-table should be so framed that each class gets at least two periods every week for extra reading. These periods should be utilized for (a) silent reading of periodicals and books, (b) guiding pupils with regard to reading materials and ascertaining whether they have gone through the books, and (c) reporting and discussing in the class about the books and periodicals read by the students.

16. The librarian should be trained, well-read and interested in children so that the requisite guidance, encouragement and help may be available to the students. In a large school there should be a library assistant to help him.

TEACHERS' RESPONSIBILITY

(1) They should develop their own love for reading which will stimulate the students to develop reading habits.

(2) They should be well-versed in children's literature so that they may suggest suitable books for the students. Generally speaking, teachers do not read children's literature with the result that they are quite ignorant of the reading needs of the students.

(3) They should adopt such methods of teaching and give assignments in such a way as the students may be encouraged to supplement their class work by extra reading.

Home environment. Environment in the home also profoundly affects the development of good study habits. A home, situated in peaceful and beautiful surroundings, where parents are educated and interested in all-round development of their children, where there are harmonious relationships among members of the family, where the individuality of the child is respected and where privacy and facilities exist for individual's study, is obviously an ideal place for the promotion of sound study habits. Good economic condition of the parents is also one of the factors for promoting in the children reading habits in the form of newspapers, magazines, story books, etc. Even parents with limited income can help their children posses their own library by presenting them books as gifts on birthdays and other festive occasions. These facts may be highlighted in parent-teacher meetings.

Meaning of supervised study. Arthur C. Bining and David H. Bining describe the meaning of supervised study as, "By supervised study, we mean the supervision by the teacher of a group or class of pupils as they work at their desk or around their tables. In this procedure, we find pupils busy at work that has been assigned to them by the teacher. When they meet a difficulty that they cannot overcome, they ask the teacher for direction and assistance. The teacher, when not called upon, walks up quietly up and down the classroom or remains at his desk watching the pupils do their work continually alert for any wrong procedures that the pupils may follow. He is always ready to direct and aid them."

Individual attention. Supervised study is an aid in helping to solve the problem of individual differences. Supervised study aids in preventing failures. The pupil works along his own mental level and at his own capacity. Assignments can be given to meet all levels of ability.

Better pupil teacher relations. Another good feature of supervised study is seen in the better pupil teacher relations that it promotes. In the usual class teaching procedure; the teacher is frequently considered a hard task master and the procedure often produces a "class versus teacher" attitude. Under the supervised study programme, he appears in the role of a helper and guide. There is greater opportunity for the display of sympathy and understanding. The teacher is able to understand the pupil and his difficulties better and in a position to spurt him on to a greater effort.

Development of skills. There are certain skills which can best be developed under this procedure. A thorough use of the supervised method would reveal weaknesses in the learner. Following skills can be developed easily.

(a) Skills as to how to read social studies material.
(b) Skills as to how to use encyclopaedias.
(c) Skills as to how to use dictionaries.
(d) Skills as to how to use maps, atlases, indexes and almanacs.
(e) Skills as to how to read graphs.

Objections to supervised study. There are some objections such as:

1. Some investigations have concluded that the weak pupil is not helped under this method suitably.

2. Supervised study requires the lengthened school day and which is not possible.
3. Supervised study is a costly method. It would necessitate and increase in the teaching force that would mean an increased cost of education.
4. Supervised study depends too much on the initiative and enthusiasm of the students which they seldom display.
5. Supervised study destroys the supremacy of the teacher as he plays a secondary role in the teaching learning process.

SIGNIFICANCE OF DIARY

Teacher's diary is a mirror of the work a teacher is doing in the class. It serves as a great guide to him as it is a record of his doing work, his plan of work with the students, what he has already done and what he intends to do in a particular period. It also contains a brief outline of the year's syllabus and other activities.

The diary contains the time-table also. The teacher records the special methods of teaching that he adopts for the development of the weak and the intelligent students.

The diary contains the records of the achievement of the students—scholastic, psychological and health etc.

The worth of a diary depends on the regularity with which it is maintained.

The head of the institution is expected to supervise the maintenance of teacher's diary and offer suggestions if needed.

SIGNIFICANCE OF TEXTBOOKS

Importance and Value of a Textbook. There can be little doubt of the value of the textbooks in the education system. Recent research has made it quite clear that the textbook is one of the most important and vital elements conducive to effective and efficient teaching-learning process. Textbooks remain essential tools for preserving and diffusing the world's storehouse of knowledge and wisdom.

Preparing Textbook Manuscripts. *A Guide for Authors in Developing Countries* (1970) has pointed out the importance of a textbook in these words, "Classroom teaching depends heavily on the textbook. In situations in which the teacher is not very well qualified, the textbook is a guide and a support to teaching. For the pupil, the textbook serves as a basis for systematic learning, for reinforcement, review and further study."

In the words of Lee C. Deighton (1971), "The ultimate objective of a textbook is to permit the student to proceed on his own, by providing the basic facts, concepts, and generalization required for further study."

According to M. Solomon (1978), "Textbooks command attention because they not only provide the basic source of school instruction but also transmit culture, reflect values and serve as springboards for the intellectual development of individuals and the nation."

Douglas Pearce (1982) observed "The importance of the role of the textbook as the least expensive and most effective way of improving academic standards is now almost universally accepted. Forecasts that textbooks would be replaced to a large extent by educational radio or television programmes, tape-recorders, and learning machines, etc., have not proved to be correct, especially in the Less Developed Countries (LDCs). In fact, although these valuable electronic aids to education have played a more prominent role in the last twenty years or so, it seems likely that they have stimulated further demand for textbook rather than replacing them."

P.G. Altbach (1983) in an article 'Key Issues of Textbook Provision in the Third World', published in *Prospects* 13 (3), has pointed out the importance of a textbook as "Nothing has ever replaced the printed word as the key element in the educational process and, as a result, textbooks are central to schooling at all levels."

According to Altbach, P.G. (1983), textbooks substitute for gaps in teacher knowledge and skills.

Beeby C.E. (1986), Murnane R.J. and Nelson, R.P. (1984) think that textbooks complement existing skills by providing more able teachers with a resource that increases their effectiveness.

Sepulveda Stuardo, M. And Farrel, J.P. (1983) are of the view that textbooks promote delivery of more complete and coherently organized curricula, particularly in situations where there is a shortage of teachers and where teacher training is limited in scope.

Walberg, H.J. (1985) is of the view that textbooks enable the teacher to make better use of time spent on teaching.

Featherstone, H. (1985) states that textbooks enable the teacher to assign higher quality home work.

Heyneman, S.P., Farell, J.P. and Sepulveda Stuardo M.A. (1981) observe that textbooks provide a basic exposure to students to written material otherwise unavailable in the environment.

Rohlen, T. P. (1983), thinks that textbooks enable students to learn independently of the teacher, particularly through completion of home work.

Thomas and Kobayashi (1987) have seen the importance of the textbook from three perspectives :

1. The most common conception of a textbook, in the eyes of both teachers and students, it that it contains authoritative knowledge. The text's content are not only true, but they are of such great value that learners should commit them to memory.
2. A second conception of textbooks is that they offer records of prior events which will influence future events, so textbooks can help learners envision the future.
3. From a third perspective, a textbook reflects a particular viewpoint or set of values from which to perceive life.

A textbook is a constant companion of a student. A textbook guides the students in learning—in the school and at home. A student uses it continuously and constantly. This feature distinguishes it from a general and reference book which a student consults once a while. Each word of the textbook has not only to be read by every student but is also expected to be understood.

A textbook is a self-teaching device. A textbook enables a student to learn through his own efforts. A textbook provides an opportunity to a student to reflect and evaluate. A student can find the specific information be needs in a book. He can review material he has read from time to time to clear up uncertainties. He can move ahead as quickly or as methodically as his individual capacities for comprehension permit.

A textbook generates educational interaction. A textbook plays a crucial role in generating educational interaction in the classroom between the teacher and the learner and also between the learner and other co-learners as a result of which learning occurs in a group.

THE PROBLEMS

1. It tends to dominate the educative process. It has dominated the method of instruction and the evaluating process. It has narrowed down the scope of the curriculum.
2. It does not provide for direct experience. The students get ready-made knowledge and, therefore, fail to assimilate to properly.
3. It introduces uniformity and rigidity for definite achievements and kills all initiative and spirit of both the pupil and the teacher.
4. A textbook is a great hindrance in the new methods of teaching like the heuristic and the inductive. The students get ready-made answers and this defeats the very purpose of introducing new methods.
5. There is every danger that the textbook may be used for the purpose of indoctrination of the ideas and beliefs of the party in power. In fact, many textbooks have been sued in some countries for the propagation of fascist and Communistic ideas. A textbooks becomes a potent instrument in the hands of the party in power to inculcate narrow nationalism and racial prejudices.

How to Use Textbooks. A textbook should be treated as a means and not an end in itself. It should be borne in mind that it is a useful means to help the child in his study. The student should never have the impression that a textbook constitutes a boundary and his task is simply to learn what it contains and no more. A textbook should serve as a basis of learning. A textbook does not provide the last word on the subject. A textbook is not to usurp the functions of a teacher. It is to supplement his work and not supplant it.

Selection of the Content. (a) Relevant content (b) Adequate coverage of the content (c) Adequate content of each topic (d) Authentic content (e) Up-to-date content (f) Integrated content (g) Content linked with life.

Organisation of Content. (i) Division into suitable units (ii) Division into suitable sections (iii) Psychological approach to the content.

Presentation of Content. (1) Attractive and appropriate title (2) Motivating presentation (3) Creative and interesting content.

Verbal Communication (Language). (a) Appropriate vocabulary (b) Short and simple sentences. (c) Correct spelling (d) Correct punctuation.

TEACHING DEVICES

In order to facilitate the learning process the teachers resort to what have been called Devices. A device implies the external mode or form which teaching may take from time to time.

According to John Mander there are five main reasons which might justify the use of these teaching expedients. They are given below:

(a) To teach something more thoroughly so that the children may retain the subject-matter taught.

(b) To teach something more quickly. This will result in 'covering more ground' in a given time, and thus gives a better chance of "getting through the syllabus".

(c) As a means of creating or sustaining interests.

(d) As a means of integrating a number of separate pieces or work already learned by other means.

(e) As a means of bringing with the experience and understanding of children something which is new to them. This often includes the inpersonating to children, in simplified form, of matters which can be appreciated fully only by adults.

John Mander explains the various devices with the help of a diagram which is shown ahead:—

Group A. This category includes both trick of verbal presentation, suited only to particular facts, and mechanical devices which illustrate single facts or process. "No book can hope to include all the advice needed by teachers in the selection and use of devices in category A." The mechanical devices of Category A include much specialised apparatus. Counters or counting sticks may be used for the teaching of elementary number combinations. Words and letter cards are used in teaching reading. Their application is only to younger children. Every fact, each sentence, offers its own opportunity for bright imagery and forceful expression.

Group B. Machines such as cinema, film strip projectors, epidiascope, etc., which may be used in the teaching of any subject are included under this heading. This device also includes devices of curriculum presentation, such as projects, which can be undertaken in any subject. Curriculum may be taken up in different forms. It may be dealt with in the traditional form. It may be taken as 'Free Activity' and without the rigid control of the teacher. It may be presented in the form of 'Topic Work' or presented in the form of projects. Some devices of teaching are termed as methods of teaching and vice versa. Examples are: The lecture method, discussion method, demonstration method, the problem method, deductive and inductive method, assignment method, supervised study. It may be noted that the use of various terms in devices of teaching is arbitrary. Devices of teaching are also categorised as natural and artificial devices of teaching. Natural devices are those wherein learning is a by-product of direct experience, e.g., in object teaching, outdoor work and school excursions, etc. On the other hand, artificial devices include oral communication through narration, explanation, exposition and illustration also.

Debate, Demonstration, Description, Discussion, Dramatisation, Evaluation, Explanation, Exposition, Lecturing, Narration, Note, Dictation, Observation, Questioning, Source Material, Story Telling, Study Habits, Supervised Study, Textbooks, Teacher's Diary.

Significance of an assignment. N.L. Bossing has observed, "The central position of the assignment in the techniques of teaching has remained unquestioned." G.H. Betts asserts, "Upon the proper assignment of the lesson depends much of the success of the recitation, and also much of the pupil's's progress in learning how to study." W.N. Drum suggests, "Teachers generally do not appreciate the importance of the assignment, and the work of the pupils probably suffers as much from hasty or careless assignment as from any other single cause." H.R. Douglass and others are of the view, "The assignment represents one of the most important phases of teaching."

Types of assignments. N.L. Bossing has listed the following types of assignment:

Page or paragraph assignment. Often thought of as the textbook assignment. This method is still widely used as recent studies have revealed.

Chapter assignment. Another form of the textbook assignment though vastly different from the page or paragraph form. Chapters usually are of a unitary nature and involve some elements of completeness within themselves.

Topical assignment. This type may or may not centre around a single chapter in a textbook. It has a wealth of possibility in the social sciences particularly.

Problem assignment. Where an arbitrary distinction is set up between a problem and a project. The type becomes very valuable form of assignment.

Project assignment. Adapted especially to the workshop, natural sciences, and some measure to the social sciences. Its special appeal is through the natural motor activity required.

Experience assignment. Most frequently used in mathematics. It represents the old traditional approach to teaching although if used in combination with other types, this form can be used very effectively.

Individual or group report assignment. Used extensively as a device to supplement other types and to provide for individual differences in interests and capacities within the class; very effective.

Unit assignment. It may apply to any extensive segment of classroom activity that presents factors of cohesion and a relatively complete additional element around which the unit may resolve itself as a core, A rather pretentious problem may serve as this unitary core.

Experimental assignment. This is a form of the problem and project types characteristic of the science laboratory. Too often in practice, it does not represent either an experiment or a problem in the true sense. It can be made a vital instrument of educational training if properly used.

Practice assignment. This type represents an assignment of repetitions of activities designed to produce mental or motor skills.

Mastery of the simple combinations in arithmetic, memorization of a poem, or practice in speed on the typewriter are examples of this type of assignment.

1. The assignment should be clear and definite.
2. The assignment should be concise but sufficiently detailed to enable each student to understand the task assigned.
3. The assignment should anticipate special difficulties and suggest ways to remove them.
4. The assignment should relate the new unit to past experience.
5. Students should understand the importance of the assignments.
6. The assignment should arouse an interest in advance work.

7. The assignment should provide for differences in the ability and interest of students.
8. The assignment should be motivated chiefly by the hope of worthwhile achievements, rather than scholastic reward or the fear of punishment.
9. The assignment should stimulate thought.
10. The assignment should provide necessary and specific directions for the study of the lesson.
11. The assignment should be adjusted to the time and opportunity of the class.
12. Materials of the assignments should be varied and adaptable to the needs and interests of the students.

Difficulties in the preparation of an assignment. Fleming and Woodring have listed the following difficulties :

1. Insufficient thought and preparation in planning the assignment.
2. Inability to obtain an acceptance by the pupil of a worthy purpose for performance of the task.
3. Stimulation of preparation of the assignments by appealing to the interests of adolescents and by providing for real needs growing out of pupils experience.
4. Prevention of loss of interest due to too long phase of time between the assignment and preparation.
5. Avoidance of assignments so long that successful accomplishment is impossible in the time available for preparation, there is consequent loss of interest.
6. Guarding against too many and too varied activities, resulting in dividing interests with consequent bad habits of work, and unsatisfactory accomplishments.
7. Difficulty in presenting work to be done so that it is clearly understood by the pupils; also, the difficulty of ascertaining whether every pupil understands.
8. Gauging the difficulty of work so that success is possible for each pupil.

9. Determining essential requirements, and differentiation of assignments to suit the various levels and types of ability existing in the class.
10. Inclusion of challenges to mental exploration by the pupil, thereby stimulating real thinking.
11. Provision for continuity of work by presenting new problems as a continuation of previous experience and anticipation of future problems.
12. Correlating with other subjects and outside activities.
13. Focusing attention on important elements in the new problem or task, and directing the attack in such a way as to increase interest rather than lessen it, to stimulate effort, and to overcome seeming obstacles to accomplishment.
14. Providing the necessary tools for preparation by training in study procedures and techniques, and in selection, organization, and use of materials, thereby developing effective habits of independent work.
15. Giving to pupils devices for checking the mastery and performance of work undertaken.
16. Evaluating the effectiveness of an assignment by the quality of response during the presentation of the assignment, and by the adequacy of pupil preparation.
17. Providing sufficient time for adequate consideration of the assignment and determining the psychological moment for its presentation.

Suggested assignment procedure. The procedure suggested for the preparation of a good assignment is as follows:

1. Analyse the nature of the learning process required in the advance unit. This is without exception the first step in a good assignment procedure. Much of what follows in any good assignment depends upon this analysis.

2. Study the various types of assignments available and select the one, or modified form of it, that appears to fit

best the learning situation. Some assignment types are admirably adapted to one form of learning for teaching but not to others.

3. Provide the essential background for the advance work where uncertainty exists that such background obtains. At this point too many teachers are likely to assume the adequacy of this background when in fact it may not exist. Scarcely can one emphasize too strongly the aperceptive preparation for the new.

4. Whether this is the next step in the assignment procedure or not, it is obvious that very early in the assignment phase the teacher must throw out a challenge to the student that will enlist his interest and maximum effort in the new unit.

5. Outline in sufficient detail the advance unit to be studied.

6. Suggest some plan of attack upon the new unit. It is well to remember one caution does not do for the student that which he may be led to do for himself. This suggests the desirability of leading the class in a cooperative discovery of desirable leads for the general attack upon the new.

7. Where reference to source material other than the textbook is necessary, this should be made, specific. The most satisfactory plan in the large unit assignment is to provide the select list of available sources in mimeographed or hectographed form with chapter or inclusive page references given.

Whether or not homework should be given to the students is a controversial point. Extreme views have been expressed regarding the usefulness of home work. The assignment of home task has been emphatically denounced by Bray. He writes, "Under normal conditions a reasonable day's work for a child has been done at the close of the afternoon and homework as it is generally organised does more harm than good as a rule in this country except perhaps from the point of view of examination success."

On the other hand, P.C. When commands the assigning of homework. An average guardian also feels that some work should be given to the student which he should do at home.

Purpose of home task. Following purposes can be stated.

1. To provide opportunities to students to work independently and thereby to develop in them self-reliance and initiative.
2. To develop habits of reading regularly among the students.
3. To provide opportunities to the students to utilise their leisure time, profitably. It is generally seen that our school children waste their precious time in loitering about or making mischief when no such work is given to them.
4. To give them an opportunity to do practice what is done in the school.
5. To finish the prescribed courses in time. The syllabus is too heavy to be finished in the classroom work.
6. To serve as a link in the parent-teacher co-operation. It enables the parents to know that regular work is being done in the school.
7. To develop permanent interests and to train the students in the profitable use of leisure.
8. To enable the child to revise his previous lesson and prepare the next one.
9. To provide remedial measure for backward children.
10. To give chance to every child to profess at his own speed.

Home Work

1. Homework in the form of solution of questions and problems which depend upon the application of the principles learnt in the school.
2. Home work in the form of written exercises in translation, grammar and composition with a view to giving practice in the work done in the class.
3. Homework in the form of verbal memorising work pertaining to curricular and co-cuirricular activities. It may take the form of cramming facts, principles, poems,

spellings, etc., or memorising work in respect of dramatics and debates etc.

4. Home work in the form of practical work, *e.g.*, preparation of maps, charts, models etc.
5. Homework in the form of advance preparation for the coming lessons.

Disadvantages and objections. These are as follows :

1. It deprives the children of participating in recreational activities when it imposes heavy demands upon them.
2. It is a great hindrance in the way of the students of enjoying family and social life.
3. It deprives children of the opportunity to help their parents in supplementing their income.
4. It imposes a great physical strain on small children and thus endangers their health.
5. It becomes a constant source of fear and worry to the students and therefore it endangers their emotional stability.
6. Children are tempted to copy whenever they find that the home task is difficult to do.
7. Sometimes children are tempted to tell a lie that due to certain reasons they have failed to do home task.
8. Unhealthy home conditions make study more harmful than profitable. There is a lack of adequate light and quietness in a large number of Indian homes and the atmosphere is not congenial for study.
9. Too much of homework develops an attitude of indifference on the part of the pupils and they become careless.
10. Lack of proper correction by the teacher, sometimes, gives rise to carelessness on the part of the pupils. It also develops wrong habits of work if the work is not properly checked.
11. Too much work is set by some over-enthusiastic specialist teachers in their subjects completely disregarding what other teachers of the same class might have set for the same day.

12. The task is generally too academic in nature and ignores those activities which are needed most for an all-round development of the personality of the child.
13. It is not properly adjusted to pupils's needs and capacities.

Principles of assigning homework. Following are the principles of assigning homework.

1. The nature of the homework should be such as it does not require any kind of assistance from a private tutor or guardian.
2. It should not be purely mechanical, *i.e.,* requiring general knowledge on the part of the child.
3. Homework should aim at developing the taste of the individual child. This purpose can be very conveniently realised if homework is in the nature of hobbies.
4. Homework should be very definite.
5. It should be supplementary rather preparatory as far as possible.
6. A single assignment for the whole class may not be considered as appropriate. It should vary according to the mental and physical makeup of the students.
7. Homework in different subjects should be coordinated. Homework time table Should be framed so as to avoid confusion.
8. While assigning homework "Principle of sliding scales" should be adapted. The primary classes might be given home task to keep them busy for about half hour or so; in the middle, secondary and senior secondary classes time involved in doing home task should not exceed one hour. Normally it should be given on alternate days.
9. Home task should not be set as a punishment.
10. Home task should be properly checked.
11. Library books should be given for reading at homes as a home task.
12. Copies of the homework time tables may be sent to the parents to seek their cooperation which is very important.

13. While assigning homework the teachers should take into consideration the home conditions of the child such as domestic employment, working condition in the home, etc.
14. 15% marks should be reserved for the evaluation of the student's work based on the assignments done through the year.

CORRECTION METHOD

1. Correction by the teacher. This is the best method and should be usually resorted to.
2. Correction with the help of the best students in the class. Sometimes it may not be possible for the teacher to correct the work himself and he may resort to the help of the bright students. It is very important that in such cases a teacher must have a cursory glance over the work and then he should sign it.
3. Correction with the help of the black-board. In language lessons this method may be used.
4. Correction by interchanging the exercise books. Dictation work is generally checked by this method and it saves a lot of time without any loss to any individual student.

Regarding the correction of the home work given, the Secondary Education commission observed, "When a great deal of home work is given and it is not properly scrutinized by the teacher, the mistakes of spelling of grammar, of expression, of involved presentation and, above all, of confused thinking remain undetected and are likely to become ingrained. That is why a little home work willingly done and carefully corrected is far better than a great deal of slipshod work reluctantly accomplished.. Here as elsewhere, quality is more important than quantity."

Parent-Teacher Cooperation in Home Work. In the words of S. Bala Krishna Joshi, "Close cooperation between the parent who is the first teacher and the teacher, who is the second parent, is the very foundation in which rests the fruitfulness of the training, imparted in our institution." Mr. George Tomlinson has stressed the need of cooperation between home and school in these words, "Let us fashion our schools with the well-being of children always in mind. In particular, remember that any clash between parents and teachers must always be harmful to the child. Harmonious working together can alone bring us the results we want." Teachers are interested in the welfare of the children; they want their pupils to develop mentally, physically, morally and socially. So is the case with the parents, hence the need for united efforts on the part of parents and teachers who are the custodians of the welfare of children.

Exercise

1. Explain the term' devices of teaching.' What useful purposes do they serve in teaching and learning?
2. Elucidate the difference between narration, description, explanation and exposition.
3. "Illustrations are good servants but had masters." Comment upon this.
4. "Though experience is the general educator, it needs textbooks to interpret and illumine our experiences." Examine this statement and explain the use of textbooks."
5. Are you in favour of home assignments? Give reasons in support of your answer.
6. "Library is the intellectual hub of school life." Explain this and suggest measures for making the best use of school life.
7. Write brief notes on:
   (i) Developing study habits in students.
   (ii) Correction of written work.
   (iii) Lecturing.

11

VARIOUS STREAMS

Teaching broadly consists of designs of instructions. The development of educational engineering has provided the scientific basis of instructional system. Educational technology has the main assumption that teaching is not only an art but also a science : teachers are not only effective by birth but they can be mode effective through training institutions.

Glaser (1968) states that professional skill and efficiency can be developed with its help of instructional designs. The expert's and specialists are, attempting to investigated the level of professional skill to be developed. L Carter (1966) found in his investigation that instructional designs were effective for developing group professional efficiency than individual. Glaser has enumerated the following functions of instructional designs:

(1) It emphasizes on structure of the task. The content is analysed for its structure and ascertaining its characteristics..

(2) The learner's responses are analysed in view of objectives and levels of learning. The entering behaviour is considered for providing new stimuli to have desired responses of the learner.

(3) The appropriate teaching strategies, techniques and tactics are selected for presenting, content so that desired

learning structure may be generated. The techniques of motivation are employed for leading the teaching.

(4) The measuring instrument is constructed for evaluating the performance level of the students and decision may be taken about the objectives of learning.

The desired objectives could not achieved on the basis of learning theories therefore, teaching learning structure, teaching theories and structure of the content have been developed. Instructional designs are the sum of these things.

THE SCIENCE

The term 'Science' and 'technology' are very confusing when -these are used simultaneously. These are two distinctive terms and have different meanings, though these are closely related to each other. The term 'Science is theoretical in nature while technology is an application to practical task for specific purpose.

The term 'Science' concerns with empirical knowledge based on experiences and observations. A micro-approach is used in science. An element is divided in molecules and atoms. An atom is further divided into electron, protons and neutrons. An experimental method is used in science. An experiment means to control to observe, and to measure. The cause-effect relationship is established in formulating theories and developing principles. The science means advancement of knowledge. It has the following characteristics:

(1) Science is an empirical knowledge based on experiences and observations.

(2) It is based on experimentation-control observe and measure.

(3) Science is based on objectivity.

(4) Science employs micro-approach to study the structure of a phenomenon.

(5) It establishes, cause-effect relationship among the variables or elements of a phenomena.

(6) Theories, principles, laws, postulates and hypothesis are the main content of science.

(7) Science is an edifice of knowledge and advance'men't of human awareness.

Technology is an application of scientific principles to practical task for specific purpose. Technology means engineering or use of machines. It has three aspects—input, process and output. The process is based on feedback theory (cybernetics). It has three functions- initiate., regulate and control. All the -machines are based on feedback system it is an hardware approach of technology. If the scientific principles applied to teaching, training and instruction for specific purpose or specific objective. It is known as software approach of technology.

THE TECHNOLOGY

The word 'technology' is derived from the Greek work technie, meaning art or skill and logia, meaning science or study. A wide definition of technology is the science of study of an art or skill. This work, technology, is differently interpreted in different contexts. Professional engineers, doctors and scientists, economists and politicians, whether they are practitioners or academicians, have their own usage. It is not surprising that teachers have difficulty in understanding the concept of technology and its place in college curriculum.

Technology is more than the academic study of materials and resources. Its importance centres around the practical application of materials - and ' resources, especially in the service of man. Technology is the purposeful use of man's knowledge of materials of different resources, sources of energy And other natural happenings. There is a close relationship between technology and society. Technology is for the benefit of the society in general or a neighbouring community. The interaction of techno logy and society is one of ends and means. The society opts for certain ends for which, the, technology provides the means. Conversely, technology influences the selection of inputs resulting in the outputs society needs and requires.

ROLE IN TEACHING

Teaching is an art as well as a science. As an art, it portrays the imaginative and artistic abilities of the teacher in creating a worthwhile situation in the classroom in which the learners learn and achieve the immediate and ultimate goal of education. As a science, it points to the logical, mechanical and procedural steps to scientific consideration of teaching has led to the evolution of a concept of teaching technology. Davies, Gage, Britner and Gagne have contributed significantly in this led to the evolution of a have contributed significantly in this area of teaching technology.

Teaching technology has certain fundamental principles on which it is based. Some of these are as follows :

1. Teaching is a scientific process and its major components are content, communication and feedback.
2. There is a close relationship between teaching and learning.
3. It is possible to modify, improve and develop the teaching learning activities.
4. The terminal behaviours of the learner in terms of learning structures can be established, by appropriate teaching environments.
5. Teaching skills can be developed and strengthened by means of feedback devices with or without sophisticated techniques.
6. Pre-determined learning objectives can be achieved by designing suitable teaching activities.
7. Use of achievement motivation techniques enhances the output of the teacher and the learner.

Davies and Glaser (1962), studied what the content of teaching technology should be and Davies presented the structure of content in four steps. The first step is planning of teaching which includes content analysis, identification of objectives and writing these in behavioural terms. Organisation of teaching comes next and it indicates the teaching strategies for achieving the objectives of teaching. In the third step, leading of teaching is mentioned whereby the communication strategies are identified in relation to teacher and student. The last one is controlling/managing of teaching, whereby the focus is placed on the assessment of the learning objectives in terms of student performance and this forms the feedback to teacher and students.

DESIGNS AS DEVICES

Unwin (1968) has given a comprehensive definition of instructional design:

"Instructional design is concerned with an application of modern skills and techniques for the requirements of education and training. This includes facilitation of learning by manipulation of media, methods and the control of environment so far as this reflects on learning."

Such type of thinking was introduced in 1950 and the different approach have been evolved for the problems of education and training but the following three approaches are most popular:

(1) Training Psychology,

(2) Cybernetic Psychology, and

(3) System Analysis.

The three approaches of Instructional Designs are not contradictory but supplementary to one another in solving the problems of education and training. They are closely related to deal with the input, output and process aspects of educational technology.

Training Psychology emphasizes on task analysis and design of interrelated training components. Cybernetic Psychology focuses on dynamic feedback and self-regulation. System Analysis focuses on system.

Designs of Instruction

	↓	↓	↓
Type–	Training Psychology	Cybernetic Psychology	System Analysis
	↓	↓	↓
Stage–	Input	Process	Output
Focus–	Task Analysis	Feedback- and Reinforcement	Development System

The chart indicates that training psychology concerns with input aspect and its main function is task analysis. It evolves the structure of teaching and learning. The second approach cybernetic deals with the process aspect of education and its major function is to provide reinforcement for leading the teaching. The third approach system analysis concerns with the development of organization and administration on the basis of output aspect of education. The meaning, principles, procedure and application of these approaches are being described in detailed in the following paragraphs.

Basic Assumptions : In planning, and designing instruction, there are certain factors which should be indicated as these are the fundamentals for proceeding with the task for designing instruction. The following are the basic assumptions:

1. Instructional design, must aim at aiding the learning of the individual. The instruction may be oriented to the individual in spite of the fact that learners may be in large or small groups.
2. Instructional design has phases that are both immediate and long range. Design in the immediate sense relates to the preparation of the design a few hours before the instruction is given. The longer range approach takes time to plan and prepare not only the design of a particular topic but the whole course itself or the entire instructional system. This approach involves more complex and varied designs. Such designs are undertaken by individual teachers, a team of teachers, curriculum planners and textbook writers.
3. Systematically designed instruction can greatly affect individual human development. A nurturing environment is not adequate to develop an individual. Planning and directing are essential aspects of learning. An instructional design should ensure that no one is educationally disadvantaged.
4. Instructional design should be conducted by means of a systems approach. Briefly, systems approach in instruction means planned and organized use of all available learning aids including instructional media,

in order to achieve the desirable learning objectives by the most efficient possible way. It focuses on the learner and his performances first and then decisions are made regarding content, learning experiences, instructional media and instructional strategies for realising the objectives.

5. Designed instruction must be based on knowledge of how human beings learn. Consideration should be given not only to what the students should learn but how they should learn. Instructional design must taken into account learning conditions.

The Functions : Instructional designs provide the scientific basis for the instructional system. It develops the professional skill and efficiency of the teachers. The sequence of teaching acts or events that a teacher plans, organises and carries out, in order to create a learning- environment for the college students is called the instructional design. Glaser (1968) has enumerated the functions of instructional designs:

1. The instructional task is analysed for the structure of the content.
2. Learner's responses are analysed in terms of objectives and levels of learning. The entering behaviours of the students are studied appropriate stimuli for better performance.
3. Teaching strategies, techniques and approaches are selected by the teachers for presenting the content so that the desired learning structures result.
4. The performance of students is assessed in order to find out if the objectives of learning have been realised.

Instructional design is, therefore, concerned with the structuring of the content to create a suitable learning' environment, the selection of appropriate teaching strategies and methods, and the assessment of the performance level of students. The different phases in instructional design are listed below:

1. Stimulating motivation.
2. Informing the learner, the objectives of learning.

3. Gaining and directing attention.
4. Activating recall.
5. Enhancing retention and transfer.
6. Providing learning guidance.
7. Eliciting performance.
8. Providing feedback.
9. Assessing performance.
10. Reviewing the process on the basis of assessment.

When a college teacher designs his instructional hours, he should be conscious of the need to motivate the students not only at the beginning of the class but right through, whenever the opportunity arises. Through motivation, attention is sought and the teacher adopts several ways to maintain it. Some of these steps may include listing the objectives of learning for the particular class or topic, enhancing retention of material learnt during the class by active questioning and providing feedback on the responses given by the students. The questions should not only aim at recall responses but also include reflective thinking, reviewing, generalising and reasoning. Selected instructional aids and media can also be used for better learning outcomes. The learning experiences thus provided may be assessed for replanning the instructional design.

Various Types : Instructional designs can be classified by viewing teaching-learning process as related to teaching skills, instructional objectives, competencies or performances, teaching strategies, teaching models, specific technology, and learning styles.

Instructional Designs : The following are classified in five categories:

1. Objective-based
2. Skill-based
3. Competency-based
4. Model-based and
5. Learning style-based

VALUE OF COMPETENCY

Competency based education, also known as performance based education is a new approach to teaching having as its core, the ideas of accountability mid competencies. With regard to accountability it is argued that teachers should be held 'accountable' for their products. This accountability is accomplished by breaking teaching into discrete competencies or behaviours which can be stated as objectives competencies or behaviours which can be stated as objectives. Mastery of these competencies, is then possible (Unwin and McAllesc 1978).

Competency-based education rests upon few assumptions which are generally shared by educationists. They are of six types as follows:

1. Learning takes place through changes in the behaviour of learners and that teaching aims at facilitating these changes.
2. Individuals achieve similar objectives but at different rates.
3. Teachers should be accountable for the learning that takes place in their students.
4. Continuous evaluation of teaching is used as a feedback for revising the instructional programme and this in turn promotes effective teaching.
5. The objectives of any educational programme bears close relationship to the educational goal.
6. Systems approach can be applied to education, especially to instructional planning and designing.

In competency-based education, competencies are spelled out so that it is possible to assess student learning through direct observation of student behaviour. The student knows in advance the extent and level of competencies to be mastered by him. The accomplishment of the learning objective can be observed mid measured in the form of specified learner behaviours. In order to facilitate this, performance goals are specified and agreed to in great detail much in advance of instruction. The teacher is held accountable, not for his students 'obtaining a passing grade' but for attaining a given level of competency in performing the essential tasks of learning. Student's progress rate depends on demonstrated competencies. The emphasis is laid on exit and not on entrance requirements. Further the focus is, being on acquisition of specific competencies by all the students. Time-becomes, variable and depending on the needs and capabilities of the learner, he is allowed to attain the competencies at his own rate and space.

Elam (1971) explains five basic features of competency-based programme:

1. Competencies to be demonstrated by the students are derived from explicit conceptions of teachers' roles and are publically stated in such a manner that students learned behaviours are related to specified competencies.
2. Criteria are to be employed in assessing competencies are stated in terms of expected levels of mastery under specified conditions.
3. Assessment of competency depends on students performance as the primary source of evidence and strives for objectivity.
4. Student's rate of progress is determined by demonstrated competencies rather than time or course completion.
5. Instructional programme is intended to facilitate the development of specified competencies.

Competency-based education is, therefore, unique in the sense that it focuses on the student's acquisition of pre-specified, agreed-upon competencies and demonstration of these specified competencies through objective assessment.

THE MODULES

Instruction is presented in modules, a module being a set of learning activities with objectives, per-requirements, per-assessment, instructional activities, post assessment and remediation. Modularization helps in self-pacing, individualisation, and independent study. The use of modules allows a much greater variety of experience than standard courses and provides a far better basis for personalised construction. Many competency-based education programmes make use of self instructional modules.

Critetion-referenced testing is an integral part of competency-based teacher-education. Criterion-referenced tests are those kinds of tests that indicate whether the learner has achieved the goal specified for the learning tasks. They do not make a reference in comparison to the performance of other learners. It is considered that the criterion-referenced tests are more sensitive than norm-referenced test for the purposes of detecting instructional efforts. They can provide the only relevant information on student's learning excellence or deficiency.

Competency-based education is unique in the sense that it shifts the emphasis from testing the memory to the demonstration of required competencies and thereby emphasizes outputs. They are not teacher-oriented but student-oriented. The principal, staff member of a concerned discipline at a particular level, under-graduate or post-graduate should evolve the academic scheme. The first step is the preparation of instructional modules suited to the level of a target group. Time is not a factor but the possibility of attaining the competencies specified by the working term, be all students at that level is more important. The prepared modules can be tried out with a small group of students. Implementation of the modules with supporting materials such as books, booklets, and cassette, slides and film strips, if necessary, will form the second stage. Students will not be permitted to proceed to the next unit of a module unless they master the competencies in that unit. A criterion-referenced test based on the pre-specified competencies should be conducted to ascertain the proficiency of the students. If the performance of the student is satisfactory they are allowed to proceed to the next lesson unit. When it is found that some of the students are lagging behind in mastering the competencies time may be given for attaining the competencies. In some cases a different set of instructional package is needed as students have different patterns of learning and communicating. In case the instructional objectives or the competencies based on them are found to be unsuitable for that particular group the whole programme needs recasting. There may be non-academic reasons such as emotional and personal problems of students that could hinder the mastery of the competencies. The different competencies that students acquire, can be more accurately reflected by a well-defined criterion-referenced test in contrast to its counterpart, the norm referenced tests.

The difficulties experienced by such students can be identified and referred to a teacher or some other qualified person for guidance and counselling. Since the personal and academic problems are intertwined and mutually interacting, cooperation between the class teacher and the counsellor when the help of such a person is requisitioned, is essential for redressing the problems the student faces.

Realising the vital role that the competency-based education could play in cognitive development of college students, teachers could make a modest beginning in preparing competency-based modules on specific topics and try them out on small groups. The instructional design based on competency-based education is yet another approach to efficient learning at college level.

LEARNING STYLE

Of recent origin is the research study on the styles of learning adopted by the learners. Students use different approaches when faced with learning tasks and problems. The way in which the students approach the learning tasks, and the, behaviour in learning situations determine their learning style, Rosenberg (1968) defines learning style as referring to an individual's characteristic pattern of behaviour when confronted with a problem. It is pointed out that the learning style of an individual has relation to factors such as prior learning experiences, openness to interpersonal and extra-personal information, physical facilities, and learning environment.

On the basis of the work of researches on learning, Rosenberg has arrived at four general learning patterns which are rigid-inhibited style, indisciplined style, acceptance-anxious style and creative style. It should be noted that when categorizing an individual as belonging to a given learning style because he exhibits the characteristic of that style, he should be considered first and foremost as an individual person rather than a member of a particular category.

Learners with a rigid inhibited style of learning require constant supervision as they get confused easily. They tend to give unrelated response to questions put forward. Changes in the class routine easily upsets them and they also exhibit signs of nervousness. They depend on the support given to them by the teacher. The behaviour of the rigid-inhibited learner is, therefore, a problem to himself and his teacher.

The indiscipline learner exhibits characteristics such as refusal to obey commands, showing disrespect to teachers, deceiving, stealing, bullying, etc. Such learners invariable leave their learning task unfinished due to lack of tolerance. They concentrated on what gives them pleasure at the moment.

The fourth type of learning style according to Rosenberg is creative style. Learners of creative style are self-confident, and able to evaluate their own performance with objectivity. They are prepared to learn from their mistakes and show divergent thinking ability. Anxiety stimulates their functioning, specialty during the learning process rather than i pair it. A creative learner continues with the learning task until .ie completes it, which gives him satisfaction. He performs well on a divergently and therefore, also prefers to work independently,

There are several other approaches to classifications of learning styles, depending on how a person looks at the whole problem. Kagan (1965) discusses about impulsive-reflective dimensions of learning style. Teachers tend to group students as obedient or disobedient, timid or outgoing, bright or dull rather than as reflective or impulsive A reflective individual may be categorised as a dull student and impulsive quick individual as bright. Both reflectiveness and impulsiveness are related to the individual's conceptual thinking. Impulsiveness may lead to meeting with difficulties such as proceeding to work out a problem without understanding it, starting an experiment without following the instructions properly, completing a reading passage without understanding the major concepts, etc. Reflectiveness is indicated in trying to comprehend material that has a variety of complex concepts in a passage above the level of students or in going over remedial work. Impassivity can result in developing anxiety and consequently being punished and ridiculed by teachers and classmates, specially when it is associated with the speed of response.

There are also learning styles characterised as dependent-indepen-dent, co-operative-non-cooperative, anxiety free-anxiety prone, competi-tive, non-competitive; study habits oriented-trial students learning styles by probing into their learning patterns some-of which can be indicated indirectly in the classroom through teacher-student's learning styles by probing into their learning patterns some of which can be indicated indirectly in the classroom through teacher-student interactions in the evaluation of academic performances and in the specific behaviour patterns.

Form the above classifications, the college teachers surmise first, the existence of different styles of learning adopted by students and secondly, the effect of these styles on the learning process. Consequently the instructional design could be based on learning styles, where the planning, preparation and conduct of a lesson emphasizes learning styles of the students. The teacher's design of instruction should provide opportunities to the students who use different learning patterns. Teachers should also make an attempt to reduce the factors that do not encourage good learning styles such as anxiety, frustration and emotional instability, dependence on teachers and parents, rote memory and convergent thinking.

TEACHING STRATEGIES

Teacher strategies aim at establishing relationship between teaching inputs and learning outcomes, mainly in terms of realising the learning outcomes. Teaching strategies include teaching methods, approaches and techniques such as lecture method, tutorial approach, case study technique demonstration method, term-teaching approach, programmed instruction,) etc. In planning and instructional design, the teacher selects a particular essential factor to base he design such as objectives, skills, competencies, models or learning styles. In doing so, he focuses attention to the type of design he is going to prepare. The teaching strategies used to elaborate the content or subject-matter of that unit or topic have to be spelled out in that particular design. Teaching strategies have been introduced in this book for large groups, small groups and individual instruction.

Teaching strategies when designed with clearly spelt-out objectives, and effective means of, achieving them with in built evaluation techniques is known as educational technology. Application of technology will ensure the achievement of objectives with the minimum effort and time required. When teaching result in effective learning of all the students taught, then any strategy that is applied to achieve this can be called educational technology. Educational technology is not deterministic, in the sense that if 'x' is done, 'y' will certainly happen. It only says that the probability of 'y' happening is very high if 'x' is done. The teaching strategies suggested have the high probability of effecting effective learning in students. Practising teachers may have to bring about some modifications, minor changes and adapt them to further increase the probability of their success in helping students learn more and better. And that is what educational technology and for the reason, and technology is for.

ROLE OF PSYCHOLOGY

Training psychology is mainly concerned with the problems of teaching learning and training. This has come up through investigation on complex problems of training. Its origin is taken from military training. The main objective of training psychology is to improve the activities in which learner performs function. The learning outcome could not be improved by learning theories, therefore, training psychology prepares an outline for task by analysing its components. The task components are organized in such a way that desired objectives may be achieved. The crucial aspect of training psychology is the Task Analysis.

It is an approach to teaching and training. It employs learning conditions in teaching learning process rather than learning theories. The main assumption of this approach is that learning is dependent variable where as teaching is the independent variable. The learning can only be improved by developing teaching tasks.

Our training institutions can not produce effective teacher with help of learning theories. Moreover, they have failed to provide substantial solution for teaching and training problems. Training psychology is an approach for these problems.

The Principles : The principles of stimulus-response of military psychology have failed to give the solution for the complex problems of training then the task analysis approach has been followed for the development of training. Robert Gagne has explained the principles of training psychology:

(1) The human task can be analysed in its elements. He further assumed that these elements are quite different from one another. The task elements can be performed by employing different tactics.

(2) The task-elements function as a mediator for last task. The functions of an element are helpful in the transfer of learning and training. The shortage of task elements reduce the transfer to zero.

Training psychology is based on three principles:

(i) The elements are identified and analysed for the performance last task.

(ii) It is assured that every task elements can be performance effectively.

(iii) The elements are organised in such a sequence which may generate appropriate learning conditions.

These statements convey the meaning to the principles of training psychology. These principles are broadly associated with task analysis.

MODELS IN EDUCATION

The teachers are prepared by determining the nature of training tasks which they perform in classroom teaching. The development of teaching concept is based on teacher-education model. The large amount of work has been done in this area during 1960's. The number of teacher-education models have been developed and these models are based on the principles of training psychology. The teacher-education models can be classified in three groups because B. O. Smith and Clark have given three types of teaching tasks. On the basis of teaching tasks, the following classification of teacher-education models has been made :

Presage Factors Models

(1) Michigan State Model of Teacher-education
(2) Florida Model of Teacher-education.
(3) Syracuse Model of Teacher-education.
(4) The Wisconssin Model of Teacher-education.

Process Factors Models

(1) Teacher College Model of TEACHERS TRAINING
(2) The Goregia Model of TEACHERS TRAINING
(3) Regional Laboratory Model of TEACHERS TRAINING.
(4) The Toledo Model of TEACHERS TRAINING

Product Factors Models

(1) Teacher for the Real World Model
(2) The North-West Regional Laboratory Model.

The presage factors models training tasks are organized in such a way that their focus is on the development of the internal abilities and efficiency of teachers. The main emphasis is given on the mastery of content and development of right-type of attitude of teaching.

The second type of teacher-education models orient the training for developing teaching skills or teacher-behaviour in the classroom interaction. The Georgia and Toledo models are the examples of this type of model. Pre-service and in-service programmes are organized in Indian conditions for developing process factor.

The third type of teacher-education models are based on out put system. These models are used for improving the outcome of learning. The Real World and -Regional laboratory models are the main examples of product factors. Such type of teacher-education internship in teacher-education programme may be employed for this purpose.

The principles of training psychology are not only useful for developing teacher-education models but also for developing instruction. Norman A. Crowder has propounded branching programme main stress is given on task analysis and difficulty of the elements is identified.

The diagnosis done for the difficulty of elements and remedial instruction is designed for such difficult elements.

The branching programme is originated from human training and from psychology principles. The task-elements are performed by each learner according to his own needs. This strategy their own requirements for each and every learner.

The training psychology has been developed for the practical problems of training and training. It has a great scope of application in the area of education and training . The principles of training psychology are being used for improving present training programme by developing models of teacher-educational in our country. The principles of training psychology may be helpful for student-teachers—

(1) To analyse the teaching task and developing competency.

(2) To identify the goal of training programme and specify learning objectives.

(3) To plan and prepare educational programmes for actual teaching.

This lesson-planning and presentation in the classroom may be greatly improved by using the spirit of training psychology.

The principles of training psychology can provide scientific basis for designing individualized or remedial instructions and development of curriculum. The curriculum and instructional material cannot be made specific and relevant to the objectives to the competence and skill to be developed in the learner.

THE CYBERNETICS

The second approach of instructional designs was evolved in second world war. The term cybernetic has come to denote discipline which is associated 'with the research of communication and control'. It suggests concern with component elements of a system and they may function together to produce the most effective integrated system. The term cybernetic is used by Norbest Wiener (1948) associated with the physical system and physics.

The Meaning : The term cybernetic has been coined from the Greek word for steerman and thus, calls to mind and first importance cybernetic concept is that of feedback.

Cybernetic is defined by W. Wiener as the science of control and communication in the animal and the machine.

Cybernetic is the sciences communication and control. In any system control is basic and key element. Control here means connectiveness, and regulation and system is a dynamic state.

Consider our school system, when the error between what the parents want their children to learn in school and they actually receive to become too great, the school policies are changed by the force of public opinions. In this way, the school systems are regulated by the modes of community. All regulatory bodies throughout of our entire society are the feedback control system.

Cybernetic Theory : Cybernetic can be considered as a branch of training psychology. It conceptualizes human beings in engineering terms considering him like an electric machine which used the process of sensory feedback to control and modify its behaviour.

Cybernetic theory views an individual as a feedback system which generates its activities in order to detect and control specific characteristics of the environment. It analyses intrinsic mechanism by which control is established an maintained of sensory feedback mechanism. The focus of the whole theory is the dynamic feedback and self-regulation.

All system include at least three basic elements : Input process and output.

The process unit acts on the material or information to modify it in any way.

The output unit consists of some techniques for discharging the results of process from the system.

The output from a system, which returned as input to control future output, is called feedback.

The system can be of two types-an open loop system and a closed loop system. The closed loop system is often referred to cybernetic system. In the open loop system the output is returned to the system and consequently affects future output of the system is one which places a boundary around the system.

The essence, then, of Cybernetic psychology rests principles of sensory-oriented feedback which are intrinsic for the individual (he 'feels' the effect of his decision) and are the basis of self corrective devices.

Instruction also can be considered as a cybernetic system. The instructional system also has three major elements. A cybernetic instructional system would also include knowledge of results to the learner and some record of students responses. Its input also consists of library material, subject matter content, learner characteristics mid objectives. Students responses function as feedback for input. The procedure controls the presentation and modifies the presentation of display and knowledge of results on the basis of students responses correspondence to the objectives. In the cybernetic system of instruction, following is the order of input, output and procedure.

The first essential input is the content or material to be presented i.e. library material or library input which is inclusive of any written material or audiovisual material programmed instruction, diagrams, charts' etc.

The most important input for an instructional system are the objectives (performance standard) by which the system is designed to accomplish.

A third input for a cybernetic instructional system is the formation concerning with the individual characteristics of the students.

Because this is a cybernetic system so the fourth type of input consists of the feedback for the learner in the form of his responses. This is an important per-without this an instructional system is not able to adjust the presentation and to produce the change in behaviour specified by the objective input. It may be noted here that in most of the instructions in schools the input of students responses is ignored.

The first essential output for an instructional system is the display of the learner, which may be oral such as lecture explanation, visual, written, and so on. A display is any stimulus situation structured and presented to the learner for the purpose of establishing some responses.

In a cybernetic system, a second output presented to learner is in form of knowledge of results.

If student's response is input to the system, a third type of output which may or may not be used in a particular instructional situation will be the record of each student's response.

The procedure is the selection mechanism which presents and displays in a linear fashion, one following the other. Movie or filmstrip presentation are good examples of such a system.

Feedback theory evaluates the techniques of self instruction according to how well they conform to principles of cybernetic design. In order to optimize feedback control of symbolic knowledge and skills original presentation should be more varied and flexible than a permitted by most of the teaching machines and programmes. Specially organized systems of reference are also important. However self instructions is useful for drill and review in specific details.

The mechanism of feedback devices are most effective for the modification of teacher-behaviour. These mechanisms are based on the principles of cybernetic.

Application of Cybernetic : Most useful concept in the cybernetic is that of feedback which has far reaching implications for teaching, learning and training. The following are the major implications of cybernetic:

(1) The principles of cybernetic are applied for classroom instruction, group as well as individual learning.

(2) It enables the teacher to understand some of the fundamental mechanism That control learning.

(3) It provides the basis for self-education. The feedback control is used to develop programmed instructional material.

(4) Cybernetic principles are used for developing remedial instruction or individualized instructional material.

(5) Teacher-education programme can be improved by employing the mechanism of feedback devices for the modification of teacher-behaviour.

(6) The innovative practices in teacher-education programme such as micro teaching, stimulated social skill and interactional analysis are based on the theory of feedback.

(7) The input, output and process units of teaching enable the teacher to understand and analyse teaching in more scientific manner.

(8) The teaching activities can be made highly structured and well organized in view of learning objectives.

The classroom instruction, a school or the programme of teaching, can be considered as a dynamic system. This stresses on the principle that teaching is a resultant activity of the combination or forces, factor and conditions. The teacher has to take in consideration all these factors to generated appropriate teaching situation. Thus, cybernetic concept is most useful for developing design of training programmes for complex behaviour.

The third approach of instructional designs which is closely related to both training psychology and cybernetic, is known as 'System Analysis'. It has emerged during second world war. It has greatly influenced management decision making 'in business, 'industry, government and military. This new technology is known by serval terms, but one term that has gained considerable standardization is, 'System Analysis.'

The Meaning : The word system has been derived from the field or engineering. A system is the sum total of agents working independently and decpendently together to achieve the required goals. The term system conveys the meaning of analysis and development. The term system from the scientific management concept. In general system analysis involves utilization of scientific mathematical techniques applied to organizational operation as a part of management decision making activities. It has the assumption that no comprehensive system development can take place without prior system analysis. It enables the administrators to use more scientific and quantitative methods for analysing management problems.

The field of educational administration is becoming with the set quantitative scientific techniques that helps the educational administrators in the decision-making process. System technology brings to educational management a scientific-quantitative approach for solving complex educational administrative problems. It is based essentially on mathematics.

The Procedure : A number of steps are followed to accomplish a System Analysis. The following steps must be utilized for conducting system analysis study—

First Step—Formulation of objectives.

The most important and difficult aspect of the entire system analysis study is to formulate the specific objectives to be achieved. To state objectives in general terms is totally inadequate. An objective may be written in behavioural terms or fiscal functions.

Second Step—Review of systems operation.

The second step in system analysis includes a comprehensive review of the systems operation. System analysis is a problem oriented and it is necessary to understand completely the systems operation. The administrators fell in some problems but these do not always turn out to be the main problem.

Under any circumstance a comprehensive review of the whole system is necessary to isolated the main problem to the solved.

Third Step—Collection of data.

The review of system for identifying the main problem yields the data within the problem area. The collection of data involves basically the statistical techniques and procedure.. In many situations the aspects as system analysis are the applications of classical statistical procedure.

Fourth Step—Analysis of data.

Analysis of data is done to make it meaningful. The analysis of data is employed to experimental paradigms to study the effect of independent variable upon dependent variable. In system analysis study, an objective analysis is made for determining the influence of variables. The investigator is concerned with the influence of variables. The investigator is concerned is to be obtain with interaction of many variables. The primary concern is to be obtain correlation not to establish cause and effect.

Fifth Step—Isolation of the problem.

The administrator does not always know, accurately the main problem therefore, it is necessary to follow earlier steps in order to isolate specific problem of the system. The collection and analysis of data helps in identifying and defining the problem.

Sixth Step—Specify operations in the problem.

After identifying specific problem, it is necessary to review the operations within problem area. It is much more comprehensive than the original review of the total operations. It helps to understand quickly the relationship of all facts of the problem to the total operating system.

Seventh Step—Block Diagram.

The problem area is a final step in the analytical stage of the system analysis. A block diagram is prepared for all functions of the subsystem that make up problem area. It denotes logical structure of the sub-system operations and similar to the block diagram.

Design : After the system analysis, the investigator attempts to design and tentative solution of the problem. A new solution of the problem is subjected to testing. A tentative solution and retesting the tentative solution continues until on analyst reaches to an optimal solution. Once optimal solution is obtained the analyst departs that loop.

Evaluation : The formal evaluation of the new solution is done for checking its work ability. It involves implementation of tentative solution in some aspect of the system. The analyst proceeds through the same steps of loop as mentioned earlier. It is advisable to evaluate all new system solutions in small scale of the required operations.

System Operations : The formal evaluation and acceptance for the solution of the problem, the new design has been implemented within the system. It involves two aspects:

(1) It concerns with implementation of new system operation.

(2) It requires the maintenance of the system where a new system is designed. It continues as monitory of the system in order to check the effectiveness of the system.

STANDARD OF EVALUATION

General criteria are included in any evaluation system performance, cost, utility and time. A general criterion is that the total system should operate in an optimal fashion. These criteria are discussed here:

Performance : The effectiveness of a system is evaluated on die basis of performance. The design of the problem solution ascertains how will the new system be effective in achieving the objectives. The performance criterion is the concept of validity of the new system. The system is valid if it does what is it supposed to do. Thus, much of the evaluation of the performance is quantitative.

Cost : Analysis of system is influenced by cost function to a major extent. The amount of resources is being put into the system function in terms of money, staff and facilities comparison are made regarding the investment of resources in the new system and old system of education. This is extremely valuable criterion for evaluation system analysis projects.

Utility : The ultimate criterion for evaluating system' project is utility of the system. The return on investment represents the utility of a given function. Many education functions require an assignment of a numerical utility.

Time : Time factors as an evaluate criterion is closely associated with effectiveness. It is particularly relevant criterion in evaluating system projects. There is high correlation between time and cost. Much of the contribution of modern electronic data processing involves time.

Application of System Analysis : The system analysis has greatly influenced the educational administration and organisation. It provides scientific and quantitative basis for studying the problems of educational system. The educational implication of system analysis have been enumerated in the following areas of education.

(1) It brings to educational management a scientific-quantitative approach for solving complex education administrative problems.

(2) It enables educational administrator to identify the actual problem and abstains a verified solution of the problem.

(3) The training programmes can also be improved with the help of system analysis. The new concept of management may be implemented in training programmes.

(4) The sub-system of eduction is analysed to understand the actual problem and tentative solutions can be verified or tested on a segment of the system.

(5) Any change in the educational system can be brought objectively, empirically and economically with great utility with the help of System Analysis.

Meaning and Definition : System approach is a rational, problem-solving method of analysing, the educational process and making it more effective. System is the process taken as a whole incorporating of all its aspects and parts, namely pupils, teachers, curriculum content, instructional materials, instructional strategies, physical environment and the evaluation of instructional objectives.

The purpose of the system analysis is to get the "Best environment in the best place for the best people at the best time and in the best price."

"The system approach in instruction is an integrated, programmed complex of instructional media, hardware and personal whose components are structured as single unit with a schedule of time and sequential phasing."

The instructional process has become complex these days because of the shift in technological focus for the classroom to curriculum planning.

The curriculum should not only specify student behavioural objectives but also suggest the strategies for helping the student to reach the objectives and evaluation instruments to measure the success. It is called the system approach.

Keshaw and Michean (1959) have defined—

"System approach is one of the techniques which aims at finding the most efficient and economically intelligent methods for solving the problems of education scientifically."

The system concept provides a framework for visualizing internal and external environmental factors as an integrated whole. This concept factors are a way of thinking which helps us to recognize the nature of the complex problems and there by provides insight which enables us to operate within the received environment.

System analysis is a systematic way of identifying goals of any system and scientifically working out different steps to more towards these goals.

The approach in general includes the following steps:

1. To analyse the existing situation.
2. To set up the goal for the desired situation.
3. To define the mechanisms to evaluate the achievement of goals.
4. To create alternative situation.
5. To select the most appropriate solution through cost benefit analysis.
6. To work out the layout of the system.
7. To design the monitory mechanisms for the system.
8. To plan for introducing the new solution.

The Components : It is a systematic attempt to coordinate all aspects of a problem toward specific objectives in education. This means planned, organized use of all available learning resources, including audiovisual media, to achieve the desirable learning objectives by the most efficient means possible. The system approach focuses first upon learner and the performance, required of him. Only then, it makes decisions regarding course content, learning experiences and the most effective media and instructional strategies for realizing the objectives.

The Instructional System employs the following steps:

1. Defining instructional objectives in behaviour terms or measurable terms.
2. Determining functions related to the achievement of the objectives by appropriate multimedia approach.
3. Defining learner's characteristics or entering behaviour.
4. Selecting appropriate instructional strategies for effective learning.
5. Selecting suitable learning experiences for available alternatives.
6. Choosing appropriate instructional aids, resources to facilitate students learning.
7. Defining and assigning appropriate personal roles: teachers of term teaching members and supporting personal students.
8. Implementing the programme : Try out with a small group of pupils in appropriate conditions.
9. Evaluating the pupils learning outcome in terms of learning objectives.
10. Revising if necessary to improve the efficiency of the system to improve student learning.

The system approach applied to educational situations includes: input, process, output and feedback. These are inter linked and interdependent stages and can be described as :

(a) Planned input and process involving learning materials and strategies suitable organised to cater the needs of a particular group of students.

(b) Explicitly stated standard of outcome performances, including sequenced behavioural objectives.

(c) Monitoring output which is used to revise, improve and evaluate the instructional system, providing feedback to the learner and teacher.

(d) A degree of inbuilt flexibility to adjust the individual situation.

The system approach can be effectively used for studying the problems of the following areas of education:

1. Instructional system or procedure.
2. School administration and supervision.
3. Examination and Evaluation system.
4. Non-formal and adult education.
5. Educational guidance system.

An example demonstrating an application of system approach is discussed in the following paragraph in an instructional system.

INSTRUCTION SYSTEM

Robb (1974) has analysed an instructional system and suggested that an instructional system can be employed into three phases : Planning, Execution and Evaluation. These phases involve eight steps and indicate the development of instructional system.

Phase First: Planning instructional system:

Step 1. Defining objective

Step 2. Pre-assessment or determining entering behaviour.

Step 3. Specifying appropriate strategies.

Step 4. Selecting materials, facilities, aids and media.

Phase Second: Execution of instruction:

Step 5. Defining and assigning personnel roles.

Step 6. Synthesising, and implementing the system of instruction.

Phase Third: Evaluation of instruction:

Step 7. Evaluation and outcome.

Step 8. Analysing, result and modifying the system.

The problem is that the development of an instructional system is for a given target population or class of students. The instructional system can be used by the following eight steps:

Defining Objectives : The objectives for the instruction are identical and written in the behavioural terms which the learners are, required to demonstrate.

Determining the Entering Behaviour : The students entry level is determined by the pre-assessment. The knowledge and skills which the learners are already equipped with, are processed.

Specifying Appropriate Method and Strategies : In this step appropriate method and strategies are specified which can suit to the nature of the students and are helpful to achieve the objectives.

Selecting Materials, Aids and Media: The learning experiences are provided with the help of appropriate material and media. The instructional strategies require the appropriate material and media to generate academic environment. Therefore, appropriate material and media are selected for providing learning experiences.

Defining and Assigning Personnel Roles : In using instructional procedure effectively, the teacher has to play various roles to assist the learner 'to achieve the objectives.'

Synthesizing and Implementing the Instructional System : This is a step of execution phase of instructional system. The system approach, strategies, material, media and roles of teachers are integrated in such way so that specified objectives may be achieved. Under this step learning experiences are provided to the learners.

Evaluation of Learning Outcome : The effectiveness of instruction is examined on the basis of post-test scores of the students. The performance of the students indicate the validity of instruction and fulfilment of the objectives.

Analysing the Result and Modifying the System : The learning outcome is analysed to ascertain die inability of the earlier steps. It provides the feedback to the designer and suggests modification and improvement in the different aspects of instructional system. It ensures the effectiveness of planning, and execution phase of the system.

Thus system analysis or approach can be applied for the development of educational administration and organisation, examination system, Instructional system, models of teacher-education, models of curriculum and educational and vocational guidance system. These three approaches can be applied simultaneously for education and training.

A comparative view of these streams of thought has been presented in the following table to make it more understandable:

Designs of Instruction

Training Psychology	*Cybernetic*	*System Analysis*
1. Exponents L. Carter Glaser and Robert Gange	Gulibod Smith and Smith Norbest-Wiener	Frank O. Banhart
2. Origin Military training Physical Science. Steering boat	Principles of	Engineering
3. Goals Task analysis Task Structure.	Feedback control Regulation	System analysis. Development
4. Assumption : Task-elements are crucial for developing Skills and competencies for his development	Human being is like a machine. Feedback is important	Management can be developed by system analysis.
5. Principles (1) Human task can be analysed its elements.	(1) Input (2) Output (3) Process.	(1) System analysis for the development.

contd.

Training Psychology	*Cybernetic*	*System Analysis*
(2) Task-elements functions as mediator for last task	It is closed loop system.	(2) It is a Scientific quantitative approach.
6. Steps (a) Goals. (b) Task Analysis (c) Organization of The elements.	(1) Stimulus in the form of environment (2) Response is the knowledge of results. (3) Confirmation. or response functions as re-inforcement.	(1) Objectives (2) Data Collection (3) Analysis of data (4) Isolation of problem (5) Design. (6) Evaluation.
(4) Task efficiency		
7. Application in Education (a) Designing instruction (b) Lesson planning (c) Teacher-education models (d) Development of teaching skills (e) Branching programme.	(1) Classroom teaching (2) Programmed instruction (3) Teaching models (4) Modification of teacher behaviour by the use of feedback devices.	(1) Educational administrative problems (2) Evolving a new system of education (3) Reform in the examination (4) Importance in teacher-education models. (5) Improvement in instructional system.

Educational Technology can be viewed from the systems approach.

A system may be defined as the assemblage of components each having its own purpose. A system is a inter-relation of parts each having a specific function. The parts mid their functions are inter-related in specific ways so that they perform adequately to achieve the purpose of the system as a whole. The whole is more than the sum of the parts. It is synergistic e.g. a bicycle, car, school, college, etc.

The educational system includes students and teachers, and refers to curriculum content, instructional materials, instructional strategy, physical environment, and the evaluation of instructional objectives.

Each component has its own functions and interactions. These functions and interaction are more important than their description.

The inputs into a system undergo some process of 'transformation into a product output' and the effects of the output on the environment care monitored so as modify future inputs. Colleges can be thought of as places where the 'process' of education works on the minds and personalities of all the members and the product is the effect of this educational process which will thus be qualitative, as well as quantitative. The 'feedback loop' represents the information on which the educational process is modified to better provide for the needs of learners who are entering the college or leaving it for work situations. The systems approach is a rational problem-solving method of analysing, process and making it more effective.

The system approach in instruction is an integrated, programmed complex of instructional media, hardware and personnel, whose components are structured as a single unit with a schedule of time and sequential planning.

It is a strategy which utilizes analysis design and management to attain the stated goal effectively and efficiently.

Exercise

1. Define the term instructional designs and enumerate its major approaches and their purpose.
2. Explain the term 'Training Psychology' and its contributions to education and teachers' training.
3. Enumerate the types of Instructional Designs. Describe competency based education.
4. Explain the term 'Cybernetic'. Describe the applications of cybernetic in education.
5. Write short notes on the following :

   (a) Competency based Education.

   (b) Learning style based Education.

   (c) Objective based Education.

   (d) Basic Assumptions.

12

TEACHER TRAINING

The progress of a country depends upon the quality of its teachers and for this reason teaching is the noblest among all professions. The irony of fate, however, is that teaching is the most unattractive profession and teacher no longer occupies an honourable position in the society. Teaching can regain its earlier noble status in case the quality of teacher-education in our country is improved. It is probably for this reason that the education commission recommends the introduction of "a sound programme of professional education of teachers". The commission further remarks that investment in teacher-education can yield very rich dividends because the resources required are small when measured against the resulting improvements in the education of millions. In the absence of other influences, a teacher tries to teach in the way in which he himself was taught by his favourite teacher and this tends to perpetuate the traditional methods of teaching in a situation like the present when new and dynamic methods of instruction are needed such an attitude becomes an obstacle in progress. He can be modified only by effective professional education which will initiate the teacher to the needed revolution in teaching and lay the foundations for their future professional growth.

BASIC PRINCIPLES

Both terms have different meanings. The term 'training' has very limited boundary while education is a very broad term under which many things come.

Training: This term is specially defined and explained in the glossary of training terms published in 1971 in London by the department of employment. In this glossary training has been defined as "Systematic, development of attitude, knowledge, skill, behaviour patterns required by an individual in order to perform adequately a given job or task."

Knowledge: 'Bruner' in "Instructional Technology" has defined the term as "Knowledge consists of facts, concepts, terms, principles, theories, generalization, etc, which are useful for a teacher."

A teacher must have knowledge of his subject, methods and techniques of teaching and factors which affect teaching and knowledge of child psychology.

For training purpose it is necessary to know which part of knowledge is essential depending upon the nature of the job.

Attitude: Attitudes are emotionalized mental state towards his job. It involves feeling about something and this feeling aspect is very important. The favourable attitude is very necessary 'in order to succeed the job. Favourable attitudes make better performance. A teacher with favourable attitude can force his students to learn more. Teacher must have positive, healthy and favourable attitude towards his job, his students, society and other related components of job; only then he can succeed in his job otherwise not.

Skills: Skills are specific behaviour or activities which an individual requires to do a particular job or task. It refers to the doing part of the human. The manner in which he has to do the work is the skill of questioning, skill of illustrating demonstrating, etc.

Behaviour Patterns: Behaviour patterns are style of functioning or working and style of functioning differs from job to job.

Training emphasizes specific attitude specific knowledge, and specific Skills. Efficient performance of the job depends upon the training. Objective of training programme is also very specific.

Education : All kinds of activities which aim at developing the knowledge, moral values and understandings required in the work of life constitute what we mean to be education.

The purpose of education is to develop well informed, well intensive and well equipped-citizen of the society. And the purpose of education is to develop the human being not an individual alone. There are qualities of general nature as the sense, that are needed by everyone in respect of the job he is engaged in. There are qualities required by everyone to live a good life, well adjusted and harmonious life. These all qualities are developed by education.

Education is a wider term that goes beyond the boundaries of one particular job. It also emphasizes knowledge, skill and attitude but these are of a general nature which may be useful in more than one job and also important from the point of view of the large community or society. Education emphasizes general, important and refinement in behaviour, development of a personality, development of a person who has interest in wider aspect of his environment. Education emphasizes development of knowledge, understanding values and behaviours which are required in all walks of life.

TRAINING IN EDUCATION

'Glaser', (1962) in his book 'Psychological Instructional Technology in Training, Research and Education' published by University of Pitsburg has pointed out that a distinction can be made in training and education on the basis of two criteria—

(a) The degree of specificity of objectives.

(b) Minimising vs. Maximising individual differences.

Training has more specific objectives and attempts to minimise individual difference while educational objectives are more general and it maximises the individual differences. It means when people are educated the difference among them are increased and when they are trained differences are minimised.

Difference between Education and Training

	Education		*Training*
1.	Education emphasised the activities which aim at developing the knowledge and moral values required in all walks of life rather than knowledge and skill relating to only a limited field of activities. Education is a process of developing integrated personality.	1.	It emphasizes on development of specific knowledge, atti-tude, skills and beha-viour patterns which an individual requires to perform a job adequately. These behaviour patterns differ from job to job. If we train a teacher we develop those skills which are needed for him to be a good teacher.
2.	The purpose of education is to provide the conditions essential for young persons and adults to develop an understanding of traditions and ideas influencing the society in which they live, others cultures and of the law of nature and to acquire linguistic and other skills which are basic to learning personal develop-ment and creativity.	2.	The Purpose of Training is to bring excellence in the specific job for which the individual is being trained. Train-ing is concerned with people learning to perform tasks fairly specific and prescribed tasks, although there are exceptions where tasks are more open-ded as in management and supervision.

Difference in education and training exits more in the context of instructional activity than the actual methods used and objectives sought. Nevertheless academically it is impossible to make clear distinction between training and education. Training is an aspect of education.

Training is necessary for efficient work in a particular job. If we appoint a person in any job after sometime through apprentice he will be quite competent for that job. If a person is trained before employing him in a job this is called pre-training. This pre-training is very important. Without providing any training if we employ a person in a job then it is risky because he does not have any knowledge about the machine, when a person fails in a job he develops negative attitude towards the job and thinks that he is not competent for that job. Therefore the pretraining is must. By having some training he will get success in his job with full satisfaction.

There is need for training in general :

1. In order to perform the job successfully and effectively.
2. It is seen that a trained person learns effectively in a lesser time than untrained person. A person can learn these things (WA/S/BP) without training also when he is in job but efforts and time will go waste and he may learn many irrelevant things also.
3. More complex jobs require more specific knowledge, attitude, and skills and behaviour patterns that more specificity is there hence training is more important in these jobs. The risk is involved if he learns on job even it may cause danger to his life also and secondly trial and error results into wastage of time and energy. A good deal of waste of efforts can be saved through training.
4. Organized and systematic programme of training makes them to learn easily in a more efficient way in lesser time.
5. If here is no specificity of objectives K.A.S.S. for a job then there is no need of training but for every job certain specific K/A/S/BP are required. Therefore, training is necessary for all kinds of job.

Certain people, who are not in favour of training hold the view that there is no need of training the teachers, only they should have mastery over the subject because there is no significant difference found in teaching of training and untrained person.

Theoretically it is not right. Training is essential for every teacher. Trained teachers can do much more than untrained teachers. There may be so many reasons for that why they do not perform their work effectively. Demand of job/profession, the objective and expectations from a teacher certify the existence of teachers' training.

To have mastery over subject matter and to communicate this to students are quite different. Many skills are needed to communicate the information effectively e.g., skill of questioning illustrating, demonstrating and explaining, etc., other skills which may be required are skill of arranging and logically sequencing the subject-matter.

Teaching is not confined to tell or to impart knowledge of subject matter to others but in wider perspective teaching aims at alround development of personality of child. But there are the things to be taught to the teacher, e.g., what his responsibilities and duties etc. are. These things or skills or attitudes can only be developed through. systematic training. Hence a systematized knowledge is required in order to achieve these skills and attitudes. For this training is must.

There is not only the knowledge of these things which are, essential for a teacher unless a person has a positive attitude towards students and his job. Attitudes are learnt through experiences. In training programme many pleasant experiences are provided to student-teacher by which he can develop favourable attitude towards himself, his job and his students.

The skills require more practice. Many specific skills have been identified which are to be developed in teacher trainees and these can only be developed by systematic programme of teachers' training.

So theoretical need for training the teacher has some rationale. The technical knowledge and skill can be developed in the teacher through training. Therefore, training is necessary for all type of teachers.

Need for training for primary and secondary teachers has been emphasized by many commissions and committees but there are few who realize the need for training the college-teachers also.

In the past it had been advocated that need for high-school and junior high-school teachers' training and for degree colleges there is no need of training. But now-a-days, a feeling is growing up in the circle of top educationists that there should be need for training for college-teachers also. The idea has been propagated by top educators particularly by N.C.T.E. But prior to this U.G.C. has also organized certain type of orientation programmes for college teachers. In the beginning there was a great resistance of this idea. Now more and more people working in universities and professional colleges are accepting this idea and advocating the need for training.

Actually, the whole universe of teachers in the country is divided into two groups—

1. Training does not make a person more effective.
2. Who have great faith in training, say if training has not produced effective teachers perhaps it might be due to several other reasons. If training is organized it must produce effective teachers. They organized seminars on different universities on teacher-education.

In 1971, U.G.C. funded a larger number of programmes of orientation teaching. U.G.C. asked various universities to hold summer course for orienting college and university-teachers.

During five year plans a huge fund is allocated for the professional improvement of college teachers by seminar, refresher courses, orientation courses, evening courses, summer courses, etc.

As a result of this, several universities with the assistance of U.G.C. have organized serval short term courses to provide orientation in teaching continuous for three years 1973, 74 and 75. As a result of this realization at Baroda University Post-Graduate Diploma Course for teaching was also started; 40 days summer course programme was also started in some universities with the assistance of U.G.C.

Relationship between training and job is helping the people to be more successful on job. If we put people on job having that knowledge and skills which are required for job, predication will be successful.

Teaching is a profession which needs training. But at what level teaching needs training, this is the questions. Teaching at any level is done with a view to impart knowledge. So far as objectives are concerned they do not vary at various levels. Only content and procedure is changed at different levels.

Besides mastery of subject many other things are developed through training. Training astonishes several things for effective teaching.

In the past few years this need has been greatly emphasized and voiced and gradually we have reached to a conclusion that some sort of training is essential for college-teachers also. All above evidences are sufficient to conclude that there must be some sort of training for college-teachers also.

TEACHERS' EDUCATION

All the teachers should be trained, but there should not be and also cannot be a specific training of teachers. This conviction is born out by observations that even the born teachers have to study the techniques of teaching craft. There are teachers who through training and experiences have acquired enormous success in teaching. There is, however, no denying the fact that much wastage in teaching-effort can be saved if the prospective teacher is subjected to teacher-education for actualization of potential in him.

A good deal of waste in teaching-efforts might be avoided by training. It is a further reason that a teacher might be trained. But a teacher is not a teaching craftsman. He has to help his students to develop certain personality traits and also to realize desirable values. This means that there should not be specific training of teachers. An era of the training teachers is past. It was born out of the necessity to bring up a literate generation and to accomplish this task. The teachers were helped to develop a narrow technique and a, highly specialised professional approach.. Today, the need is to bring out a 'sophisticated' and 'cultured' generation, and to accomplish this task a new type of men and women are demanded. The very phrase "the trainee teacher" is out of date. Training is commonly associated with adhoc preparation for an absolute content or with teaching tricks for animal or with a narrow vocationalism.

The schools of today generally lay emphasis on an integrated and balanced personality of the teacher as a whole man. The teacher of today, must be the teacher of a whole man, and he can never be this unless he himself is a complete man. We teach more by our actions than by our preaching.

Training cannot be a matter of teaching professional tricks, and the student who comes to the training institution should try his best to learn these tricks. A narrow vocationalism is wholly out of tune with modern educational thought, and it is antipathetic to those generous sympathies and that consciousness of being one member in a self education community which is generally demanded from teachers.

Many teachers' training institutions are producing humanly illiterate teachers who are not able to cope up with the aspirations of rising generation of youth who will be required to meet the human encounters. The new teacher will have to integrate the skills of teaching with his life style and also to help the students to develop not only intellectually but also emotionally.

The tragedy is that teacher in general adopt little real character or work of whom we entrust to bring up children in an ideal way.

Teachers are a section of community sharply segregated from the rest of the community preparing themselves for their life's work in institutions where their fellow students will be preparing themselves for developing human attributes. They have little opportunity and less encouragement to share in the enjoyment of things by which a man lives. The teacher-education system as it exists today may succeed in the training of teachers, but it has entirely failed to educate the human beings. This is what we have tended to do. The trained teacher has been too often the untrained human being. This process, therefore, must be reversed. Our aim must be the education of the right human beings for work in our schools. If we can succeed in this, the trained teachers will follow. An era of the training of teachers is past; our concern 'today' is with the education of the educators.

Then, who is the human being that we need? His chief characteristic, if there is any thing in him, must be wholeness of personality, mind and wholeness of experience. With proper type of education to the prospective teacher, he will be in a more favourable position to correlate his knowledge with experience, to see life steadily and to see it as a whole. His mature study of child's growth process will strengthen his intellect. The only means of strengthening one's intellect Keats has said, is to let the mind be a thoroughfare for all thoughts, not a selected party. From this open-mindedness, sympathy, tolerance, intellectual adaptability and that width of interest will spring the attributes which are essential for successful living and to deal with children. But all this requires, a comprehensive goal to deal with. This implies a philosophy of life and education, a map by which the future teacher may see himself in relation to other teachers as well as other human beings activities. It means that he must be given time and opportunity during his training course to think about education because he will have little time to think about education after completing his training. After the completion of his teacher-education course, he will be engaged in the all absorbing tasks of the classroom and the common life.

The prospective teacher, therefore, must be offered opportunities frequently to associate with the best minds and thereby to develop a disciplined intellect as well as the quality of appreciation of culture into all forms. This implies that he will have an emotional life developed to a fine sensitivity but held in a strict control.

The need of today's teacher is such a philosophy which is primarily concerned with human beings to interact with each other. In our humanistic programme for teacher-education we are attempting to develop a human teacher who possesses such qualities as spontaneity, acceptance, creativity and self-realization. This programme should give and opportunity to the prospective teacher in order to relate theory to practice to search for greater personal understanding of himself and for the learning process of children'.

It should help him to develop compassion for weakness in individuals and sensitivity for the needs of human beings. The most important product of such an approach will be a teacher who will be true for his feelings and he will be in a position to know how to help children to realize their potential. It is hoped this humanistic approach to teacher-education will produce teacher who will be able to halt the continued process of education of human potential in our schools.

Though methods can never be taught, but the methods adopted by other teachers can be studied. Such knowledge which is gained and combined with other considerations, the student will be able to try out various approaches to his work and afterwards during the practical work of the course. This is so because a practising teacher generally evolves and polishes his own method. It should be indeed in practice and not in the lecture-room in order to acquire technical skills.

The teacher should possess such skills and competencies so that his task may be easy, useful and effective. He should know the techniques and procedures which should be adopted in his profession. He should think about the effective performance' of his duties. The important task of education for the future is to improve the intellectual and technical competence in teachers.

Competence and professional skills are the very heart of the programme of teacher-education.

For this purpose, the following operations are needed to be taken

1. Providing professional educated entrants to the profession in adequate numbers.
2. Maintaining or increasing the quality of entrants for the profession to satisfy society's needs. Whereas the first aim is quantitative, the second one is qualitative.

Professional education should focus on the person as an individual who is in practice and seek to broaden his human, that is his mental, moral and emotional capacities. The teacher should have a sound philosophy of education. He should have the knowledge of an adequate functioning of psychology. He should also have a dynamic sociological perspective.

The education which we want to provide to the teacher should be such which will be helpful in developing their inner capacity and power. Only such teachers will be capable in relating theoretical insight to practice and will be able to improve preparation programme. Besides this they will be effective practitioners in their profession.

The aim of teacher-education is to develop such competencies in the prospective teachers which will be useful for them in becoming a successful teacher.

It tends to increase the ability of the teacher to deal with a range of individual differences. Many teachers presently believe that their job is to develop certain basic skills in a group of youngsters at a given level of achievement. This type of teacher is no longer useful for the school.

The teacher of tomorrow should be one who can design a teaching situation which is conducive for the growth of pupils' mental health and develops in them a commitment to a set of values that is creativity and enquiry skill.

Now-a-days a teacher is in the urgent need of certain skills and competencies to develop and he is also in need of a new type of knowledge to development in knowledge and attitude, atmosphere and facility so that he may be in a position to make this task easy, fruitful and confirming for the demands of the students. His education, therefore, should be according to the necessities of the time and needs, of the society.

Some of competencies which need to be developed in the teacher are as below:

1. The, ability to relate with the learning of one student, this includes diagnosis and individual instruction.
2. The ability to analyse group development interaction and to perform a leadership role in a group.
3. The ability to communicate with the individual as well as the group.
4. The ability to acquire knowledge and skill in a disciplined manner.
5. The ability to structure the acquired knowledge, this competency will enable the teacher to choose from his specialisation, the type of knowledge that is important for a particular individual or group. It should be commensurated with pupil's growth.

In the end, it can be said that teaching is based upon scholarship. Scholarship will be of little use unless the teacher will communicate his scholarship to his student. Today, the chief task of education should be to upgrade the intellectual and technical competence of the teacher. The teachers of today are in need of such an education which is new, constructive spontaneous and which is based upon new philosophy of life. This education should also emphasize on social urgency, social ideal and social livings.

Education helps in the development of an individual's cognitive, conative and affective abilities. Teacher-education programmes are designed to prepare effective teachers by providing theoretical awareness of teaching and developing teaching competency and teaching ability.

The present level of performance of an individual on a test will indicate the growth of his ability.

Teacher-education covers those theoretical aspects through which knowledge, pertaining to specific subjects and transmitted to students and teachers, is prospected.

All those activities,.operations and event through which the prospective teachers are to be made aware to the latest trends of subjects and teaching as well as pertaining to the theory related to learner's behavioural changes and behavioural management as well as subjecting them to situations—formal, and informal dealing to the development of communication of teaching skills. Finally, teacher-education is provided to prospective teachers consequent to which they develop interest in teaching.

The purpose of education is not only to acquaint him with certain skills and abilities but also developing his interest in-teaching is necessary. Because if a teacher is interested he will continue to acquire new knowledge and shall put better and still better.

Teaching goes in the class with the intention that his pupils will learn something. For this purpose planning is required that is done with the help of mind i.e., central nervous systems. Planning is based on certain rules, planning analysis, planning teaching learning activities and evaluation. Teacher through his mind prepare a theoretical hypothetical model which is translated in the class. Motivational activities are done so that the pupils are interested. The result is the pupil's behaviour. Now the pupil's behaviour is changed. If the pupils have learned there will be feedback to the pupils. If the teacher is dissatisfied with his teaching there will be not a change in teacher's perception and he has to change his strategy. But if he is satisfied there will be confirmation to his activities and he will try to employ the same strategy in his further teaching. We have to learn that best can help our pupils to learn. What are these teaching practice and strategies, which should be in a successful teaching?

In all teacher-education theory, curriculum as well as practical curriculum, there are objectives. To achieve these objectives there are certain programmes. Teacher is assigned some course to teach. Schedule for a activities prepared. In planning it is not merely the case to help the student teacher to plan his lesson but to help him to become an educator. Through particular experience the ST is helped to know the role of educator.

This is the co-operation plan of teacher-education (T.E.) as well as Student-teaching (S.T.). It will deliver the plan in the class and the T.E. will supervise the S.T. As the teacher-educator will see whatever the student-teacher has developed the desired skills or not, it will give him feedback, while, the student-teacher will see whether his pupils have learnt.

Teacher-education refers to all those programmes, strategies tactics as a result of which a prospective teacher is able to help his pupils to acquire learning-cognitive psychomotor and affective.

The following are the general objectives of teacher-education programmes:

1. Teacher-education has the general objectives of develop Gandhian values of non-violence, truthfulness, self-discipline, self-reliance and dignity of labour.
2. Perceives the role as an agent of social change in the community.
3. Not only acts as a leader of the student community but also as guide to the wider community.
4. Established a liaison between the school and the community by employing ways and means for integrating the resources as a life of the community with school life.
5. Not only uses but also helps in the conservation of environmental resources and life and preservation of historical emoluments and other cultural heritage.

6. Develops a warm and positive attitude towards the growing children their academic socio-emotional and personal problems.
7. Develops an understanding of the objectives of student-teaching in the Indian context and awareness of the role played by school in achieving the goals of developing a democratic, secular and socialistic society.
8. Develops understandings, interests, attitudes and skills which will enable him to foster the alround growth and development of the children under his care.
9. Develops competency to teaching on the basis of accepted principles of learning and teaching.
10. Develops communication, psychomotor skills and abilities conducive for human relations which will enable him to promote learning inside and outside the classroom.
11. Keeps abreast with the latest trends in the knowledge of the subject he teaches and the techniques of teaching the same.
12. Undertakes investigations and action research projects.

The following are the basic assumptions for the objectives and teacher-education:

1. Since the objective of education is to build a man who can help in the development of a secular, democratic and socialistic society. Therefore, teacher-education must ensure the man-making process.
2. The man-making process is start right from infancy to adulthood, therefore, all levels of teacher-education will help to develop such teacher-education in which ensures continuity on the one hand and diversity in terms of the learners characteristics and social demands.
3. The continuity aspect of teacher implies that teacher-education should have a core curriculum. The core curriculum will be called to all the teacher-education namely pre-primary, primary, secondary and college level.

4. The diversity aspect of teacher-education programme implies that teacher-education programme for each needs stage be designed in the context of children's developmental and national goals.
5. Teacher-education programme of each stage should merge into a teacher-education programme of higher stage in the progressive order.
6. All teacher-education programmes irrespective of difference teacher-education levels should have the following three integral components—
   (a) Pedagogical course.
   (b) Working with the community.
   (c) Content-cum-methodology course and practice-teaching courses.
7. The pedagogical components working with community component and content of methodology component will vary in their proportionate weightage from stage to stage in the total teacher-education programme.
8. The three components stated above should form the nucleus of teacher-education for reasons as under—
   (a) The prospective teacher must be familiarized with the work why and how of teacher behaviours, the answer to these questions have to be supplied to him on the basis of accepted principles of pedagogy, psychology and sociology.
   (b) The prospective teacher must be an agent of social change, leader of the students and guide to the society.
   (c) The prospective teacher will have to be a master over the subject and an expert in the teaching methodology of the subject of his teaching.
9. Consequent to the integral components of teacher-education the prospective teacher will act inside and outside the classroom situation on the basis of scientific knowledge, positive attitude and convictions he will apply those techniques of modifying and managing

learning behaviours which will be of use in actualizing learners's potentials.,

10. To be effective, a teacher needs to have a close understanding of the characteristics of the society, of the community in which he lives and also be equipped with social skills through which he may help in community development and desirable social change.

11. Teacher-education programme will be valid to the extent oral experiences are reinforced by visual, factual and motor experiences.

    The teacher-education programme therefore needs to be vivid, varied and comprehensive.

12. Teacher-education being an on-going process needs to have three basic characteristics, namely flexibility, relevance and inter-disciplinary.

13. Teacher-education programme should, embrace two types of courses namely content or subject courses and method courses. The content courses should including learning experience pertaining to the subject of teaching the teacher after completion of training is expected to teach. The method courses should impart knowledge and help in the development of two types of skills.

    (a) Core teaching skills common to all stages of teacher-education.

    (b) Specific teaching skill meant for a specific group of teachers at a specific level of teacher-education pre-primary primary, secondary and collegiate.

    (c) Theory course should be drastically cut to include only suck theoretical concepts as are of significance in the understanding of the learner and in the modification of his cognitive, psychomotor and effective behaviour.

VARIOUS LEVELS

It has been assumed that, teacher who will be educated in the pre-primary teacher institution, will generally teach children between 3 to 8 years of age. This age group is considered psychologically to be the most important formulated years of an individual's life span.

Freud believed that foundations of personality of an individual are made in the first five years of his age. This being so, teacher at pre-primary level need to be the best equipped in terms of his ability to help in laying, down strong foundation for a normal human personality and also the competencies which may enable him to actualize an individual's inherent potentials. However, little care in the country till date has been made in designing a teacher-education curriculum which may develop knowledge, skills and attitudes among the prospective teachers to help in the personality building process as well as in naturalization of young children's potentials.

National Council of Educational Research and Training (NCERT) broucher has laid down the following objectives of teacher-education at pre-primary stage:

1. Acquires theoretical and practical knowledge of childhood education.
2. Understands the major principles of growth and development of the children.
3. Applies theoretical and practical knowledge to the education of the, children in Indian context-rural, urban an industrial.
4. Develops understanding, skills, attitudes and interests which will enable him to foster alround growth and development of the children under his care.
5. Develops skills to help in the physical and emotional health of the children by providing a conducive environment.
6. Develops communication skills such as story telling explaining situations, etc.
7. Develops skills to provide a variety of learning experiences through organization of musical, rhythmic grammatic activities, play, worth experience, creative art and games.

8. Develops skills to provide visual aids with the help to waste of indigenous material.
9. Understands the home environment of the child and develops amicable home-school relationship.
10. Understands the role of the school and the teacher in changing the society.

The learner at the primary stage has a better developed cognitive, psychomotor and affective abilities. He has a better capacity in comparison to the learner at the pre-primary stage to make abstractions, to think, to reason out, to draw inference, to manipulate words, to communicate, to develop proper relationship with peers, social group, home, neighborhood and the society to conform to social norms, to control his emotions and express his feelings. Consequent these developments and also according to social expectations' because of origin of new problems, new perspectives, new dimensions, in his life the teacher's talk at this stage is no less crucial and significant than what it was during pre-primary stage. To be successful as a teacher, the prospective teacher should acquire, the following behavioural changes—

1. Possesses knowledge of the first and second, language topics related to social and natural sciences related to environmental studies.
2. Develops skills to identify, select and organize learning experiences pertaining to subjects mentioned above and also the skills to conduct them.
3. Possesses theoretical and practical knowledge in respect of the child's health, physical and creational activities, work experiences, play', games creative art and music and the skills to conduct these activities.
4. Develops understanding of the major psychological principles pertaining to growth and development of the children under his care.
5. Possesses theoretical and Practical knowledge in respect of childhood education including integrated teacher.
6. Develops, understanding of the major principles of learning in formal and informal situations.

7. Conducts action research.
8. Understands the role of the school, the peer group and the community in shaping the personality of the child and also develops an amicable home school relationship.
9. Understands the role of the school and teacher in changing the society.

The following are the basis for the objectives:

1. The child is at the adolescent stage and has problems.
2. All mechanism of growth and development.
3. Child's interests at this stage become crystallized in their interaction with varied situation.
4. Child, after the completion of adolescence, is ready to choose vocation and pursue it upto his optimum level.
5. Child's interests in religion, society, politics, nation and work at large trends to be manifested.

The following are the main objectives:

Possesses competency to teach subject of his specialization of accepted principles of teaching and learning in the context of new school curriculum-

Terminal Behaviours—The following are the terminal behaviours—

(a) Depth of his understanding of the concept pertaining to his discipline.

(b) Makes an internal and external judgement of the quality of an article through ideal of principles against a criterion.

(c) Locates the deficiencies, short falls and errors committed by an author.

(d) Suggests solutions for overcoming the falls and observes deficiency and pitfalls.

(e) Knows the ways through which adolescent learns.

(f) Understands the concept of work and experience.

(g) Appreciates the rationale of 10+2 curriculum.

(h) Possesses the skills to teach.

Develops understandings, skills, interests and attitude which would enable him to foster the alround growth of the child.

Terminal Behaviours—The following are the terminal behaviours—

(a) Understands the total concept of personality.

(b) Knows the various techniques through which total personality development takes place.

(c) Understands the significance of enabling the child to make wholesome personality development.

(d) Possesses communication mental and social skills to interact with pupils.

(e) Manifests his psychomotor- skills in formal and inform institutional situations.

(f) Shows a positive and warm attitude about the optimum physical intellectual, emotional and social development of the child.

(g) Shows interests in the development of the child indicated by—

  (i) intrinsic and extrinsic reading pertaining to adolescent growth problems and needs,

  (ii) organization of socio-cultural functions and excursion terms,

  (iii) conference with the adolescent.

Possesses sufficient theoretical and practical knowledge about an adolescents's health and physical education programme, work experience and rercreational activities.

Terminal Behaviours—The following are the terminal behaviours:

(a) knows the sources institutional home neighbourhood and the local of the institution which influence health,

(b) knows the structure and functioning of various bodily systems,

(c) knows about the system causes infection and contagious disease,

(d) knows about the role of the P.E. games and recreational activities in the health of an adolescent is able to detect causes showing health disorders,

(e) he is able to make a healthy guess about the nature of bodily disorder and the type of techniques on as whom needs,

(f) applies first aid techniques on as whom needs.

Develops skills in identifying selecting, innovating and organising learning experience pertaining to the subject to his specialization.

Terminal Behaviours—The following are the terminal behaviours:

(a) understands the concept of learning experience,

(b) identifies learning experience by—

  (i) analysing the learning content into its elements,

  (ii) developing specific objectives of teaching units,

  (iii) specifying each unit of objectives into behaviour,

  (iv) conceiving activities which may develop the specific behaviour,

(c) uses only essential learning experience out of a mass of experience,

(d) modifies learning experience into light of research conducted,

(e) presents the learning experience in a logical and psychological sequence,

(f) subjects to the situation evoking their initiative voluntary effective participation, ego involvement and raising the level of aspiration.

Develops understanding about the psychological principles of growth and development, individual differences and similarities and cognitive, conative and attitudinal learning.

Terminal Behaviour—The following are the terminal behaviours:

(a) understands the concept of growth and development,

(b) understands the principles of physical, intellectual, social and emotional growth,

(c) defines each ability into specific learning output,

(d) understands the concept of ability and types of ability,

(e) knows the behaviours associated with cognitive psychomotor abilities.

Develops skill in guiding and counselling the learners in academic and vocational subjects growth as well as in their academic and personal problems.

Terminal Behaviours—The following are the terminal behaviours—

(a) understands the concept of guidance and counselling,

(b) elicits, cooperation from institutional personal, community, experts and personality data,

(c) applies guidance and, counselling techniques on problematic children deficient in their academic achievement in relation to their intelligence,

(d) organizes a guidance clinic,

(e) elicits cooperation from institutional personal community, experts and personality data,

(f) applies experimental behavioural treatment and its effect by finding out the magnitude of improvement.

Understands the role of school home and peer groups, in shaping the personality of the child and also develops a relationship between school and home to their mental benefit.

Understands the role of schools and teacher in changing the society.

Understands action research/experimental research projects or investigatory projects to improve his own teaching, effectiveness in enable children to develop their capacities.

The following are the basis for the objectives—

1. Learner at college stage is at the transitional adulthood stage.
2. The learner is ready to lead an independent life by vocational and social adjustment.
3. Aptitudes are by and large hardest and stable, habits are enduring and style of work and personality undergo very little change.
4. Learner is able to acquire more abstract concept able to reasonable to test it under able to propound his own theory and conducive learning conditions.

Objectives. The main objectives ate as follows:

(1) The future teacher for collegiate stage should possess competency to teach the subjects of his specialization on the basis of accepted principles of teaching and learning also by striving to keep himself abreast with, the latest knowledge in the subject of his specialization' and methodology of teaching.

(2) Develops understanding of the aims and objectives of education in general and of higher education in particular and is also aware of his role in building up a democratic secular and socialistic society in Indian context.

Terminal Behaviours—The following are the terminal behaviours—

(a) understands the various philosophical, sociological, psychological interpretation of concept of education,

(b) discrimination between aims and objectives of education,

(c) recalls the objectives of education in general and those of higher education,

(d) discriminates between gentler and specific objective of higher education,

(e) understands the behavioural pattern: associated with secular, democratic and socialistic society or an individual,

(f) knows, the, operations and activities which need to be taken for building up a society of the democratic, secular characterisation.

(3) Develops skills psychomotor and cognitive to teach the subject of his specialization, i.e., vocational and academic subject.

(4) Develops skills to make use of educational technology in the teaching of the subject of his specialization, i.e., vocational and/or academic subjects.

Terminal Behaviours—The following are other terminal behaviours—

(a) understands the concept of educational technology,

(b) discriminates between educational and instructional technology,

(c) appreciates the role of educational technology in maximising learning,

(d) analyses the educational content,

(e) frames micro lessons, programme instruction and applies them into actual classroom situation,

(f) understands the differences among different types of teaching models,

(g) conducts his teaching-on the basis of specific models.

(5) Understands the bio-psycho-social needs of adolescent and he is also aware of problem arising out of the

infulfilment of these needs and develops skills to help the adolescent to solve his academic and personal.

Terminal Behaviours—The following are further terminal behaviours—

(a) understands the concept of need,

(b) recalls the basic needs,

(c) discriminates between the efforts caused by the non-fulfilment of each of the personal needs,

(d) discriminates between biosocial and psychological needs,

(e) knows the significance of guidance to adolescent,

(f) understands, the sequential steps of guidance and counselling procedure,

(g) possesses skill to administer tests gives the instruction score responses sheets treats data satisfactorily,

(h) uses psychotherapy in cases which require it.

(6) Undertakes investigation research project, action research, experimental research project to solve problems pertaining to pupil behaviour, modification in and outside the classroom.

(7) Understands the role of teacher and the school in changing the society.

Exercise

1. Explain the meaning of teachers' training. Differential between teachers' training and teacher-education.
2. Enumerate some of the competencies which are needed to develop among teachers.
3. Different between teachers' training and teacher-education.

4. Need of teacher-education for different stage of education.
5. Differentiate between objective and ability. Describe the Brown Model and Argyle's Model of teaching.
6. Enumerate the basis assumptions for the objects of teacher-education. Describe the objective at primary level.
7. Describe the objectives of teacher-education at secondary stage and specify some of important objectives in behavioural terms.